Central Serbia
Pages 64–75

Eastern Serbia
Pages 100–111

Southern Serbia
Pages 112–121

EYEWITNESS TRAVEL

SERBIA

EYEWITNESS TRAVEL

SERBIA

Author **Matt Willis**

DK

Produced by Bigmetalfish Design Services
Project Manager and Designer Sunita Gahir
Project Editor Ankita Awasthi Tröger

Author Matt Willis
Illustrators Peter Bull Art Studio, Sunita Gahir, Arun Pottirayil

For Dorling Kindersley Ltd
Publishing Director Georgina Dee
Publisher Vivien Antwi
Managing Editor Sally Schafer
Executive Editor Michelle Crane
Senior Executive Cartographic Editor Casper Morris
Cartography Manager Suresh Kumar
Senior Cartographer Mohammad Hassan
Executive DTP Designer Jason Little
Executive Picture Researcher Ellen Root
Picture Researcher Susie Peachey
Picture Research Assistant Lucy Sienkowska
Jacket Designer Richard Czapnik
Production Controller Stephanie McConnell

Printed and bound in China

First published in Great Britain in 2016
by Dorling Kindersley Limited
80 Strand, London WC2R 0RL

A CIP catalogue record is available from the British Library.

ISBN 978 0 24124 717 4

Floors are referred to throughout in accordance with European usage; ie the "first floor" is the floor above ground level.

The information in this DK Eyewitness Travel Guide is checked regularly.

Every effort has been made to ensure that this book is as up-to-date as possible at the time of going to press. Some details, however, such as telephone numbers, opening hours, prices, gallery hanging arrangements and travel information are liable to change. The publishers cannot accept responsibility for any consequences arising from the use of this book, nor for any material on third party websites, and cannot guarantee that any website address in this book will be a suitable source of travel information. We value the views and suggestions of our readers very highly. Please write to: Publisher, DK Eyewitness Travel Guides, Dorling Kindersley, 80 Strand, London, WC2R 0RL, UK, or email: travelguides@dk.com.

Front cover main image: The Cathedral Church of St Michael rising above Belgrade's riverfront

Contents

How to Use this Guide **6**

The enormous dome of the Temple of St Sava on Vračar Hill, Belgrade

Introducing Serbia

Discovering Serbia **10**

Putting Serbia on the Map **14**

A Portrait of Serbia **16**

Serbia Through the Year **28**

The History of Serbia **32**

A 16th-century fresco of holy warriors, Poganovo Monastery, Southern Serbia

◀ Hills and forests surrounding Lake Spajići, set on the southern fringes of Lake Zaovine in Tara National Park, Western Serbia

Conifer- and juniper-forested mountains surrounding Lake Zaovine in Tara National Park, Western Serbia

Serbia Area by Area

Serbia at a Glance **40**

Belgrade **42**

Central Serbia **64**

Western Serbia **76**

Northern Serbia **88**

Eastern Serbia **100**

Southern Serbia **112**

Exquisite stonework in the rosette window of Žiča Monastery, Western Serbia

Travellers' Needs

Where to Stay **124**

Where to Eat and Drink **130**

Shopping in Serbia **140**

Entertainment in Serbia **142**

Sports and Outdoor Activities **144**

Survival Guide

Practical Information **148**

Travel Information **158**

General Index **166**

Acknowledgments **172**

Phrase Book **174**

Metal weathervane with cardinal directions in Petrovaradin, Novi Sad, Northern Serbia

The magnificent 15th-century Manasija Monastery, Central Serbia

HOW TO USE THIS GUIDE

This Dorling Kindersley Travel Guide helps you to get the most from your visit to Serbia. It provides detailed practical information and expert recommendations. *Introducing Serbia* maps the country and its areas, places them in their historical and cultural context, and describes events through the entire year. *Serbia Area by Area* is the main sightseeing section, which covers all the important sights, with numerous photographs, maps and illustrations. Information on hotels, restaurants, shopping, entertainment and outdoor activities is found in *Travellers' Needs*. The *Survival Guide* has advice on everything from visas, personal security and health to getting around, money and communications.

Serbia Area by Area

The country has been divided into six areas, each with a separate chapter. The most interesting places to visit have been numbered on a *Regional Map* at the beginning of each chapter.

1 Introduction
The landscape, history and character of each area is described here, showing how the region has developed over the centuries and what it offers the visitor today.

2 Regional Map
This shows the road network and airports and gives an overview of the entire region. All the sights are numbered here and there are also useful tips on getting around.

Sights at a Glance lists all the chapter's sights, following the numbering on the *Regional Map*.

A suggested route for a walk is shown with a dotted red line.

Stars indicate the sights that no visitor should miss.

3 Street-by-Street Map
This gives a bird's-eye view of a key area covered in the chapter. The numbering of the sights matches the fuller descriptions on the pages that follow.

4 Detailed Information

All the important towns and other places to visit are described individually. They are listed in order, following the numbering on the *Regional Map*.

Each area of Serbia can be quickly identified by its colour coding, shown on the inside front cover.

Story boxes highlight a special feature or interesting story about the town or sight.

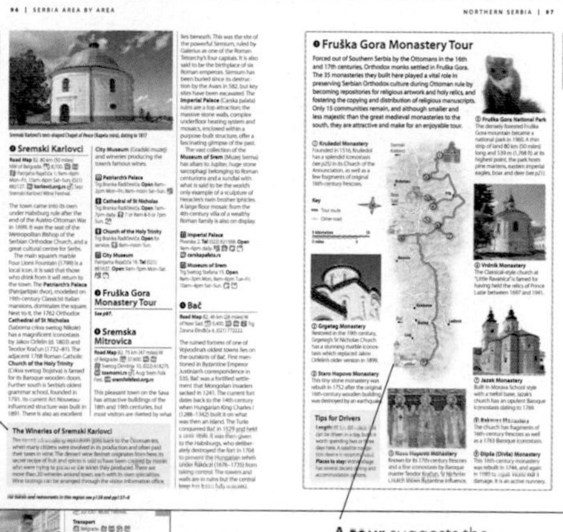

A tour suggests the best route covering all the sights in an area of natural beauty or historical interest.

5 Town Map

Major towns have a map showing the main sights, each of which is described in detail. The map also shows the town's transport hubs.

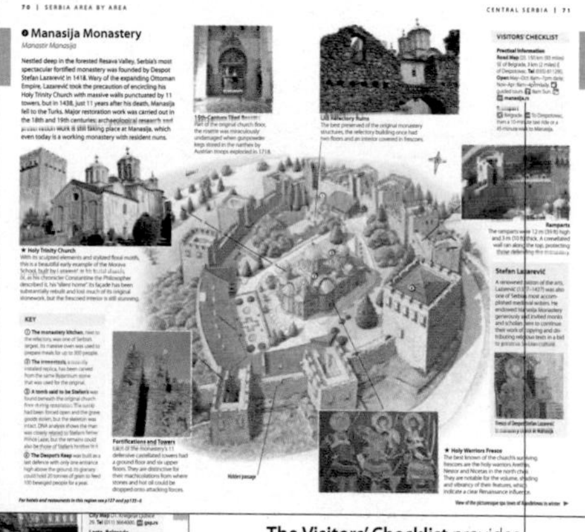

6 Serbia's Top Sights

These are given two full pages. Places of interest are shown from a bird's-eye view, with specific sights and features picked out and described, and accompanied by images.

Numbered circles point out major features of the sight listed in the key.

The Visitors' Checklist provides all the practical information needed to plan your visit.

Directories contain contact details for all the organizations or companies mentioned in the text.

7 Practical Information

The *Travellers' Needs* and *Survival Guide* sections offer information on practical aspects such as visas and paperwork, responsible travel, health, money, hotels, restaurants, entertainment, activities and shops.

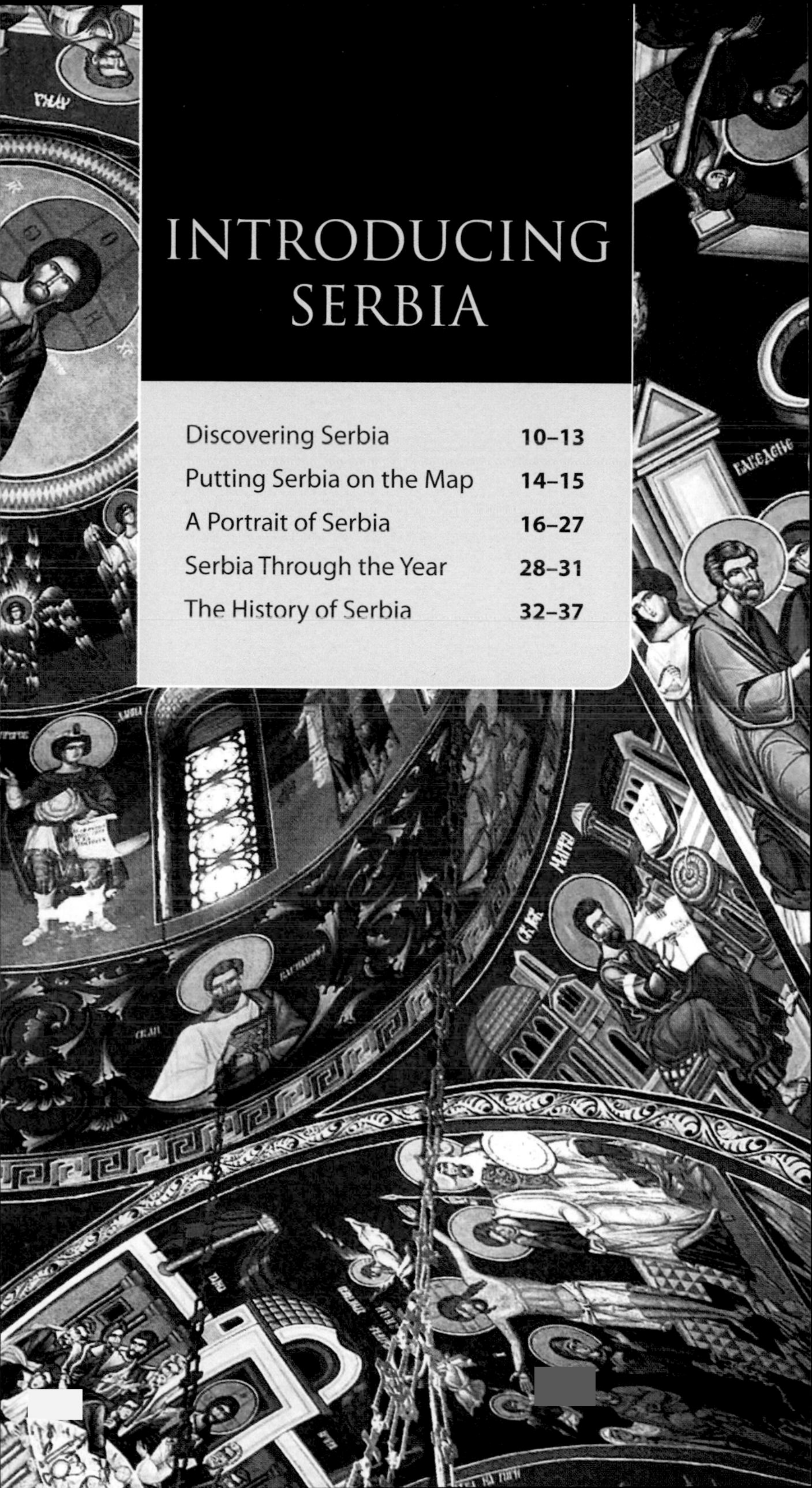

INTRODUCING SERBIA

Discovering Serbia 10–13

Putting Serbia on the Map 14–15

A Portrait of Serbia 16–27

Serbia Through the Year 28–31

The History of Serbia 32–37

DISCOVERING SERBIA

The following tours have been designed to take in as many of Serbia's highlights as possible while keeping long-distance travel to a minimum. First is a two-day route around the country's historic capital Belgrade, which can be extended to four days by adding excursions to nearby attractions. The ten-day itinerary begins with an exploration of the capital, followed by eight days covering Serbia's must-see sights in the south, north and centre. The number of days required are based on visitors travelling independently with a hire car; allow a couple of extra days if you plan to rely on public transport.

Skadarlija, Belgrade
Skadarska and the smaller streets around it forming the old bohemian quarter are popularly known as Skadarlija. After World War II the area was partially modernized, but in the 1960s the cobblestones, fountains and streetlamps were reinstated, restoring much of the area's old-fashioned charm.

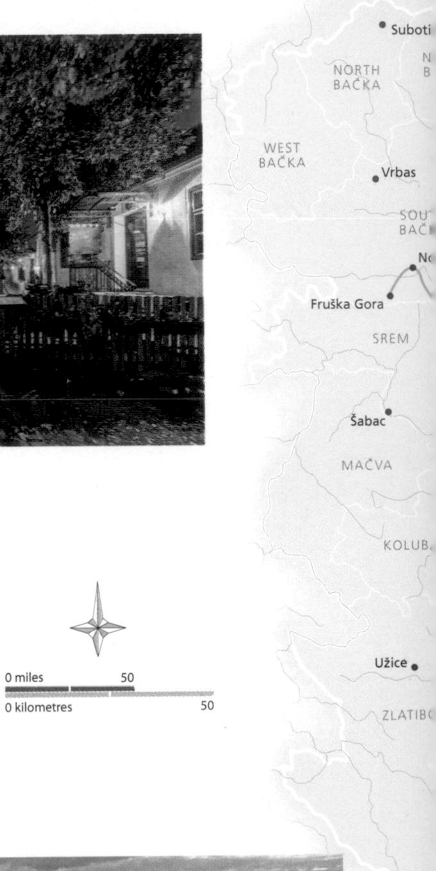

NORTH BAČKA
WEST BAČKA
Vrbas
Fruška Gora
SREM
Šabac
MAČVA
Užice

0 miles 50
0 kilometres 50

Novi Sad
Serbia's second city and capital of Vojvodina, Novi Sad has a delightful historic core and plays host to the internationally acclaimed EXIT Music Festival, held annually in the mighty Petrovaradin Fortress on the banks of the Danube River.

◀ Frescoes painted on the dome of St Sava's Church, next to the Temple of St Sava in Belgrade

Karađorđe Mausoleum Church of St George, Topola
This stunning church in Topola, clad in white marble, boasts a monumental portal with a mosaic of St George slaying the dragon. The saint is depicted with the face of Karađorđe, symbolizing the liberation of the Serbs.

Skull Tower, Niš
A town whose history stretches back to the Romans, Niš is home to the grim Skull Tower, which stands testament to the long and often bloody war waged by the Serbs for their freedom from the Ottoman Empire.

Key

— Ten Days in Serbia

Ten Days in Serbia

- Be amazed by the sheer size of **Smederevo Fortress**.
- Try not to get spooked by the macabre **Skull Tower** in Niš.
- Marvel at the astonishing fortifications of medieval **Manasija Monastery**.
- Pamper yourself with some therapeutic spa treatments at **Prolom Banja**.
- Contemplate the eerie shapes of the rock formations at **Devil's Town**.
- Admire the resplendent mosaics covering the interior of the **Karađorđe Mausoleum Church of St George** in Topola.
- Soak in the view of the Danube and the fine architecture of Novi Sad from the ramparts of **Petrovaradin Fortress**.

Two Days in Belgrade

Belgrade's busy riverfront and vibrant nightlife make the city an exciting point of arrival. The capital is also home to one of the country's most fought-over strongholds, Kalemegdan Fortress.

- **Arriving** Set at the western edge of Belgrade, Nikola Tesla Airport is a 30-minute drive from Republic Square (Trg republike).
- **Moving on** Nikola Tesla Airport serves domestic as well as international flights. The Central Bus and Railway Stations are in Savski venac, a 15-minute walk south of Kalemegdan Park.

Day 1

Morning Start with a tour of the **Old Town** *(see pp46–7)* to admire its eclectic mix of architectural styles. Most of the buildings date to the 19th century, when the city became Serbia's capital, but the many gaps left after the destruction of the World Wars have been filled with modern replacements. The **Palace of Princess Ljubica** *(see p49)* is one of the city's few remaining Ottoman-influenced buildings and makes for an enjoyable visit. Afterwards get to grips with the country's tumultuous history by spending a couple of hours at the **National Museum** *(see p51)*, with its absorbing exhibitions.

Afternoon Lunch at one of the Old Town's outdoor restaurants, such as Smokvica *(see p135)*, or enjoy fantastic city views from Ebisu on the rooftop of Square Nine Hotel *(see p135)*. Then follow Knez Mihailova for a visit to **Kalemegdan Fortress** *(see pp52–3)*, without which no trip to Belgrade is complete. From its hilltop battlements there are wonderful views of the confluence of the Sava and Danube Rivers, and of Great War Island where invading armies used to gather before advancing on the fort. The excellent Military Museum in the fort is worth a visit. In the evening dine at an atmospheric traditional *kafana* (tavern) in **Skadarlija** *(see p51)*.

Day 2

Morning Devote the morning to museum hopping. Take a quick look at the colourful folk outfits at the **Ethnographic Museum** *(see p48)* before visiting the **Nikola Tesla Museum** *(see p55)*, Serbia's most popular museum, to see demonstrations of some of Tesla's creations. Car enthusiasts should not miss the excellent collection at the **Automobile Museum** *(see p54)*, which includes Tito's Cadillac.

Afternoon The splendid **Royal Palaces** *(see p59)* in Dedinje are among Belgrade's highlights, but are only open at weekends. A good alternative that is only closed on Mondays is the site of Tito's tomb, the **House of Flowers** *(see p58)*. The **Museum of Yugoslav History** in the same complex has a good exhibition on pre- and post-war Yugoslavia and is a great place to buy retro Socialist-themed souvenirs. If the weather is warm, cool off at **Ada Ciganlija** *(see p59)*. In the evening, head back to the city centre for dinner at one of the smart new riverside restaurants at the Beton Hala development.

To extend your trip...
The medieval fortress at **Smederevo** *(see p68)* is an easy day trip from Belgrade. **Novi Sad** *(see pp92–3)*, only 94 km (58 miles) to the north, is another option but it has plenty to see so be sure to get an early start.

Ten Days in Serbia

- **Airports** Arrive and depart from the Nikola Tesla Airport in Belgrade.
- **Transport** This itinerary can be followed using the bus and rail network, but hiring a car will allow easier and more flexible travel.

Days 1 and 2: Belgrade
Follow the two-day itinerary detailed for Belgrade.

Day 3: Smederevo Fortress and Viminacium
Follow the Danube River east from Belgrade towards the huge, impressive fortress at

The White Palace's arcaded corridor overlooking the gardens of the Royal Palaces in Dedinje, Belgrade

For practical information on travelling around Serbia, see pp160–65

Church of the Holy Dormition at the 13th-century Žiča Monastery near Kraljevo, painted red to represent the blood of Christian martyrs

Smederevo *(see p68)* where the medieval Serbian state was crushed by the Ottomans in 1459. From here it is an hour's drive to the archaeological site at **Viminacium** *(see p104)*, with its fascinating Roman ruins.

The Holy Trinity Church and Despot's Keep at the 15th-century Manasija Monastery

Day 4: Manasija Monastery and Resavska Cave
The A1/ E75 offers a smooth link south to **Manasija Monastery** *(see pp70–71)*, whose formidable medieval fortifications make it one of Serbia's most spectacular monasteries. Later, tour the cool depths of **Resavska Cave** *(see p68)* before continuing south.

Day 5: Niš
Spend a day exploring historic **Niš** *(see p116)*. Niš Fortress is an obvious starting point, but there is also the former Nazi concentration camp that now houses the thought-provoking Red Cross Camp Museum, the grim Skull Tower and the interesting remains of Constantine's summer villa at Mediana.

Day 6: Devil's Town
Drive two hours southwest towards Kuršumlija to enjoy a pleasant walk through the leafy nature reserve that contains **Devil's Town** *(see p120)*, Serbia's most intriguing rock formations. From here it is a long hike or a short drive to **Prolom Banja** spa *(see p120)*, where the hotel is a wonderful place to relax.

Day 7: Kruševac, Ljubostinja Monastery and Kraljevo
A picturesque country road leads north from Prolom Banja to **Kruševac** *(see p69)*, a pleasant town that was the capital of Serbia in the medieval era; its excellent museum and Lazarica Church make a brief stop here worthwhile. If time permits, stop at **Ljubostinja Monastery** *(see p69)* on the way to **Kraljevo** *(see pp80–81)*, an enjoyable town with several good places to stay and a lively riverside social scene during the summer.

Day 8: Kragujevac and Topola
Kragujevac *(see p74)* to the northeast is a sprawling industrial city with a 19th-century core that is a legacy of its heyday as the first capital of the modern Serbian state. Spend the morning at its central sights; save time for the moving October 21st Memorial Museum, dedicated to the civilians massacred by the Nazis in 1941. In the afternoon head to **Topola** *(see p75)* to see the remarkable Karađorđe Mausoleum Church of St George. Either stay here overnight or continue north towards Belgrade.

Day 9: Novi Sad
Northwest of Belgrade on the A1/E75 lies **Novi Sad** *(see pp92–5)* with its fine architecture and museums, as well as the imposing Petrovaradin Fortress across the Danube. The main sights could detain you for a couple of days but, if time is short, they can be managed in a day.

Day 10: Fruška Gora
The wooded hills of Fruška Gora are a short drive south. Spend a leisurely day driving or hiking to the region's pretty **monasteries** *(see p97)*, with lunch at Krušedol or Vrdnik. Alternatively, plan a tasting tour of a few of the area's 60 or so wineries before enjoying therapeutic treatments at the Banja Vrdnik spa. Head back to Belgrade via the A1/E75.

Corridor decorated with a religious icon at Fruška Gora's Grgeteg Monastery

Putting Serbia on the Map

Located in southeastern Europe, Serbia is a landlocked country covering 77,474 sq km (29,913 sq miles) with a population of around 7.2 million. It is bordered by Hungary, Romania, Croatia, Bosnia and Herzegovina, Montenegro, Macedonia and Bulgaria. The Danube, the country's largest river, separates the northern plains of Vojvodina from the rest of Serbia and forms a border with Romania to the east and Croatia to the west. The Stara planina, Rhodope and Carpathian Mountains run along Serbia's eastern border with Bulgaria and Romania while the southwest is dominated by the Dinaric Alps. Belgrade, the capital, is Serbia's largest city and stands at the confluence of the Danube and Sava Rivers.

For additional map symbols *see back flap*

HUNGARY
Hódmezővásárhely
Szeged
Arad
Nădlac
Subotica
Radna
Brad
Vinga
Ilia
Deva
Senta
Bačka Topola
Balint
Kikinda
Timișoara
Lugoj
Tisa
Bretea-Română
Novi Bečej
Vrbas
ROMANIA
Tamiš
Zrenjanin
Deta
Gătaia
Caransebeș
Bačka Palanka
Novi Sad
Reșița
Carpathian Mountains
Sremski Karlovci
Kovačica
Vršac
Inđija
Padinska Skela
Uljma
Batajnica
Bela Crkva
Pančevo
Motru
Belgrade
Šabac
Sava
Danube (Dunav)
Orșova
Drobeta-Turnu Severin
Smederevo
Požarevac
Kladovo
Derdap National Park
Koceljeva
Kučevo
Lazarevac
Lajkovac
SERBIA
Majdanpek
Klokočevac
Valjevo
Aranđelovac
Krespoljin
Topola
Svilajnac
Negotin
Great Morava
Kučaj Mountains
Kragujevac
Bor
Timok
Vidin
Borač
Jagodina
Zaječar
Užice
Čačak
Požega
Paraćin
Gledić Mountains
Dimovo
Mokra Gora
Boljevac
Kraljevo
Rtanj 1,565 m
BULGARIA
Tornik 1,496 m
Ibar
West Morava
Sokobanja
Novo Selo
Ivanjica
Kruševac
Aleksinac
Knjaževac
Vinishte
Prijepolje
Svrljig
Rhodope Mountains
Uvac
Stara planina
Raška
Pančićev vrh 2,016 m
Prokuplje
Niš
Kopaonik
Pirot
Kuršumlija
South Morava
Novi Pazar
Bijelo Polje
Leskovac
Dimitrovgrad
Mojkovac
Podujevo
Grdelica
MONTENEGRO
Mitrovica
Tran
Vladičin Han
KOSOVO
Priština
Pernik
Vranje
Vukël
Maja e Jezercës 2,693 m
Bujanovac
Zelenčev vrb 1,574 m
Izvor
Kyustendil
Prizren
Kačanik
Kriva Palanka
Kumanovo
Shkodër
Pukë
Kukës
Tetovo
Skopje
Kočani
Delčevo
ALBANIA
MACEDONIA
Lezhë
Gostivar
Štip
Milot

A PORTRAIT OF SERBIA

Serbia's stunning scenery and temperate climate make it an ideal year-round tourist destination whose tremendous potential is only just beginning to be fully realized. The capital, Belgrade, is a bustling urban centre with a thriving cultural scene and some of the best nightlife in the Balkans, and the country's wealth of broad rivers, rugged mountains and picturesque rural landscapes combined with its rich heritage of sublime monasteries, mighty fortresses and Roman remains make it a rewarding destination where visitors can expect a warm welcome from a people known for their hospitality and open-heartedness.

From prehistoric cave dwellings, Mesolithic settlements and entire Roman cities that lie just beneath the surface to dramatic hilltop fortresses, Serbia's archaeological heritage is remarkably diverse and has filled its award-winning museums with artifacts dating back thousands of years.

The mountain ranges covering two-thirds of Serbia's territory dominate the south and provide spectacular backdrops to towns and villages where shepherds still graze their flocks and farmers rear pigs in lush foothills and valleys. The country's picturesque rural heartlands produce plums to make *šljivovica* – the national drink – together with an abundance of fruit, dairy and meat products for which Serbia is renowned. The great northern plains of Vojvodina, where corn and wheat fields stretch for miles in all directions, are known as Serbia's bread basket. Here, and across the rest of the country, harvest and folk festivals that have been enjoyed for centuries continue to be celebrated with vigour. Subotica's wheat harvest festival is famed for its colourful folk traditions, the nation's wine-producing regions are noted for their week-long festivities and several towns host lively annual folklore events.

The music festivals of Serbia are equally important, attracting visitors from across the world. Hundreds of thousands of people swamp the tiny village of Guča in Western Serbia during its legendary trumpet festival, while Novi Sad's award-winning EXIT music festival and the Niš and Belgrade jazz festivals showcase performers from all over the globe.

Zasavica Special Nature Reserve near Fruška Gora, one of Serbia's best preserved wetlands and a major wildlife refuge

◄ Naïve art depicting a harvest scene, painted by the well-known Slovak artist Zuzana Chalupova from Kovačica

People and Society

While much has changed in Serbia's cities, where Ottoman-era skylines of minarets have long since been replaced by modern European architecture, the pace of life remains slower than in the West – people tend to wake early and linger over coffee and cigarettes in cafés before a mid-afternoon finish and an evening spent with friends in the very same cafés. Serbs are known for being open, relaxed and quick to make friendships. Having borne the brunt of economic sanctions and NATO bombs in the recent past, they are often curious to know how they are viewed by the outside world and are keen to communicate their side of the story.

Of the country's 7.2 million inhabitants, 85 per cent are Orthodox Christian Serbs. Muslim Bosniaks form the majority in the southwest and Serbs, Catholic Hungarians, Croats and Bunjevci live in the north along with small minorities of Romanians and Slovaks. Many Orthodox Serbs visit monasteries and churches to light candles and venerate icons and relics, but few take religion seriously enough to embark on the 40-day fasts before Christmas and Easter. All Orthodox Serbs do, however, honour their family's patron saint each year by inviting their friends over for the *slava*, a large, uniquely Serbian celebratory feast which was added to the UNESCO Intangible Cultural Heritage List in 2014.

Serbians relaxing with friends at a café in Sokobanja, Eastern Serbia

Ravanica Monastery fresco of St Trifun, patron saint of viticulture

Cultural Influences

Lying at the crossroads of Europe, Serbia has been a major meeting point of Eastern and Western cultures and faiths for hundreds of years. The revered Serbian saint Sava (1175–1235) gloomily noted in the 12th century that Serbs were "doomed to be the East in the West and the West in the East", a point vividly illustrated by the 13th-century Raška School of church architecture, which combined Roman motifs with Byzantine frescoes and structure. After the nascent Serbian medieval state was crushed by the Ottoman Empire, Oriental culture dominated for several hundred years; its impact can still be seen today, most obviously in its influence upon Serbian cuisine.

Baroque tendencies were borrowed from the Habsburgs in the 17th century, particularly in Vojvodina by Serbians who had fled from the Ottomans during the Great Migrations. Many Serbs returned to Belgrade after its liberation in the 19th century and helped to replace its Oriental architecture with a European cityscape. Western trends were followed until Tito and his Communists took power in 1945, but the Soviet Realism they adopted was abandoned when Tito fell out with Stalin in 1948. During the 1960s and 70s the country became one of the more Western-leaning of the Balkan nations, with the latest rock, pop and jazz music freely available and European fashions in vogue.

Government and Economy

From pariah state under the single-party rule of Socialist Slobodan Milošević in the 1990s to parliamentary democracy and aspiring EU member, Serbia has come far in recent years. Crippling economic sanctions combined with the damage caused by NATO air strikes in 1999 left Serbia's economy just half the size it had been in 1990. Milošević was forced to resign in October 2000 after massive, widespread protests against election fraud. His successor, a prominent opposition leader named Zoran Đinđić, was assassinated in 2003; this was followed by several years of political instability. It was only after the arrests of Bosnian Serb war criminals Radovan Karadžić in 2008 and Ratko Mladić in 2011 that significant progress was made towards EU accession talks. In 2012 Serbia received full EU candidate status; the next year it took steps towards normalizing relations with Kosovo to facilitate the start of its EU entry talks. In 2014 the EU agreed to open negotiations on Serbia's accession. The Kosovo issue is still unresolved, and although talks began in late 2015 it seems unlikely that Serbia will enter the EU before 2020.

The country currently suffers from a high unemployment rate of around 19 per cent, but International Monetary Fund loans are likely to continue funding infrastructure projects, and trade liberalization and direct foreign investment have rejuvenated some of its industrial sectors. A major fruit exporter, Serbia is the world's second-largest producer of plums and raspberries, although its most successful export by far is tennis champion Novak Đoković.

Tourism and Outdoor Activities

Alongside its wealth of sights, Serbia offers a wide range of activity holidays. The country's picturesque mountain regions entice a stream of outdoor enthusiasts who come for hiking, biking, canyoning and paragliding. The meandering rivers are perfect for kayaking and rafting, and pony trekking and off-roading are also catching on. The national parks harbour an abundance of flora and fauna; several pairs of endangered eastern imperial eagles are among the species that attract keen bird-watchers from all over the world.

Those in search of less demanding adventures can opt for a heritage steam train ride high into the mountains at Mokra Gora or visit the wine-producing regions of Negotin, Vršac or Fruška Gora for a vineyard tour. For complete relaxation, a trip to the natural hot springs at one of the many spa resorts is a must. Serbia's tourism infrastructure has seen significant investment in recent years, so whatever you choose to do, staff at the country's outstanding network of visitor information centres will be able to assist. The locals are usually keen to help too, and the warmth of their hospitality will remain in visitors' memories as long as images of the country's magnificent monuments and splendid landscapes.

The gooseneck meanders of the West Morava River *(meandri Morave)*, Ovčar-Kablar Gorge, Western Serbia

Landscape and Wildlife

The largely unspoilt and little visited landscapes of Serbia encompass a broad range of habitats that are home to a remarkable 80 per cent of Europe's bird species and around 65 per cent of European mammals, while 50 per cent of the continent's freshwater fish species can be found in its rivers. With several well-run national parks and nature parks, the country is a veritable paradise for nature lovers and adventure sports enthusiasts.

A climber on Trem, the highest peak on Suva planina mountain near Niš in Southern Serbia

Northern Lakes

The north is strewn with lakes and wetlands. The ancient Lakes Ludaš and Palić, with their meandering streams, are often called the "pearls of the plains". The small islands of Palić and the reedy surrounds of Ludaš are home to marsh birds such as herons, bitterns and bearded reedlings.

The European otter *(Lutra lutra)*, the most widely distributed of otter species, can be found all across the Danube River basin.

The ferruginous duck *(Aythya nyroca)* is a diving duck that inhabits shallow expanses of water rich in submerged vegetation.

The lax-flowered orchid *(Anacamptis laxiflora)* is native to western and southern Europe. It blooms from April to June and can reach up to 60 cm (27 in) in height.

Mountains

South of Belgrade the land is predominantly mountainous, with the Dinaric Alps in the west and Stara planina in the east. Kopaonik in the south is Serbia's largest massif, with some of the country's highest peaks set amidst a mixture of broad grasslands and dense forests.

Golden eagles *(Aquila chrysaetos)* are renowned for their hunting skills and can be easily identified by the distinctive way they spread out their wingtip feathers like fingers when gliding.

Edelweiss flowers *(Leontopodium alpinum)* are covered in dense white hairs that protect them from the cold at high altitudes.

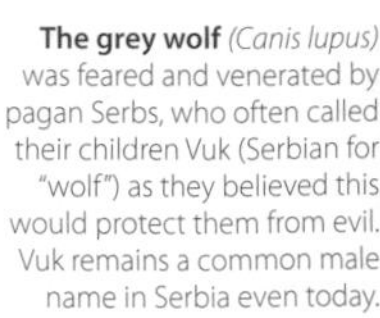

The grey wolf *(Canis lupus)* was feared and venerated by pagan Serbs, who often called their children Vuk (Serbian for "wolf") as they believed this would protect them from evil. Vuk remains a common male name in Serbia even today.

Bird-watching in Serbia

Deliblato Sands (Deliblatska Peščara) in the Vojvodina region is particularly popular with bird-watchers due to its abundance of bird species and its proximity to Novi Sad and Belgrade. Once part of a prehistoric desert, it is now a sandy region with 330 sq km (127 sq miles) of grasslands, agricultural land and mixed forests fringed by the Danube, Karaš and Tamiš Rivers. Resident birds include saker falcons, lesser spotted eagles, black kites, eastern imperial eagles and sand martins. The area is also known for its large population of grey wolves.

A male ortolan bunting *(Emberiza hortulana)*

Rivers

Most of Serbia falls within the drainage basin of the mighty Danube, which flows for 588 km (365 miles) through the country. Its most spectacular stretch is at the Iron Gates, Europe's longest river gorge, where ancient beech and oak forests shelter wolves, jackals and bears.

Beluga sturgeon *(Huso huso)* populations in the Danube have dropped significantly since the construction of the Đerdap Dam blocked their migration route.

Lilacs *(Syringa vulgaris)* are usually a light shade of purple, but white, pale yellow, pink and even burgundy blooms are also commonly seen.

Longhorn beetles *(Cerambycidae)* can commonly be found in woodland along the Danube, which also serves as an ideal home for a variety of other beetles including stag and bark.

Arable Plains

The vast fertile plains north of the Danube are known as the bread basket of Serbia. They cover 21,500 sq km (8,300 sq miles) of the Pannonian Basin, of which 85 per cent is planted with fields of wheat, maize, soybean and sugar beet as well as sunflowers, grapes, walnuts and other crops.

Roe deer *(Capreolus capreolus)* live in woods and grasslands and are primarily crepuscular. When alarmed, these small deer make a hoarse barking sound.

Wild boar *(Sus scrofa)* are sociable animals with an acute sense of smell and hearing, and can be spotted in forests and marshlands across the region.

The eastern imperial eagle *(Aquila heliaca)*, once the heraldic animal of the Austrian monarchy, is now classified as vulnerable on the IUCN Red List. It is close to extinction in much of Europe, and there are just four or five breeding pairs left in Serbia.

Serbian Orthodox Church

Firmly established during the golden age of St Sava and the Nemanjić dynasty from the 13th to the 15th centuries, the Serbian Orthodox Church went on to suffer centuries of oppression under Ottoman rule before experiencing a revival in the 19th century. Spectacular medieval monasteries and cathedrals across the country attest to the important role of the church in Serbia and in the daily lives of the people.

Icon of the patron saint Nicholas

Elements of the Orthodox Church

An element unique to the Serbian Orthodox Church is the slava. *Each family has a patron saint, regarded as a protector and passed from father to son and husband to wife. The* slava *is the family's annual celebration of their saint's feast day; this can sometimes last two or three days. Frescoes and icons, common in Orthodox churches, are viewed as reminders of the presence of God and, in the days when congregations were largely illiterate, were used to communicate a visual story that could be universally understood.*

Holy Mother of God, an early 12th-century fresco of the Constantinople School, Studenica Monastery

Illuminated Manuscripts
Monasteries encouraged the creation of illuminated manuscripts in an effort to preserve Serbian culture and religion. Miroslav's Gospel (c. 1185) is considered one of the most important Serbian works.

Iconostasis
These rich icon-covered screens separate the apse from the naos, where the liturgy takes place.

Altar
Set in the apse, altars are traditionally covered with brocaded cloth. Relics are often placed within them.

Holy Relics
The bodies of saints are thought to be transformed by divine grace, and the veneration of their relics is an important aspect of Orthodox Christianity. Ravanica holds the relics of Prince Lazar.

Serbia's Orthodox Churches and Monasteries

Orthodox churches in Serbia are oriented east, symbolically facing the light of God and the eschaton. They generally have a large central dome representing the heavens, where an image of Christ can be found gazing down upon the congregation. The floorplan is usually rectangular, symbolizing the Ark of Salvation, or cruciform, embodying the Cross. The building is traditionally divided into the narthex, nave and altar (or sanctuary); the latter is separated from worshippers by an iconostasis and cannot be approached without the permission of the priest.

Crna Reka Monastery
This small monastery was built into an inaccessible rock face in the 16th century to isolate its monks from the distractions of the outside world and to protect them from the Turks.

Temple of St Sava, Belgrade
One of the largest Orthodox churches in the world, this monumental cathedral is built on a Greek cross plan and is 91 m (299 ft) from east to west and 81 m (266 ft) from north to south.

Sts Peter and Paul, Novi Pazar
Serbia's oldest intact church, built in the 9th century, features a circular interior with three radial apses and several old frescoes. It was once the seat of the bishops of Raška.

Religion in Serbia

The Serbs began to convert to Christianity in great numbers in the 7th century. Rome and Constantinople tussled for primacy until the Eastern Orthodox Church broke with Rome in 1064. In the early 13th century, the Serbian church became an autocephalous body within the Eastern Orthodox Church. Around 85 per cent of the population are Serbian Orthodox Christians today. Six per cent are Roman Catholics from ethnic groups such as the Croats, Hungarians, Bunjevci and Roma who live in northern Vojvodina; this religiously and ethnically diverse area also includes German Protestants, Hungarian Calvinists, Slovak Lutherans and Greek-Catholic Ukrainians. During Ottoman rule, many Serbs converted to Islam and today make up 5 per cent of the population, living mostly in the southwest, especially around Novi Pazar. The country's once thriving Jewish community was decimated during World War II, and there are only about 800 Jews left in Serbia.

The Altun-alem Mosque in Novi Pazar

Serbian Art

Renowned for their medieval church frescoes, Serbia's monasteries are its oldest art galleries. The country's artistic output continued to be almost exclusively religious until the late 18th century when Western influences had an impact on creative trends. Galleries across Serbia have fascinating exhibitions of 19th- and 20th-century pieces by local artists, and Belgrade's Museum of Contemporary Art in Zemun holds a superb collection of modern works.

Depiction of Christ Pantocrator in a 13th-century fresco at Žiča Monastery

Medieval Art

Serbia's church art dates back to the medieval state's formal adoption of Christianity in the 9th century, and some of the earliest examples can be seen at Novi Pazar's Sts Peter and Paul Church. Although Serbian art preserved its Orthodox character and Byzantine iconographic compositions for centuries, artists started to experiment with more expressive styles that led to the monumental paintings at Sopoćani Monastery. At Studenica a Western-influenced move towards Classicism enhanced the emotional character of compositions, but these developments were cut short by the fall of the Serbian Empire in the 15th century.

A pair of angels gaze down upon the Crucifixion from Heaven.

Isaiah, one of the four major prophets, is also shown in Heaven.

Studenica Monastery Frescoes
The monumental Crucifixion scene is on the west wall of the Church of the Virgin Mary. It was painted by an unknown master from Constantinople.

A moving depiction of the Virgin Mary emphasizes her deep sorrow.

Jesus on the Cross is a remarkably realistic portrayal of the human body.

St John the Baptist is portrayed next to Jesus with an expression of grief.

Baroque Art

The Great Migration of the Serbs to Vojvodina in 1690 was a crucial turning point for Serbian art as it brought exposure to Western trends. The 18th-century artists Teodor Kračun and Stefan Tenecki transformed traditional Orthodox icons into Baroque portraits; this became one of the key elements of a distinctive new Serbian culture. Kračun's iconostasis at Sremski Karlovci's Orthodox cathedral and Tenecki's landscapes at Krušedol are among Serbia's finest Baroque masterpieces.

Krušedol Monastery Landscapes
In 1756 Tenecki painted Baroque landscapes under the church's choir windows at this early 16th-century Fruška Gora monastery.

19th-Century Art

Landscapes and portraiture detailing social change, such as Arsa Teodorović's work, and Đura Jakšić's Romantic art were popular until the late 19th century, when artists such as Đorđe Krstić adopted Realism. Their monumental paintings showed idealized versions of Serbian history, supporting the emergence of a national ideology.

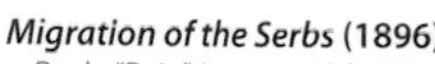

***Migration of the Serbs* (1896)**
Painted by Pavle "Paja" Jovanović (1859–1957), one of Serbia's greatest Realists, this depicts Serbs fleeing the Ottomans in 1690.

Modernism

Early 20th-century Serbian art was heavily influenced by Munich and Paris trends. Impressionist Milan Milovanović's work tended to be more subdued than that of French artists, while Nadežda Petrović developed a distinctive Expressionist style after discovering Van Gogh and Munch's art. Avant-Garde's local version, Yugo-Dada, was founded by Dragan Aleksić, while Surrealism also had its Serbian adherents.

Detail, *Drunken Boat* (1927)
Sava Šumanović's (1896–1942) early masterpiece showing a debauched party caused an uproar when it was painted. His bold style was influenced by Cubism and Fauvism.

Post-War and Contemporary Art

Social Realism dominated after World War II, but Tito's break with Stalin led to state acceptance of alternative genres and the creation of the December Group (1950s), who focused on geometric abstract art. The Black Wave cinema of the 1960s saw directors such as Želimir Žilnik rejecting official optimism and exposing the dark side of socialism; Abstract Expressionism, Constructivism and Suprematism emerged soon after. By 1970 conceptual art was established in Belgrade and Novi Sad, but despite this the cultural scene remained limited by official policy; it was finally freed from the constraints of a closed society after the fall of Communism.

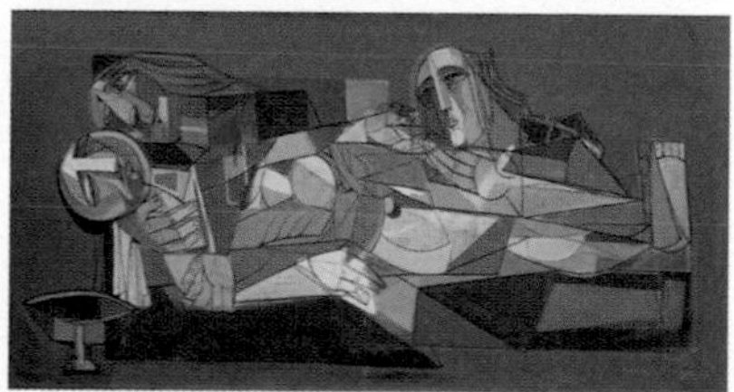

***Pieta* (1956)**
Heavily influenced by Cezanne's Realism and Picasso's Blue Period, Lazar Vozarević (1925–68) was a leading Modernist who strove to express the relationship between the conscious and subconscious.

Architecture

The country's development of elegant church architecture was abruptly curtailed by centuries of Ottoman rule that favoured the proliferation of mosques and Turkish culture. Until the mid-19th century the urban skylines of Serbia were dominated by minarets, but the demise of the Ottoman Empire precipitated a nationalistic rush to Westernization through the construction of the fine Neo-Renaissance buildings that define most Serbian towns and cities today.

The Church of the Virgin Mary, Studenica Monastery

Medieval Church Architecture

Early Byzantine church architecture developed into the Romanesque-influenced Raška style that produced Studenica Monastery. A resurgence of Oriental influences lead to the Serbo-Byzantine style, which was superseded by the Morava School of church architecture in the 14th century.

Ravanica Monastery
With a trefoil plan, intricate stonework and decorative elements, the monastery is said to have been the birthplace of the Morava School.

Ottoman Architecture

Much of Serbia's Ottoman heritage was destroyed after the departure of the Turks in the mid-19th century, but some fine examples have survived. Among these are the 16th-century Bajrakli Mosque in Belgrade and the early 18th-century Ottoman fortress in Niš. Belgrade's Palace of Princess Ljubica exemplifies the crossover between Ottoman and Western design styles, while Novi Pazar has retained a distinctly Oriental atmosphere and boasts some of the best-preserved Ottoman architecture in the country.

Niš Fortress, Istanbul Gate
Built in 1723, the massive fort contains the Ottoman arsenal, a Turkish hammam and the Bali-beg Mosque.

National Theatre, Belgrade
Designed in 1869 by prolific Serbian architect Alexander Bugarski, this was modelled on Milan's La Scala. The original façade was destroyed in World War I and replaced in 1922.

Neo-Renaissance Architecture

In order to create the fine city centres necessary to signal its transformation from an Ottoman vassal into a contemporary Westernized country, Serbia drew upon all the trends of 19th-century European architecture. The combination of Classicist, Romanesque, Gothic, Baroque and Renaissance influences resulted in the broad Neo-Renaissance style that would later be supplanted by Eclecticism. Splendid examples include Belgrade's National Theatre, Novi Sad's 1895 City Hall by Geörgy Molnàr and Sremski Karlovci's 1892 Patriarch's Palace by Vladimir Nikolić.

Art Nouveau Architecture

The Vojvodina region of northern Serbia was heavily influenced by Western architectural styles, which resulted in the renowned Art Nouveau architecture of Subotica. The Raichle Mansion is perhaps the country's best example of the style, while the spectacular City Hall building blends elements from Hungarian folklore with the organic lines and unusual colour combinations typical of Art Nouveau.

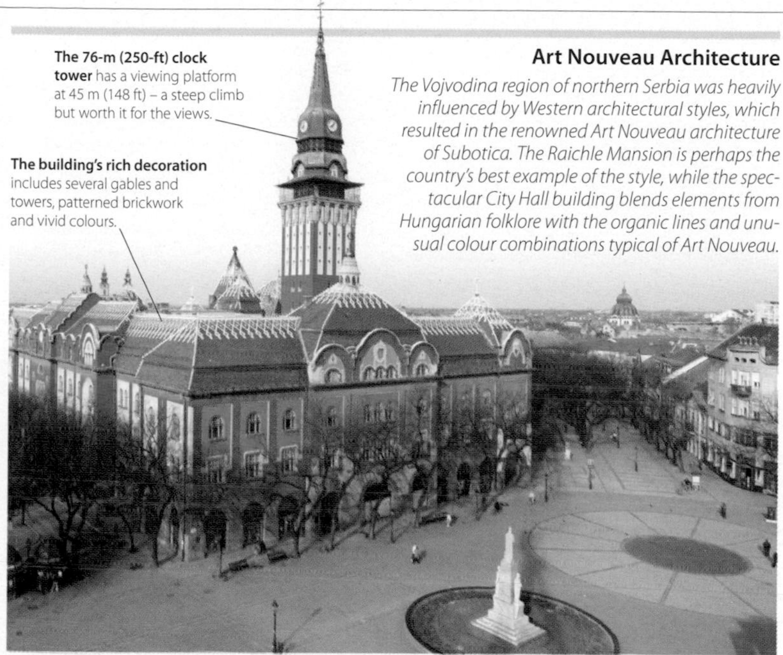

The 76-m (250-ft) clock tower has a viewing platform at 45 m (148 ft) – a steep climb but worth it for the views.

The building's rich decoration includes several gables and towers, patterned brickwork and vivid colours.

Subotica's City Hall, designed by Hungarian architects Marcell Komor and Dezső Jakab and built in 1910

Modern Architecture

Tito's early split with Stalin meant that very few Social Realist public buildings were built in the country. Belgrade's Museum of Contemporary Art, built by Ivan Antić and Ivanka Raspopović in 1965, is a Modernist take on the Socialist style; Genex Tower, built by Mihajlo Mitrović in 1980, is the city's most striking example of Brutalism. The Belgrade city skyline has been transformed in recent years by major new landmarks such as Ada Bridge, designed by Viktor Markelj and Peter Gabrijelčič in 2012.

Ada Bridge, Belgrade
Also called Sava Bridge, this impressive single-pylon, cable-stayed bridge cuts across Ada Ciganlija and took three years to complete.

Street Names

It is common for streets in Serbia to be known by multiple names, yet only the latest version will be listed on maps. Squares and roads were often renamed to reflect political circumstances, particularly during the turbulent 20th century with the victory of Communism after World War II and its collapse in the 1990s. Kralja Petra, one of the oldest streets in Belgrade, was originally called Dubrovnik; in 1904 it was renamed Kralja Petra to honour the newly installed King Peter I; in 1946 its name was changed to 7th July by the Communist Party to mark the 1941 partisan uprising against the Nazis; in 1997 it reverted to Kralja Petra. Another Belgrade street started off as Dva Bela Goluba in 1872 and was changed to Svetogorska in 1896, Bitoljska in 1922, Georges Clemenceau in 1930, Svetogorska again in 1943, Lola Ribar in 1946, and Svetogorska yet again from 1997 onwards.

SERBIA THROUGH THE YEAR

Serbia has four distinct seasons with a mild spring, a long and hot summer, a pleasant autumn and an icy winter. The holidays of the Serbian Orthodox Church are tied to the Julian calendar so Christmas falls around two weeks later than in the West, but all non-religious dates follow the Gregorian calendar. Cultural events throughout the year attract visitors, performers and artists from all over the world. There is something for everyone, with events ranging from puppet theatre, food fairs and local folklore shows to flower carnivals, boat shows and internationally renowned music festivals. In fact, the summer festival calendar can get so packed that the only difficulty is deciding which event to visit.

Spring

Serbia is at its most beautiful in spring when temperatures are pleasant, the lush countryside is blooming with flowers and the mountains are still capped with snow. Many Serbians observe Lent, the year's most important fast, before Easter. Spring also sees the start of the concert festival season in Novi Sad.

March

Great Lent (Vaskršnji post) *(Feb/Mar/Apr)*, nationwide. The Great Lent fast lasts for 40 days before Easter. Most Serbians see this as a time of self-restriction, but only the strictest Orthodox Christians fully participate through religious confession and shunning meat and dairy products for the whole period.

April

Orthodox Easter (Pravoslavni uskrs) *(Mar/Apr/May)*, nationwide. On Easter Sunday Serbians go to church and greet one another with the phrases *Hristos vaskrse* ("Christ has risen") and *Vaistinu vaskrse* ("Truly He is risen"). A popular Easter ritual involves a game where participants take it in turns to tap their decorative hard-boiled eggs together. The owner of the last unbroken egg wins the game.

NOMUS (Novosadske muzučke svečanosti) *(mid-Apr)*, Novi Sad. Classical music aficionados can enjoy over a week of concerts at various venues, including the synagogue *(see p93)*.

May

Cubanero *(late May)*, Novi Sad. Serbia's largest salsa dance festival involves performances, parties and workshops.

International Festival of Children's Theatres (Međunarodni festival pozorišta za decu) *(late May)*, Subotica. This enormously entertaining festival of puppetry and theatre, held at various venues, lasts a week. Check dates online in advance.

Sunflowers, widely farmed across Serbia in summer

Jazz Fest Valjevo (Valjevski džez festival) *(late May)*, Valjevo. This four-day event attracts musicians from Europe and beyond.

Summer

Serbia's summers are packed with cultural events that take place all around the country, from major international music festivals to folklore gatherings.

June

Tour de Serbie *(May/Jun)*, various cities. International cycling race across Serbia. The route varies each year but generally includes Belgrade.

International Pančevo Carnival (Internacionalni Pančevački karneval) *(mid-Jun)*, Pančevo. Major festival with parades, concerts, and street entertainers from all over the Balkans.

Arsenal Fest *(late Jun)*, Kragujevac. A high-energy rock festival in the city's disused industrial zone with bands from Serbia and the former Yugoslav states.

Flower Carnival (Karneval cveća) *(late Jun)*, Bela Crkva. First recorded in 1852, this annual flower carnival is among Europe's oldest.

Belgrade Calling *(late Jun)*, Belgrade. Held in Kalemegdan Fortress, this rock festival has been headlined by international legends such as Judas Priest.

St Vitus's Day (Vidovdan) *(28 Jun)*, nationwide. Although not a public holiday, it is of special significance to Serbs as the Battle of Kosovo *(see p34)* took place on this date in 1389.

Danube Day *(29 Jun)*, nationwide. Watersports, excursions and exhibitions take place across the Danube River basin.

July

Belgrade Boat Carnival (Beogradski karneval brodova) *(Jul/Aug)*, Belgrade. A huge riverside party and traditional decorated boat parade on the Sava and Danube.

Costumed crew on a decorated boat taking part in the Belgrade Boat Carnival

Merry Downriver Ride (Veseli spust) *(early Jul)*, Kraljevo. About 3,000 boats float down the Ibar from Maglič Fortress to Kraljevo.
EXIT Music Festival *(mid-Jul)*, Novi Sad. Festival of rock, pop, electronic, metal, punk and alternative music *(see p95)*.
Jazzibar Festival *(mid-Jul)*, Kraljevo. International jazz players perform in this city set on the banks of the Ibar River.
Wreath of Vršac (Vršački venac) *(mid-Jul)*, Vršac. A colourful festival focusing on international folklore.
Palić European Film Festival *(late Jul)*, Subotica. Film screenings at indoor and outdoor venues at the lake resort of Palić.
Hillsup Festival *(late Jul)*, Zlatibor. Music and activities to promote healthy living.
ParkFest *(late Jul)*, Užice. Acts from Serbia and the former Yugolav states feature in this rock festival.
Gitarijada *(late Jul)*, Zaječar. Guitar talent is showcased at this well-established festival of guitar music.

Souvenir from the Guča Trumpet Festival

August

Serbian Youth Culture Festival (Festival kulture mladih srbije) *(early Aug)*, Knjaževac. Youth art, poetry, music and performance.
Old City Music Festival (Muzički festival "Stari Grad") *(early Aug)*, Novi Pazar. Rock music festival.
World Music Festival (Muzički festival "Svet muzike") *(early Aug)*, Sirogojno. Traditional Balkan music is performed at this open-air museum village.
International Folk Festival (Međunarodni folklorni festival) *(early Aug)*, Pirot. Five days of lively parades and concerts.
Guča Trumpet Festival (Dragačevski sabor trubača) *(early Aug)*, Guča. This renowned brass band festival attracts well over 600,000 visitors.
Srem Folk Fest *(mid-Aug)*, Sremska Mitrovica. Folklore festival lasting five days.
Dužijanca *(mid-Aug)*, Subotica. During this harvest festival, traditionally costumed participants ride carriages decorated with wreaths woven from wheat sheaves.

The Roy Hargrove Quintet performing at Nišville International Jazz Festival

Nišville International Jazz Festival (Internacionalni džez festival) *(mid-Aug)*, Niš. The town's biggest festival is held in its huge Ottoman fortress.
Sokobanja Accordian Festival (Prva harmonika Sokobanje) *(mid-Aug)*, Sokobanja. Serbian and Macedonian artists compete for the top accordion prize.
Belgrade Beer Fest (Beogradski festival piva) *(late Aug)*, Belgrade. This week-long event is visited by around one million people.
Interetno Festival *(late Aug)*, Subotica. Gathering of international folklore groups.

Climate

Most of the country has a temperate climate, but the southwest borders on subtropical and continental. There are good levels of year-round sunshine. Low-lying areas can be stiflingly hot in summer, and autumn is warmer than spring. The continental rainfall pattern means higher volumes in the warmer months, except for the southwest, which sees most rain in autumn.

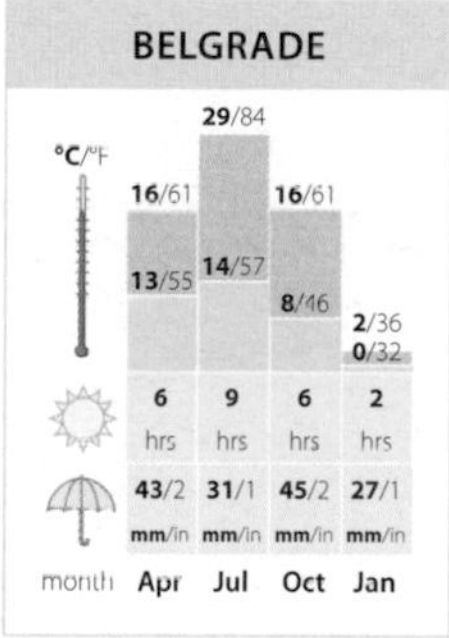

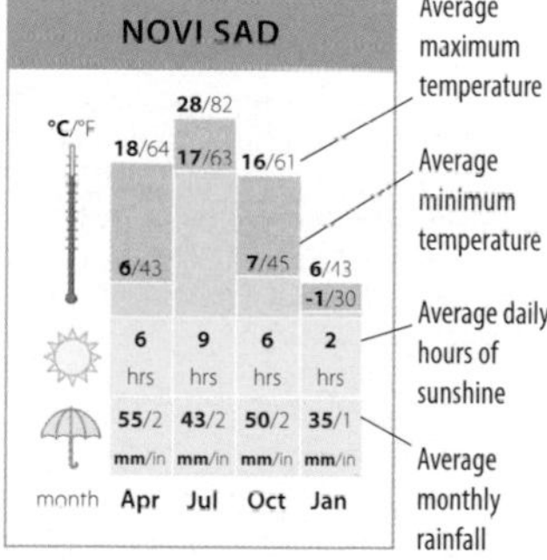

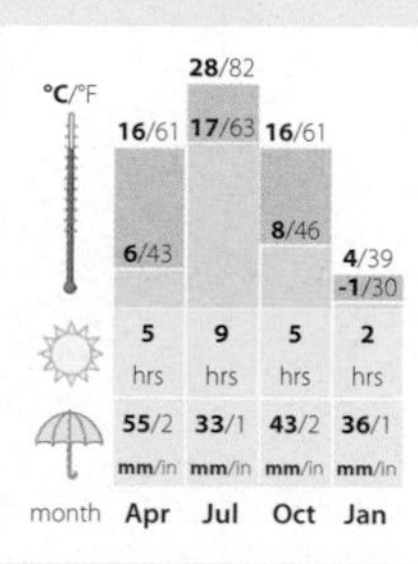

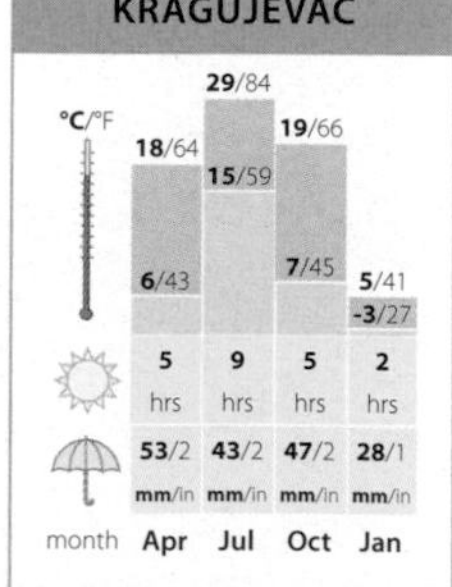

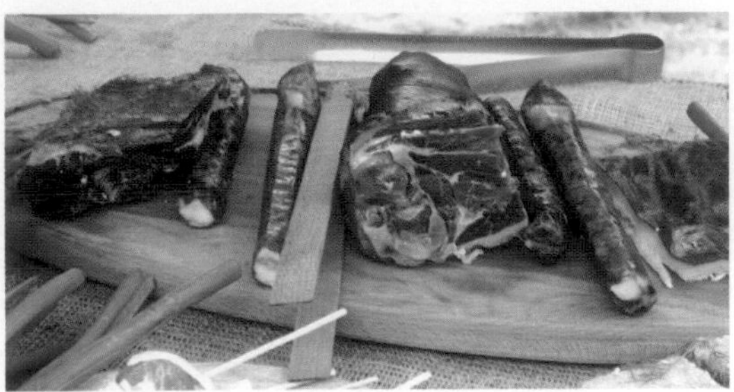

Kobasice prepared for the Leskovac Grill Festival (Roštiljijada) in September

Autumn

Autumn is a pleasant season in Serbia. With warm weather and little rainfall, it is a great time to explore the mountainous regions of the country. September is the month of the grape harvest, with a host of lively festivals to celebrate it. The cultural season continues well into November with music and dance festivals.

September

Leskovac Grill Festival (Roštiljijada) *(Aug/Sep)*, Leskovac. This legendary carnivorous festival attracts over 700,000 visitors across five days *(see p132)*.

Kraljevo Film Festival (Kraljevski filmski festival) *(first week of Sep)*, Kraljevo. Competitive festival dedicated to international and Serbian short films.

Autumn in Smederevo (Smederevska jesen) *(first week of Sep)*, Smederevo. A celebration of the year's grape harvest and a showcase for the rich medieval history of the town.

International Festival of Orthodox Film (Međunarodni festival pravoslavnog filma) *(first week of Sep)*, Kruševac. This unique event screens films from Orthodox Christian countries.

Street Musicians Festival (Festival uličnih svirača) *(first week of Sep)*, Novi Sad. Two days of street performances by local and international artists.

Burek Days (Dani bureka) *(early Sep)*, Niš. Several calorific days devoted entirely to the production and consumption of Niš's favourite pastry *(see p132)*.

Ljubičevo Equestrian Games (Ljubičevske konjičke igre) *(early Sep)*, Požarevac. A week of horse exhibitions, equestrian skills and races, plus fireworks, bands and medieval contests of skill.

Belgrade International Theatre Festival (Beogradski internacionalni teatarski festival) *(mid-Sep)*, Belgrade. Highly regarded festival with performances at several independent theatres.

Days of Mokranjac (Mokranjčevi dani) *(mid-Sep)*, Negotin. Festival of choral music honouring the legacy of Stevan Stojanović Mokranjac and featuring several Serbian and international choirs.

Sremski Karlovci Wine Festival (Karlovačka berba) *(mid-Sep)*, Sremski Karlovci. Lively event to mark the grape harvest with wine, food and music.

Vršac Grape and Wine Festival (Vršačka berba Grožđebal) *(mid-Sep)*, Vršac. This celebration of the grape harvest offers fireworks, a parade and a concert.

October

Pork Crackling Festival (Festival duvan čvaraka) *(mid-Oct)*, Valjevo. Butchers demonstrate 200-year-old methods of making the town's famed pork crackling.

Belgrade Music Festival (Beogradske muzičke svečanosti) *(late Oct)*, Belgrade. Founded in 1969, this is Serbia's oldest classical music festival.

November

Belgrade Book Fair (Beogradski sajam knjiga) *(first week of Nov)*, Belgrade. A week-long celebration of the written word.

Belgrade Jazz Festival (Beogradski džez festival) *(first week of Nov)*, Belgrade. Founded in 1971, Serbia's oldest jazz festival offers world-class music.

Novi Sad Jazz Festival (Novosadski džez festival) *(mid-Nov)*, Novi Sad. Hot on the heels of Belgrade's jazz festival, this event also attracts musicians from around the world.

Dance Fest Novi Sad *(mid-Nov)*, Novi Sad. Three days of multi-discipline performances.

Serbians picking grapes as part of the harvest celebrations in one of Serbia's wine-producing regions

New Year fireworks over Kalemegdan Fortress reflected in the waters of the Sava River, Belgrade

Winter

Winter sees thick snowfall in Serbia's mountainous regions that is perfect for winter sports. The ski season usually lasts from early December to April with the help of artificial snow machines. It is also the time of the Orthodox Nativity Fast and the complex rituals practised at Christmas, while New Year's Eve sees the biggest party of the year across the country.

December

Nativity Fast (Božićni post) *(Dec–Jan)*, nationwide. As with Easter, strict Orthodox Christians observe a 40-day fast leading up to Christmas.

Open Heart Square (Trg otvorenog srca) *(mid-Dec)*, Belgrade. Christmas market on Republic Square with plenty of grilled sausages, mulled wine, Christmas gifts and children's entertainment.

Christmas market sweets, Open Heart Square, Belgrade

New Year's Eve (Doček Nove godine) *(31 Dec)*, nationwide. Despite the Serbian Orthodox Church following the Julian calendar, Serbians celebrate 31 December with much more vigour than the Serbian New Year, which falls on 13 January according to the Gregorian calendar. The new year (Nova godina) is heralded throughout with copious eating, drinking, partying and firework displays. The celebrations continue with equal gusto the next evening.

January

Orthodox Christmas Eve (Badnje veče) *(6 Jan)*, nationwide. Men leave home early in the morning to look for a *badnjak*, an oak log that is to be burnt in the evening; following Serbian tradition, they fire their guns as they set off. In cities, the logs are sold at street stalls. The Christmas Eve meal is strictly vegan, to honour the last day of the Nativity Fast, and is followed by a visit to the local church, where the bells are rung at midnight.

Orthodox Christmas Day (Božić) *(7 Jan)*, nationwide. In Serbia it is not customary to exchange gifts on Christmas Day. The very first visitor a family receives on Christmas Day is known as the *položajnik* – he or she is thought to bring well-being and is often chosen in advance. Rural Serbs will often roast whole pigs or sheep for Christmas dinner; others will have a rich meal of roast pork or lamb. Family members each break off by hand a piece of the *česnica*, a decorative Christmas loaf with a coin inside; it is believed that whoever receives the money will have good fortune that year.

St Sava's Day (Sveti Sava) *(27 Jan)*, nationwide. The day dedicated to Serbia's first archbishop is not a public holiday but Serbs mark it by visiting churches consecrated to him.

Küstendorf International Film and Music Festival (Međunarodni filmski i muzički festival Kustendorf) *(late Jan)*, Drvengrad. A festival organized by the renowned Serbian film director Emir Kusturica in the small village built by him.

February

FEST Belgrade International Film Festival (Medunarodni filmski festival) *(late Feb)*, Belgrade. This respected festival has screened around 4,000 films since its inception in 1971.

Public Holidays

New Year (Nova godina) (1–2 Jan)

Orthodox Christmas Day (Božić) (7 Jan)

Statehood Day (Dan državnosti Srbije) (15–16 Feb)

Orthodox Good Friday (Veliki petak) (late Apr or early May)

Orthodox Easter Monday (Vaskrsni ponedeljak) (late Apr or early May)

International Workers' Day (Praznik rada) (1–2 May)

Armistice Day (Dan primirja) (11 Nov)

THE HISTORY OF SERBIA

Serbia's contemporary culture is deeply rooted in its medieval history, when a strong national consciousness was forged through the adoption of Orthodox Christianity and the establishment of the first Serbian kingdom. Medieval Serbia had conquered most of southeastern Europe before succumbing to the Ottomans in the 15th century; subsequent centuries saw it become the battleground for wars between the Habsburg and Ottoman Empires, both of which left their mark on the country before it was liberated in the 19th century. The Yugoslav Wars of the late 20th century were a dark time for Serbia, but it has since re-established itself and looks set to join the EU in the future.

The earliest evidence of human civilization in Serbia dates back as far as 9,000 BC when Mesolithic tribes settled beside the Danube at Lepenski Vir. Thracians, Illyrians and Dacians arrived around 1,000 BC, and in the 2nd century BC the Romans began their subjugation of the region. In the 6th and 7th centuries, Slavic tribes from east of the Carpathian Mountains and hordes of rampaging Huns and Avars swarmed across the Danube, overrunning much of the Balkan Peninsula. The Croatian Slavs headed west while the Slavic tribes that would later be known as Serbs made their way south and occupied parts of what are now Serbia, Montenegro and Bosnia and Herzegovina.

Orthodox missionaries from Byzantine Constantinople gradually converted the pagan Serbian tribes to Christianity. This paved the way for the emergence of a common culture, but feuding continued until the 12th century when a sense of Serbian national identity finally began to take shape during the Nemanjić dynasty. Stefan Nemanja (r. 1166–96), the first in a long line of powerful Nemanjić rulers, took advantage of a Byzantine Empire weakened by war with the Hungarians and extended Serbia's territory south into Montenegro and Kosovo. His youngest son, Sava (1174–1236), became a monk. It was through the skilful diplomacy of Sava that Serbia was recognized as a kingdom and his brother Stefan II (r. 1196–1228) crowned its first king in 1217. In 1219 Sava became the first archbishop of a newly independent Serbian Orthodox Church, achieving political and religious autonomy for the country.

King Stefan II was succeeded by several generations of capable rulers. His great-great-grandson, Stefan Dušan the Mighty (r. 1331–55), conquered Bulgaria, Macedonia and northern Greece, became emperor of the Serbs and Greeks in 1346 and had even set his sights on Constantinople, but his untimely death in 1355 left Serbia suddenly bereft of a great leader and vulnerable in the face of the expanding Ottoman Empire.

9000 BC Mesolithic tribes settle beside the Danube at Lepenski Vir

200 BC The Roman Empire begins its subjugation of the territory that later became known as Serbia

Tablet of Trajan

AD 600 Slavic tribes, Huns and Avars overrun much of the Balkans

AD 1217 Serbia is recognized as a kingdom; in 1219 Sava becomes archbishop

9000 BC | **6000 BC** | **3000 BC** | **AD 1** | **AD 450** | **AD 900**

Prehistoric figurine found at Lepenski Vir, made from sandstone cobbles and dating to around 7000 BC

1000 BC Thracians, Illyrians and Dacians settle in the area

AD 395 The region becomes part of the Roman Empire

7th–9th century AD Serbian tribes begin to accept Christianity

Staro Hopovo Monastery

AD 1346 Stefan Dušan is crowned emperor

◀ **A 13th-century fresco depicting Emperor Constantine at Mileševa Monastery, Western Serbia**

Ottoman Rule

After the death of Stefan Dušan, quarrels between local lords undermined the nation's unity and in 1371, following its defeat at the Battle of Maritsa, Serbia lost Macedonia and parts of Greece to the Turks. The severely weakened Serbs fell back as the Ottomans pushed north. Prince Lazar (r. 1362–89) attacked them in 1389 at the Battle of Kosovo where both he and the Ottoman Sultan Murad I (r. 1362–89) were killed. Despite heavy losses on both sides, it was Serbia that suffered most as the Ottoman Empire had far greater resources and was able to continue its relentless expansion into the Balkans. The Serbs held out for a few more decades, but finally lost their empire when the Ottomans took Smederevo Fortress in 1459.

Thousands of Serbs fled northwards to Vojvodina and beyond, many were carried off as slaves and those who remained in Serbia became second-class citizens or converted to Islam to make life easier. Christianity was tolerated by the Turks and it was through the Orthodox religion that the national spirit was preserved, but many of the great monasteries were plundered and Serbian towns Islamized with mosques that dwarfed and outnumbered churches.

Serbian Uprisings

After several hundred years under Turkish rule, Serbs had become dissatisfied with the increasingly corrupt behaviour of the Ottoman janissaries (soldiers). *Hajduci* (Serbian rebels) began small-scale rebellions that laid the ground for the First Serbian Uprising of 1804, led by Đorđe Petrović (1762–1817), better known as Karađorđe *(see p75)*. The rebels killed the Ottoman governors, landowners and janissaries, and, with the help of the Russians, defeated the Ottoman army sent to quell their rebellion. Much of the country was liberated and concerted efforts were made to revive the medieval Serbian Empire, but disaster struck in 1812 when Russia made peace with the Ottomans. In 1813 a vast Ottoman army destroyed the rebels and set up a new government in Belgrade's Kalemegdan Fortress; Karađorđe escaped across the Danube to Austria.

An 1838 portrait of Prince Miloš Obrenović by Emile Desmaisons

The Second Serbian Uprising in 1815 was led by Miloš Obrenović (1780–1860), whose military successes against the Turks persuaded them to grant Serbia autonomy under Ottoman suzerainty. Prince Miloš organized the new Serbian state, distributed land to peasants and implemented an education system to bridge the cultural gap left by Ottoman rule. By 1833 he had negotiated complete autonomy for Serbia, and in 1878 Serbia's independence was recognized at the Congress of Berlin.

Gazimestan, marking the Battle of Kosovo

1389 Prince Lazar is killed during the Battle of Kosovo against the Ottoman Empire

1459 Smederevo Fortress falls to the Ottomans, signalling the end of the Serbian Empire

The defensive towers and mighty ramparts of the imposing Smederevo Fortress

1360 | **1455** | **1550**

1371 Serbia loses Macedonia and parts of Greece to the Ottomans after being defeated at the Battle of Maritsa

1456 The Byzantine Empire collapses. The Siege of Belgrade, one of the greatest medieval crusades, takes place as Sultan Mehmed II besieges the city with 150,000 soldiers and over 100 ships

Ottoman Sultan Mehmed II (1432–81), known as Mehmed the Conqueror

The Balkan Wars

Despite Serbia, Montenegro, Bulgaria and Greece having gained independence, large areas of the Balkan Peninsula were still under Ottoman control in the early 20th century, so the four countries formed the Balkan League and attacked the Ottomans in 1912. The First Balkan War was a huge success for the league and within months the Turks had lost most of their European territories and were forced to concede Kosovo and Macedonia to Serbia in May 1913. Bulgaria, however, was unhappy with Serbian gains in Macedonia and in June 1913 it started the Second Balkan War when it attacked Serbia and Greece with disastrous consequences. Its army was quickly repelled and Serbia and Greece entered Bulgaria. The Turks also took advantage of the situation to reclaim the Bulgarian territories they had lost. Romania joined the fray by marching on Bulgaria's capital, Sofia, to settle its own territorial disputes. Two months later, a much chastened Bulgaria accepted a treaty ceding western Macedonia and parts of western Bulgaria to Serbia, almost doubling Serbia's territory in the process.

World War I

Russia was supportive of Serbia's increased size, but the Austro-Hungarians were dissatisfied with their neighbour's growing strength and links to Russia. When Gavrilo Princip, a Bosnian Serb nationalist, assassinated Archduke Franz Ferdinand, heir to the Austro-Hungarian throne, in Sarajevo in June 1914, Austria-Hungary blamed Serbia. Its declaration of war triggered World War I. Serbia defended itself heroically before the overwhelming might of the German, Bulgarian and Austro-Hungarian armies forced its army to retreat. Regrouping in Greece, the Serbs returned to fight alongside the Allies on the Macedonian Front, achieving the liberation of occupied Serb territories in September 1918. The Serbs had regained their country but had lost an estimated one million people, around a quarter of their pre-war population.

A 1915 colour print showing Serbs fighting Austrians in World War I

The Kingdom of Yugoslavia

The Kingdom of Serbs, Croats and Slovenes was created by the Treaty of Versailles in 1918 as a monarchy ruled by Alexander I Karađorđević (1888–1934). From the start, Croats were displeased with the choice of a Serbian monarch and refused to vote on the new constitution of 1921. The conflict over perceived Serbo-centric policies came to a head in 1928 when a Montenegrin Serb politician assassinated the Croatian Peasant Party leader. In response, Alexander abolished parliament and the constitution in 1929 and took full control of the country, renaming it the Kingdom of Yugoslavia.

Karađorđe Monument opposite the Temple of St Sava, Belgrade

1804 The First Serbian Uprising against the Ottoman Empire is led by Đorđe Petrović, better known as Karađorđe

1740

1815 Prince Miloš Obrenović, a veteran of the First Uprising, leads the Second Serbian Uprising against the Ottoman Empire

First Balkan War (1912–13)

1835

1878 Serbia's independence is acknowledged by the international community at the Congress of Berlin

1912–13 The First and Second Balkan Wars take place, throwing the region into turmoil

1914 Gavrilo Princip's assassination of Archduke Franz Ferdinand triggers World War I

1929 King Alexander abolishes parliament and renames the nation the Kingdom of Yugoslavia

Tito making a speech on 1 May 1945 in Belgrade

World War II

In the run up to World War II, Hungary, Bulgaria and Romania joined the Axis, and, under pressure from Hitler, Yugoslavia's Prince Paul (1893–1976) followed in March 1941 in his capacity as regent for the teenage King Peter II (1923–70). This provoked angry public demonstrations throughout the country and a British-backed military coup replaced Paul with Peter, who withdrew all support for the Axis. Hitler was outraged and began a ferocious aerial attack on Belgrade, followed by a land invasion that conquered the city within days and forced Peter into exile in London. Yugoslavia was divided up between the Axis powers, with Croatia and Bosnia and Herzegovina becoming the Independent State of Croatia run by the Croatian army, which set about purging the state of Serbs, Jews and Roma.

Two Yugoslavian resistance groups with opposing ideologies soon emerged: the royalist Četniks under Draža Mihailović (1893–1946) and the Communist partisans led by Josip Broz Tito (1892–1980). Brutal Nazi reprisal massacres forced Mihailović to curtail Četnik raids, but Tito's refusal to compromise, coupled with British logistical support, proved far more effective. By September 1944, the partisans, with Soviet Red Army support, had forced the Germans to retreat beyond Yugoslav borders and were close to liberating Yugoslavia.

Yugoslavia Before and After Tito

Elections in 1945 saw the Communist Party win 90 per cent of the vote. Tito abolished the monarchy and set up a single-party state with six republics – Serbia, Croatia, Macedonia, Slovenia, Montenegro and Bosnia and Herzegovina. Land was redistributed, industries nationalized and a five-year economic plan implemented in line with Stalinist policies; however, in 1948 Tito severed relations with the Soviets in favour of his own brand of socialism based on the motto "Brotherhood and Unity". While wach republic had autonomy for its internal affairs, nationalist politics were completely suppressed as Tito understood this was the greatest threat to Yugoslavian unity. Despite his autocratic tendencies, he was a popular leader at home and abroad – the record number of delegates at his 1980 state funeral made it the largest ever held.

Despite Tito's posthumous plan for the Yugoslavian presidency to rotate between the republics every year to prevent power from being concentrated in any one region, it wasn't long before nationalist politics appeared as each republic focused on its own interests. Economic stagnation and rising inflation put the country deep in debt as living standards fell dramatically and unemployment rose.

The young King Peter II Karađorđević of Yugoslavia, 1940

1948 Tito severs relations with Stalin to follow his own brand of socialism

1981 Kosovan Albanians ask for the recognition of the State of Kosovo; riots erupt among the community

1930 | 1945 | 1960 | 1975

1941 Prince Paul, the regent of Yugoslavia, joins the Axis powers

1945 Tito's partisans liberate Yugoslavia with the help of the Red Army; free elections held at the end of 1945 bring Tito to power

Sculpture of Josip Broz Tito (1892–1980)

1980 Josip Broz Tito dies in Ljubljana at the age of 88; ethnic tensions rise across the country following his death

The Yugoslav Wars

In June 1991 Slovenia and Croatia declared independence from Yugoslavia, triggering the Ten-Day War. Soon after, Croatia's War of Independence began, with Croatian president Franjo Tuđman (1922–99) speaking of defeating "Greater Serbian imperialism" and Serbian president Slobodan Milošević (1941–2006) reminding Serbs of Croat atrocities during World War II. By the time of the UN ceasefire in January 1992, when the international community recognized the Republic of Croatia as a sovereign state, hundreds of thousands of Croats and Serbs had been displaced and the term "ethnic cleansing" had entered the English language for the first time. While Macedonia separated peacefully from Yugoslavia in 1991, the Bosnian War and the infamous Siege of Sarajevo were the tragic result of Bosnia and Herzegovina's declaration of independence in 1992. The republic's complex ethnic mixture of Orthodox Serbs, Catholic Croats and Muslim Bosniaks made this the bloodiest of the Yugoslav Wars and the hardest to resolve. The war ended in November 1995 with the autonomous Serbian Republika Srpska established within Bosnia and Herzegovina.

The two remaining Yugoslav republics, Serbia and Montenegro, had joined to form the Federal Republic of Yugoslavia in 1992. Following accusations of war crimes during the Yugoslav Wars, the republic was under EU and UN sanctions that caused a severe economic downturn and rampant inflation. In 2006, after Montenegro voted for full independence, Serbia became an independent state for the first time since 1918.

Belgrade buildings damaged by the NATO bombing strikes of 1999

Kosovo and Post-Milošević Serbia

Since his election in 1989, Milošević had supported Kosovan Serbs in their ongoing conflict with the Albanian majority. In 1998, after reports of Kosovo Liberation Army reprisal attacks on Serbs, Milošević sent in the Yugoslav army. NATO, convinced that he was intent on ethnically cleansing Kosovo, bombed Serbia in 1999 until the Yugoslav army withdrew. In 2008, Kosovo declared independence, which has been recognized by the US and most EU nations, although not yet by Serbia.

Milošević was ousted after accusations of election fraud in 2000. He was arrested in 2001 and tried for war crimes at a Hague tribunal, but died before the trial ended. Sanctions were relaxed after his departure; in 2006 Serbia joined NATO's Partnership for Peace framework and in 2015 agreed to a NATO Individual Partnership Action Plan covering areas such as gender perspective, defence planning and public information. In 2009 the country formally applied for EU membership, and finally began the process of accession talks at the end of 2015.

1990 – **2005** – **2020**

1991 Macedonia separates peacefully from Yugoslavia but war breaks out as Slovenia and Croatia declare independence

1992 Croatia is recognized by the international community; Montenegro and Serbia form the Federal Republic of Yugoslavia; the Bosnian War begins, lasting until 1995

1999 NATO launches air strikes against Serbia

2000 Milosević is ousted from power

Slobodan Milošević

2006 Serbia joins NATO's Partnership for Peace

2008 Kosovo declares independence from Serbia

2009 Serbia officially applies for membership of the EU

2015 Serbia starts the process of EU accession talks at the end of the year

2016–20 The World Bank plans to lend Serbia $2.2 billion to strengthen its economy and support its EU accession

SERBIA AREA BY AREA

Belgrade	**42–63**
Central Serbia	**64–75**
Western Serbia	**76–87**
Northern Serbia	**88–99**
Eastern Serbia	**100–111**
Southern Serbia	**112–121**

Serbia at a Glance

Lying at the geographical and political crossroads of Europe, Serbia stretches from the Dinaric Alps in the west to the Carpathians in the east. Between them flows the mighty Danube, dividing this small country in two. Beyond the obvious allure of Belgrade, historic ruins, sublime medieval monasteries and great expanses of untouched nature are among the many attractions of this fascinating country. Its mountains and rivers offer plenty of scope for active adventures, from skiing, hiking and biking to paragliding, kayaking and canyoning, while in summer Serbians compensate for the country's lack of beaches by transforming riverbanks into "seasides" for swimming and sunbathing.

Kalemegdan Fortress *(see pp52–3)* in Belgrade contained the entire population of the capital for hundreds of years until the city began to spread beyond the fortress walls during the 19th century.

Studenica Monastery *(see p81)* contains frescoes that date back to the 13th century and are thought to be among the finest in Serbia. Along with Sopoćani Monastery and the Stari Ras complex, Felix Romuliana and the Kosovo monasteries, Studenica is one of the four UNESCO World Heritage Sites in Serbia and its autonomous province of Kosovo.

◀ Belgrade's colourful Sava riverfront, with the Cathedral Church of St Michael dominating the skyline

Subotica *(see p98)*, in the far north of Serbia, boasts a splendid array of Art Nouveau buildings. Most were designed by Hungarian architects when the city was part of the Austro-Hungarian Empire.

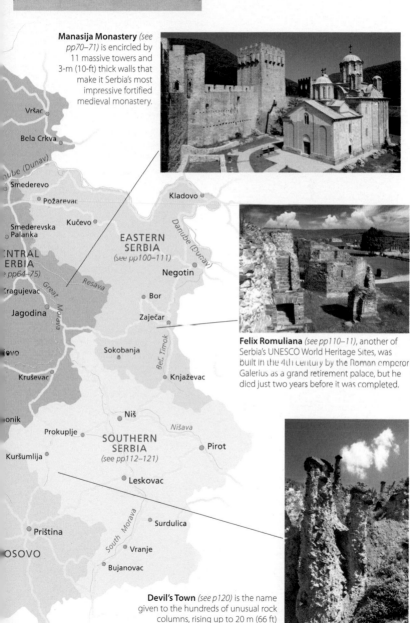

Manasija Monastery *(see pp70–71)* is encircled by 11 massive towers and 3-m (10-ft) thick walls that make it Serbia's most impressive fortified medieval monastery.

Vršac
Bela Crkva
Danube (Dunav)
Smederevo
Požarevac
Kladovo
Kučevo
Smederevska Palanka
EASTERN SERBIA
(see pp100–111)
Danube (Dunav)
CENTRAL SERBIA
(see pp64–75)
Negotin
Resava
Kragujevac
Great Morava
Bor
Jagodina
Zaječar
Beli Timok
Sokobanja
Kruševac
Knjaževac
Niš
Nišava
Prokuplje
SOUTHERN SERBIA
(see pp112–121)
Pirot
Kuršumlija
Leskovac
South Morava
Surdulica
Priština
Vranje
KOSOVO
Bujanovac

Felix Romuliana *(see pp110–11)*, another of Serbia's UNESCO World Heritage Sites, was built in the 4th century by the Roman emperor Galerius as a grand retirement palace, but he died just two years before it was completed.

Devil's Town *(see p120)* is the name given to the hundreds of unusual rock columns, rising up to 20 m (66 ft) high, formed by natural erosion on the slopes of Mount Radan.

BELGRADE

From high above the confluence of the Danube and Sava Rivers, Belgrade's breathtaking river views are among the most spectacular of any city in Europe, yet it has only lately begun to emerge as a popular tourist destination. This sprawling city tends to underwhelm at first, yet rapidly draws visitors in. Its captivating vibrancy is evident from early in the day, when cafés fill with locals enjoying leisurely coffees, until well past midnight in lively bars and clubs where the nightlife rivals that of any modern Western capital city.

Belgrade's commanding position on the natural boundary between the East and the West was coveted by competing empires for millennia. Having been ravaged and rebuilt on at least 30 occasions and bombed four times in the 20th century alone, it is little surprise that the city is not renowned for its historic architecture, although a few gems stand out.

Kalemegdan Fortress once contained the whole city within its walls; it has been battered countless times and has finally found peace as a tranquil park frequented by promenading locals. During Ottoman rule, the city spread well beyond the ramparts of the fortress, but of the 200 mosques that were built only one survived the destruction visited first by the Austro-Hungarians during their brief occupation and later by Serbs who arrived following the Turkish withdrawal from Belgrade in 1867. Nineteenth-century Serbian buildings such as the mansions of Princess Ljubica and Prince Miloš demonstrate the tentative influence of Western culture that was soon to be fully embraced as the city gradually expanded along King Alexander Boulevard and Prince Miloš Street.

The world-class collections at the city's National Museum and the Museum of Contemporary Art are a major draw, as is the small but enormously popular Nikola Tesla Museum. Belgrade even has its own "seaside" on the riverbank at Ada Ciganlija where locals gather in their thousands to cool off during the scorching summers.

Sunset over the confluence of the Danube and Sava Rivers, viewed from the bastions of Kalemegdan Fortress

◀ The cupolas and domes of Belgrade's beautiful 19th-century Cathedral Church of St Michael

Exploring Belgrade

Kalemegdan Fortress is a good starting point for any tour of Belgrade. Both the Sava and Danube Rivers are accessible via steep pathways from its ramparts and many of the city's main sights are within easy reach. At the heart of the Old Town (Stari grad) is bustling pedestrianized Knez Mihailova, with cafés, shops and street entertainers, while nearby Skadarlija offers traditional cuisine in atmospheric 19th-century *kafanas*. Central Belgrade's easternmost attraction is the Temple of St Sava; Topčider Park and the House of Flowers are in the southern suburbs. It is possible to visit the Museum of Contemporary Art by walking across Brankov Bridge (Brankov most) into New Belgrade. The city's famous boat bars are moored a short distance from the bridge.

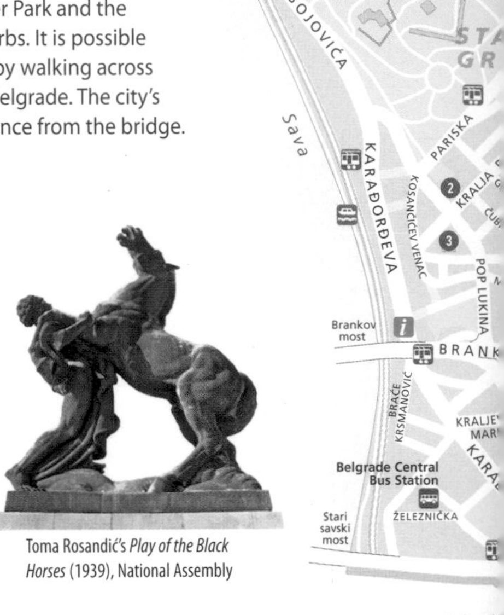

Getting Around

Belgrade's Old Town is small enough to be explored on foot, and modern Belgrade is also walkable even though it lacks pedestrianized zones. Sights that lie further afield can be reached by bus, tram, trolleybus or taxi. Hiring a bicycle or joining a bike tour is a wonderful way to explore the city, especially along the purpose-built cycle tracks beside the Danube and Sava Rivers that go as far as Zemun and Ada Ciganlija. Driving in the city can be stressful due to heavy traffic, road conditions and limited parking.

Toma Rosandić's *Play of the Black Horses* (1939), National Assembly

Boats moored at Ada Ciganlija, with Ada Bridge in the background

Sights at a Glance

Museums and Historic Buildings

1. Ethnographic Museum
3. Palace of Princess Ljubica
4. Fresco Gallery
5. *Kalemegdan Fortress pp52–3*
7. Jewish Historical Museum
11. National Museum
12. Automobile Museum
16. Nikola Tesla Museum
18. National Library of Serbia
20. Museum of Contemporary Art
21. House of Flowers
23. Royal Palaces

Cathedrals, Churches and Mosques

2. Cathedral Church of St Michael
6. Bajrakli Mosque
8. Church of St Alexander Nevsky
14. Church of St Mark
17. Temple of St Sava

Parks, Squares and Streets

9. Skadarlija
10. Republic Square
13. King Alexander Boulevard
15. Prince Miloš Street
19. Zemun
22. Topčider Park
24. Ada Ciganlija

For hotels and restaurants in this region see pp126–7 and pp134–5

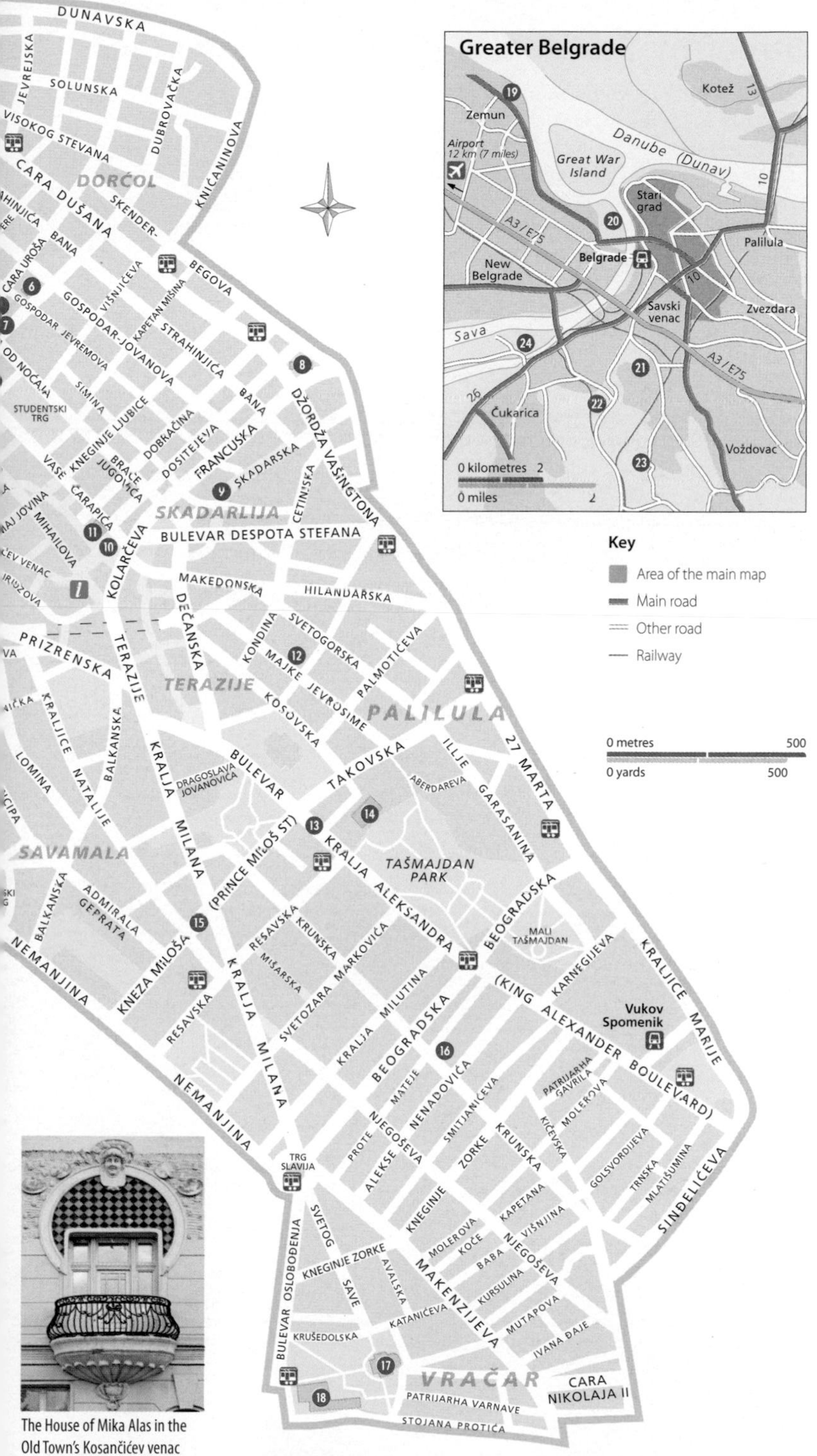

The House of Mika Alas in the Old Town's Kosančićev venac

Street-by-Street: the Old Town (Stari grad)

Belgrade's most characterful quarter, the Old Town was the heart of the city's rapidly increasing Serbian community in the mid-19th century. Prince Miloš Obrenović built his first city residence here in 1831 – now known as the Palace of Princess Ljubica – and was soon joined by the wealthy merchants of the city who erected fine mansions with river views. Much of the Old Town was devastated during the catastrophic wars of the 20th century, but the neighbourhood has retained its period charm.

Kosančićev venac
This winding cobbled street was once home to some of Belgrade's wealthiest citizens. Following the line of the old city walls and boasting wonderful river views, it is a reminder of how the city looked in the 19th century.

Key

— Suggested route

★ Embassy of France
Designed by French architect Roger-Henri Expert in 1928, this is regarded as one of the city's finest Art Deco structures. Sitting atop the edifice is French sculptor Carlo Sarrabezolles's bronze statue of three women symbolizing *liberté, égalité, fraternité*.

❷ ★ Cathedral Church of St Michael
Built by Prince Miloš in 1841 on the site of an 18th-century church, the Classical-style cathedral boasts an impressive iconostasis. Opposite, the Museum of the Serbian Orthodox Church was founded during World War II to preserve artifacts collected from Serbia's churches for safekeeping.

PARISK
KNEZ
KOSANČIĆEV VENAC
KRALJA P
ZADAR
Sava

★ Kralja Petra
Kralja Petra, one of Belgrade's oldest streets, was also one of the most important in the 19th century. Until Knez Mihailova was laid out in the 1860s, Kralja Petra was a busy shopping area. Pause at nos. 39 and 41 to admire this pair of fine Art Nouveau buildings dating from 1907.

Belgrade Central Railway and Bus Stations ↓

0 metres 50
0 yards 50

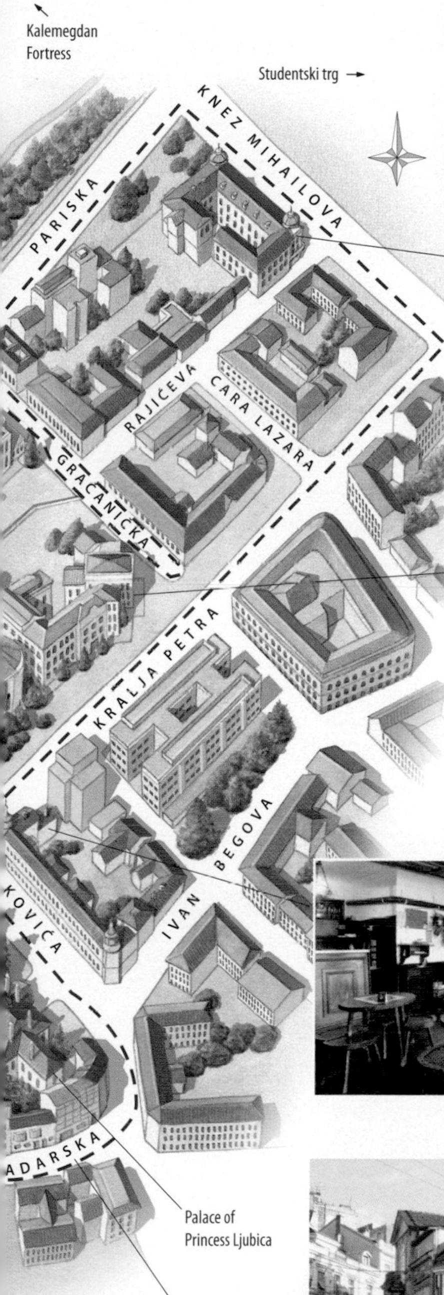

Kalemegdan Fortress

Studentski trg →

KNEZ MIHAILOVA

PARISKA

RAJIĆEVA

CARA LAZARA

GRAČANIČKA

KRALJA PETRA

BEGOVA

IVAN

KOVIĆA

ADARSKA

Faculty of Fine Arts and Knez Mihailova
With a range of stores, Knez Mihailova is the city's main pedestrianized shopping street. At no. 53–55 stands the Faculty of Fine Arts. Built in 1889 for lawyer Marko Stojanović, the Neo-Classical building was taken over by the faculty in 1937.

Kralja Petra School
Located on the site of an old Serbian school founded in 1718, Kralja Petra is Belgrade's oldest school. The current building dates to 1906 and was designed by Serbia's first woman architect, Jelisaveta Načić.

★ Kafana Question Mark
Belgrade's oldest *kafana* (traditional tavern) has had its unique name ever since its owner was forced to rename it in 1892 *(see p134)*. Built in 1823, the *kafana* boasts its original interior.

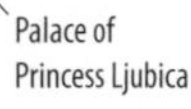

Palace of Princess Ljubica

★ Zadarska
This narrow cobbled residential street has plenty of historic character and is often used as a backdrop for period films.

❶ Ethnographic Museum

Etnografski muzej

City Map C2. Studentski trg 13. **Tel** (011) 3281888. No. 28, 29, 31, 41. **Open** 10am–5pm Tue–Sat, 9am–2pm Sun.
W **etnografskimuzej.rs**

Housed in a somewhat grim 1934 Functionalist building that was once the Stock Exchange, the Ethnographic Museum gives visitors a colourful introduction to Balkan folk traditions and houses a treasure trove of vivid Balkan folk costumes that reflect both the ethnicity and social status of the wearers.

Split into regions, the ground floor collection emphasizes the stylistic differences that often came about due to local circumstances. The vast Dinaric mountain region of Southern and Western Serbia, Bosnia-Herzegovina and continental Montenegro was almost completely dependent upon cattle and sheep breeding, so its folk dresses, examples of which are on display here, were made of homespun wool and heavy cloth. Yarn coloured with herbal dyes was used to embroider geometric and floral decorations specific to regions, villages and families. There are also a few silver chest plates known as *toke* that were attached to the outfits of Dinaric men – worn in combination with a flintlock pistol tucked into a broad leather belt, they were considered heroic and manly.

The Functionalist exterior of the Ethnographic Museum in Belgrade

The Cathedral Church of St Michael and the Museum of the Serbian Orthodox Church

Central Serbia's Morava and Raška regions saw a mixture of styles worn by farmers and herdsmen. These are notable for the elaborate headdresses for women, while the collection of garments from the northern region of Vojvodina have incredibly detailed embroidery even on simple everyday outfits such as shepherd's jackets. Several of the wedding dresses on display feature aprons and headdresses made of silver coins, which were thought to bring prosperity to the newly married couple.

Upstairs is an exhibition of ecclesiastical paraphernalia and above that are some splendid dioramas of 19th-century rural and urban dwellings alongside early examples of agricultural machinery and implements.

❷ Cathedral Church of St Michael

Saborna crkva svetog Mihaila

City Map B2. Kneza Sime Markovića 3. **Tel** (011) 2636684. **Open** 7am–8pm daily. 7.30am & 5pm.

Construction of the cathedral was begun by Prince Miloš Obrenović (1780–1860) in 1837, just a few years after he gained Serbian sovereignty from the Ottomans and they relaxed their ban on the building of churches. Dedicated to the Archangel Michael but known simply as the Orthodox Cathedral, this Neo-Baroque structure boasts a fine gilt iconostasis by the sculptor Dimitrije Petrović. Dimitrije Avramović, one of the best known 19th-century Serbian Romanticist painters, also worked on the icons and church frescoes.

The relics of Prince Lazar, the most powerful ruler of medieval Serbia, were kept here from 1954 to 1989, after which they were returned to Ravanica Monastery *(see p69)* in time to mark the 600th anniversary of the Battle of Kosovo. Prince Miloš is buried here along with his son Mihailo (1823–68). Vuk Karadzić (1787–1864), the philologist and linguist who standardized the Cyrillic alphabet and wrote the first Serbian dictionary, is buried outside, as is Dositej Obradović (1739–1811), linguist, philosopher and first Serbian education minister.

Visitors wearing short skirts, shorts or skimpy tops will be expected to cover up with black cloth wraps that can be borrowed from the small gift shop just inside the entrance.

❸ Palace of Princess Ljubica

Konak kneginje Ljubice

City Map B2. Kneza Sime Markovića 8. **Tel** (011) 2638264. **Open** 10am–5pm Tue, Wed & Fri, 10am–6pm Thu, noon–8pm Sat, 10am–2pm Sun. **W mgb.org.rs**

In the early 19th century Kneza Sime Markovića street was at the heart of Serbian Belgrade and it was here that Prince Miloš Obrenović chose to have his palace built. It became his official residence in 1831, but he never felt comfortable with its proximity to the Turkish garrison in nearby Kalemegdan Fortress and soon moved away to his Topčider estate. Princess Ljubica, his wife, was left to live here with their children. She stayed here until 1842, when her son Prince Mihailo was deposed. Although few of the objects currently on display are directly related to her, most have been sourced from that era.

Designed by Nikola Živković (1792–1870), the architect of the Church of St Mark *(see p54)*, the mansion has an Oriental exterior that illustrates how the ruling class were still heavily under the influence of Ottoman culture despite having gained sovereignty in 1830. The interior plan is also typically Levantine with separate male and female areas occupying the bay windows on the upper and lower floors and a marble-floored hammam (Turkish bathhouse) below. However, the creeping influence of Western culture is apparent in rooms that contain Oriental rugs and Turkish coffee jugs alongside hefty Baroque furniture imported from Paris, Budapest and Vienna.

Reproductions of frescoes and casts of monuments at the Fresco Gallery

❹ Fresco Gallery

Galerija fresaka

City Map C1. Cara Uroša 20. **Tel** (011) 2621491. **Open** 10am–5pm Tue, Wed & Fri, noon–8pm Thu & Sat, 10am–2pm Sun. **W narodnimuzej.rs**

A branch of Belgrade's National Museum *(see p51)*, the gallery features striking, monumental copies of medieval frescoes and casts of architectural details from former Yugoslavian monasteries and churches. The collection began in 1950 with a popular exhibition of fresco copies in Paris called Yugoslav Medieval Art, and has since grown to over 1,300 fresco replicas and 300 casts. The stunning centrepiece is a cast of the entrance to the 13th century Catholic cathedral in Trogir, Croatia. Its elaborate depictions of Biblical scenes include sculptures of Adam and Eve riding lions. Other exhibits include reproductions of New Testament scenes from the monastery churches of Studenica *(see p81)* and Sopoćani *(see p83)*, a massive medieval monastery door key and a cast of a trifora window from Studenica.

While it is true that a visit to the gallery is no substitute for viewing the frescoes in situ, the collection provides a thrilling introduction to the region's wealth of medieval art and to the Orthodox Christian culture that thrived in the area before the Ottoman occupation, and is perfect for those visitors who lack the time for extensive tours of Serbia's splendid monasteries.

The Oriental façade and minaret-like chimneys of the Palace of Princess Ljubica

5 Kalemegdan Fortress

See pp52–3.

The minaret and dome of Belgrade's 17th-century Bajrakli Mosque

6 Bajrakli Mosque

Bajrakli džamija

City Map C1. Gospodar Jevremova 11. **Tel** (011) 2622428. **Open** 7am–8pm daily.

Of the more than 200 mosques built in Belgrade during the Ottoman era, this is the only one to have survived. It is also the oldest extant centre of worship in the city. Endowed by a wealthy textile merchant in the late 17th century, it was set in the centre of the Turkish quarter. The mosque's name – *bajrak* is Turkish for "flag" – references the banner that was hoisted from its minaret to signal prayer time to all the surrounding mosques.

Unlike most Ottoman edifices during the second period of Austrian rule from 1717 to 1739, the Bajrakli Mosque escaped destruction because its occupiers converted it into a church and installed a bell tower in the minaret. After the Ottomans were expelled from Serbia, the mosque stood empty until 1868 when Prince Mihailo Obrenović commanded its renovation in order for the city's Muslims "not to be without religious consolation". Today the squat stone structure is hemmed in by modern apartment blocks and still serves the city's small Muslim community.

7 Jewish Historical Museum

Jevrejski istorijski muzej

City Map C1. Kralja Petra I 71/1. **Tel** (011) 2622634. **Open** 10am–2pm Mon–Fri. **Closed** Public holidays. **jimbeograd.org/en**

Opened in 1960 after almost two decades spent gathering artifacts, the museum has an absorbing collection that documents the Jewish history of the former Yugoslavia in comprehensive detail. Running chronologically, it begins in the Roman era with the migration of the first scattered communities of Jews to the region that would later become known as Yugoslavia. Ashkenazi Jews arrived in the 13th century and were joined in the late 15th century by Sephardic Jews expelled from Portugal and Spain and welcomed by the Ottomans. More Ashkenazi Jews followed in the 18th and 19th centuries to escape persecution in Poland and Russia. Exhibits include original documents, paintings and items of clothing alongside a multitude of religious artifacts such as examples of the nine-branched hanukiah candelabra and a rare 18th-century scroll containing the Jewish holy texts. Black and white images portray thriving Jewish communities throughout Yugoslavia during the early 20th century, but these are followed by ominous anti-Semitic Nazi newspaper articles and propaganda dating from the 1930s.

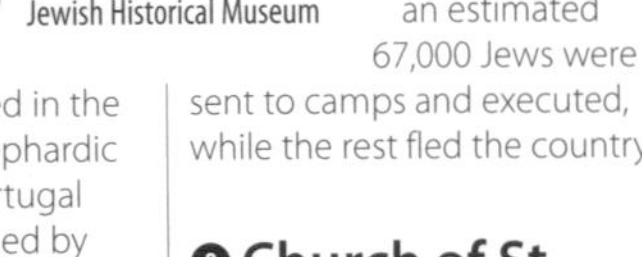

17th-century Torah, Jewish Historical Museum

The final hall of the exhibition is dedicated to the tragic events of the Holocaust. Concentration camps were set up around the country, carrying out their grim functions so efficiently that within a few months of their occupation from 1941 to 1945, Nazi officers reported to high command that Belgrade was "free of Jews". Yugoslavia's thriving Jewish community was decimated during the war; from a pre-war population of around 82,000, an estimated 67,000 Jews were sent to camps and executed, while the rest fled the country.

8 Church of St Alexander Nevsky

Crkva svetog Aleksandra Nevskog

City Map D1. Cara Dušana 63. **Open** 7am–7pm daily.

Numerous Orthodox churches and cathedrals have been dedicated to St Alexander Nevsky (1221–63), a medieval Russian prince renowned for his military prowess who was later canonized and venerated by soldiers in particular.

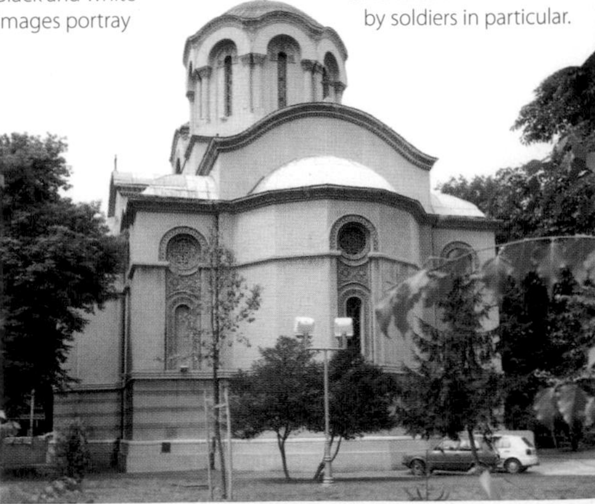

The Church of St Alexander Nevsky, influenced by the Morava School of church architecture

Republic Square and the equestrian statue of Prince Mihailo, with the National Theatre in the background

The Church of St Alexander Nevsky was built on the site of a field church dedicated to the saint and left behind by departing Russian troops who had supported the Serbs in the Serbian-Ottoman War of 1876–77. Heavily influenced by the 15th-century Morava School of church architecture and topped by a hefty pair of belfries, the church was finally completed in 1929 after building work was delayed by World War I. The striking white marble iconostasis inside was a gift from King Alexander I Karađorđević who had originally intended it for Topola's Karađorđe Mausoleum Church of St George *(see p75)*.

❾ Skadarlija

City Map D2. Skadarska.

One of Belgrade's most famous attractions, Skadarlija is the city's old bohemian quarter centred around Skadarska, a sloping cobbled street of gift shops, galleries and charming eateries decked out with cascades of colourful flowers in summer and scented with the smell of grilled meat throughout the year. The atmospheric street dates back to the early 19th century when it was part of a Roma district packed with shabby drinking dens that were gradually replaced by more respectable restaurants and *kafanas*. By the 1850s it had started to become the haunt of artists, actors, musicians, writers and poets who gathered for wine and song at quirkily named establishments that remained popular throughout the 20th century. Among these were the Three Hats (Tri šešira), the Golden Jug (Zlatni bokal) and the Two Stags (Dva jelena), which are still open today. These days the street is as much an attraction for locals as it is for tourists, and it is the best place to sample the country's typical cuisine while being serenaded by a Roma band.

❿ Republic Square

Trg republike

City Map C2. 

Known by locals simply as Trg, Belgrade's bustling central square is the city's main focal point. It was here that Serbs celebrated the liberation of Belgrade in October 1944 and the formation of their first post-war government in March 1945. Half a century later it was the site of daily student protests against Milošević's regime. Today the square still sees occasional demonstrations but is more likely to be used as a venue for outdoor exhibitions. When Serbs arrange to meet *"kod konja"* ("by the horse") in Belgrade it is understood that they will see one another at the equestrian statue of Prince Mihailo Obrenović on Trg republike. Erected in 1882, it portrays the prince pointing south towards the Serb lands still to be liberated from the Turks. In 1868, just a few days before his death, Prince Mihailo gave his permission for the National Theatre (Narodno pozorište) to be built facing the square. Originally boasting a stunning façade modelled on Milan's La Scala, it was later destroyed during World War I and rebuilt in 1922 *(see p26)*.

⓫ National Museum

Narodni muzej

City Map C2. Republic Square 1a. **Tel** (011) 3306000. **Open** 10am–5pm Tue, Wed, Fri; noon–8pm Thu, Sat; 10am–2pm Sun.
narodnimuzej.rs

Dominating Republic Square next to the National Theatre stands a strikingly grand Neo-Classical building, dating from 1903, which originally housed a bank before becoming the home of the National Museum in 1951. Founded in 1844 and recently reopened following years of protracted renovations, the museum boasts a vast collection covering many floors. It begins with stone and bone tools dating back over half a million years to the Palaeolithic era, and subsequent rooms trace the complex history of the region through the Mesolithic, Neolithic, Bronze and Iron Ages. The highlights of the collection include gold jewellery from a Bronze Age tomb and the famous Dupljaja Cart, a three-wheeled model chariot led by a pair of ducks. Further rooms focus on the Roman era, the arrival of the Serbs, their medieval kingdoms that fell to the Turks and the eventual establishment of modern Serbia.

❺ Kalemegdan Fortress

Kalemegdanska tvrđava

Dominating the confluence of the Danube and Sava Rivers, the formidable Kalemegdan Fortress (from *kale* meaning "fortress" and *meydan* meaning "field") was one of the most fought-over strategic points in southeastern Europe. It was first settled by the Celts, then the Romans, and then refortified by the medieval rulers of Serbia and expanded during the Ottoman and Austrian occupations, slowly evolving into an extensive complex of buildings blending various architectural styles. Today, it is Belgrade's most popular park, offering views of the Danube from its bastions.

Kula Nebojša (Nebojša Tower)
Also called the "daredevil tower", this 15th-century hexagonal structure was used as a dungeon under the Ottomans.

★ The Victor (Pobednik)
One of the best-known works of Croat sculptor Ivan Meštrović, *The Victor* was erected in 1928 to honour Serbian victories in the Balkan Wars (1912–13) and World War I. From here, the confluence of the Danube and Sava is visible.

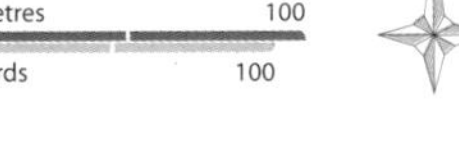

Military Museum
Built in 1924, the Military Museum resembles a medieval fortress. Tanks, cannon and World War II machinery are on display. The casemates below the bastion on which the museum sits are open to the public and can be explored.

KEY

① **Gate of Emperor Charles VI**, a triumphal arch, was built by the Austrians to celebrate the capture of Belgrade in 1718.

② **Belgrade Planetarium** is housed within the old Turkish hammam.

③ **Despot's Gate** is the only one to have kept its medieval appearance.

④ **Leopold Gate**, on the east side of the fortress, was built in honour of Austrian Emperor Leopold I, who held Belgrade from 1688 to 1690.

⑤ **Stefan Lazarević Monument**

⑥ **Grand Vizier Ali Paša's Tomb**

⑦ **Sahat Kula**, a distinctive clock tower, was built by the Austrians in the 18th century.

⑧ **The Cvijeta Zuzoric Art Pavilion** is named after a celebrated poet and beauty from 16th-century Dubrovnik.

⑨ **The Gallery of the Natural History Museum** is based in the 1835 Turkish guardsmen's building.

⑩ **The Great Ravel** is a V-shaped fortification used for theatrical performances on summer evenings.

⑪ ***Struggle* by Simeon Roksandić** (1874–1943), a Serbian sculptor, portrays a fisherman wrestling a snake.

For hotels and restaurants in this region see pp126–7 and pp134–5

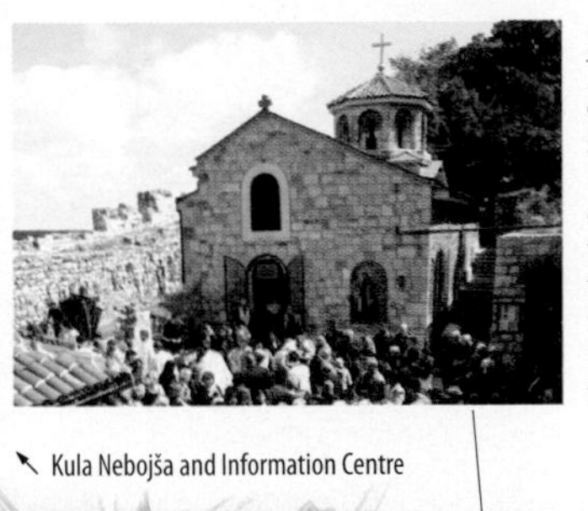

★ Chapel of St Petka
This 1937 chapel stands on the site of a sacred spring said to have healing powers and is dedicated to St Petka, protector of families, women, the sick and the poor. St Petka's relics were kept in a church here from 1417 to 1521.

↖ Kula Nebojša and Information Centre

↗ Belgrade Zoo

VISITORS' CHECKLIST

Practical Information
City Map B1. (011) 2620685. **beogradskatvrdjava.co.rs**. Belgrade Planetarium: **Open** 9am–4pm Tue–Thu, 2pm–10pm Sat. **adrb.org**. Gallery of the Natural History Museum: **Open** Summer: 10am–9pm Tue–Sun (to 5pm in winter). **nhmbeo.rs**. Military Museum: **Open** 10am–5pm Tue–Sun. **muzej.mod.gov.rs**. Kula Nebojša: **Open** Jun–Sep: 11am–7pm Wed–Sun (10am–6pm in winter). **kulanebojsa.rs**. Sahat Kula: **Open** 11am–7pm daily.

Transport
No. 31. No. 2. No. 19, 21, 22, 28, 29, 41.

★ Zindan Gate
This massive 15th-century fortified gate was used as a *zindan* (prison) by the Ottomans. Its two barrel-like towers offer good views of the Danube.

Monument of Gratitude to France
The bronze sculpture of a woman by Ivan Meštrović represents France rushing to Serbia's aid and honours the troops who played a major role in liberating the country in 1918.

Vintage car at the Automobile Museum

⓬ Automobile Museum

Muzej automobila

City Map D3. Majke Jevrosime 30. **Tel** (011) 3034625. **Open** 9.30am–8pm daily. **Closed** Public holidays. **automuseumbgd.com**

Housed in Belgrade's first public garage, which was built in 1929 and a decade later used to store racing cars for the city's first and only Grand Prix, this fascinating museum is crammed with a small but dazzling collection of cars. Among the gems are a supercharged 1947 Fiat 500B, an immaculate 1969 Triumph TR6, a replica of the fur-upholstered Robin Reliant from the British television series *Only Fools and Horses* and Tito's prized Cadillac. Put together by the Serbian film director Bratislav Petković, the collection boasts about 100 vehicles in pristine condition; the oldest is a French 1897 Marot-Gardon racing tricycle with a De Dion-Bouton engine.

⓭ King Alexander Boulevard

Bulevar kralja Aleksandra

City Map D3.

Flanked by broad pavements thronged with pedestrians, this impressive six-lane boulevard is one of the city's longest roads and busiest shopping streets. Named after King Alexander I Obrenović, the street begins at Trg Nikole Pašić, running east between the Neo-Classical National Assembly building and the Pionirski Park gardens, which once belonged to the Obrenović royal family, before continuing on past the Church of St Mark and Tašmajdan Park. Its route follows the ancient Via Militaris, which was built by the Romans in the 1st century to connect Constantinople with Belgrade and which was later used by the Ottoman army as a link between Istanbul and Kalemegdan Fortress. In 1944 the Red Army and Tito's partisans fought their way into the city against fierce resistance from the Nazis along this very boulevard, earning it the name Bulevar Revolucije (Revolution Boulevard) during the era of Communist rule.

⓮ Church of St Mark

Crkva svetog Marka

City Map D3. Bulevar kralja Aleksandra 17. No. 25, 26, 27, 32. No. 6. **Open** 8am–7pm daily.

Designed by architects Petar and Branko Krstić, who were best known for their Modernist buildings, St Mark's was inspired by the 14th-century monastery church at Gračanica in Kosovo, which was a typical example of the Byzantine School of church architecture. Much larger than Gračanica, St Mark's was finished in 1940 but the fresco painting was interrupted by World War II and never completed. The comparatively bare interior of the church highlights the glittering mosaic of the Last Supper set in the iconostasis. An engraved copper sarcophagus on a block of black granite holds the relics of the powerful medieval king Stefan Dušan (1308–55). The bodies of King Alexander I Obrenović and Queen Draga, who were assassinated in 1903, are interred in the crypt. Prince Milan (1819–39), the son of Prince Miloš, is also buried here.

⓯ Prince Miloš Street

Kneza Miloša

City Map C4.

Midway through his first reign, Prince Miloš Obrenović's unease at Belgrade's proximity to the Ottoman forces in Kalemegdan Fortress prompted him to relocate the city centre a safe distance from their cannon. Connecting Miloš's mansion in Topčider Park *(see p59)*, with New Belgrade, Kneza Miloša became the new centre's focal point upon completion in 1842. The street grew into the city's most fashionable after affluent citizens were invited to build suitably impressive homes next to the grand embassies and

The Church of St Mark, with its layered stonework inspired by medieval churches

government offices that had sprung up along it. After World War II, Tito continued the trend by adding important buildings and using the street for state processions; the last would be for his own funeral in 1980.

The government buildings of Belgrade were targeted by NATO during the three-month bombing of Serbia in 1999. The Ministry of Internal Affairs and the Ministry of Defence on Kneza Miloša were among those hit by cruise missiles, and today they remain derelict as a stark reminder of the impact of NATO's controversial decision.

Belgrade's Nikola Tesla Museum, housed in an early 20th-century mansion

⓰ Nikola Tesla Museum

Muzej Nikole Tesle

City Map E4. Krunska 51. **Tel** (011) 2433886. No. 26, 27. No. 7, 12. **Open** 10am–6pm Tue–Sun. **Closed** Public holidays. **W tesla-museum.org**

Venerated as a Serbian national hero, Nikola Tesla (1856–1943) appears on the 100-dinar bank note and has had the city's international airport named in his honour. One of the geniuses of the modern age, he is best known for his pioneering work on x-rays, radio transmission, induction motors, wireless communications and alternating current electricity supply – the latter is now used around the world. He registered over 700 patents during his lifetime, and in 1960 the international unit for measuring magnetic fields was named after him. Despite spending most of his adult life in the US, Tesla asked that his ashes be brought to Belgrade after his death; this memorial museum was established in 1952 to house them.

Hugely popular, the museum receives more visitors than any other in Serbia. Set in a grand mansion built in 1929, it exhibits Tesla's diaries, writings, project drafts, personal effects and a gold-plated spherical silver urn holding his ashes, as well as models of his various inventions. The hourly lectures in English are a must for visitors as they provide a fascinating insight into the workings of many of Tesla's inventions.

⓱ Temple of St Sava

Hram svetog Save

City Map D5. Karađorđev Park. **Tel** (011) 3445177. **Open** 7am–8pm. **W hramsvetogsave.com**

Set in an elevated position on Vračar Hill, visible from all over Belgrade, the cathedral is dedicated to Sava (1174–1236), the Serbian prince and saint who was the founder of Serbia's Orthodox Church. Clad in gleaming white marble with a 70-m (230-ft) high central cupola, it is one of the world's largest Orthodox churches, with space for 10,000 worshippers.

The temple's foundations were laid in 1939, but building work was suspended during the Communist era and the exterior wasn't completed until 2004; work on the interior is still underway. The adjacent church was built in honour of St Sava in 1895 to mark the 300th anniversary of the day the Ottoman military commander Sinan Paša exhumed Sava's remains and burnt them on a pyre on top of Vračar Hill. Furious at the success of a Serbian uprising in Vršac in 1594 where rebels had marched under St Sava's banner, Sinan Paša intended this gruesome display to rob the saint of his mythical powers.

⓲ National Library of Serbia

Narodna biblioteka Srbije

City Map D5. Skerliceva 1. **Tel** (011) 2451242. **Open** 1pm–2pm Tue & Fri with guide (advance reservation required). **W nb.rs**

Serbia's National Library, along with its collection of over half a million books, was destroyed by Nazi air raids during World War II. It was reopened in 1947 with manuscripts gathered from all over Yugoslavia; the old building was replaced in 1973 by the current Modernist edifice that stands next to the Temple of St Sava. Designed by Ivo Kurtović (1910–72), a prominent post-war architect, the concrete structure is representative of the peak of the Belgrade School of modern architecture with its emphasis on a central inner core that expands outwards in all directions.

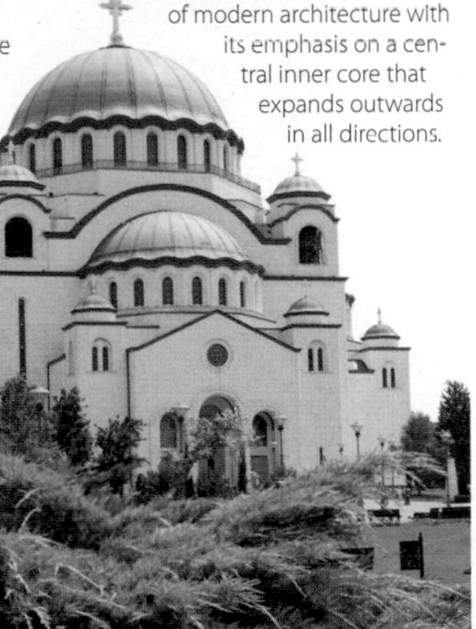

The Temple of St Sava with its huge 12-m (39-ft) tall golden cross topping the dome

Basement of the Royal Palace in Dedinje, richly decorated in the style of the Terem Palace in Moscow's Kremlin ▶

The 18th-century Baroque-style Karamata House on Karamatina street, Zemun

⑲ Zemun

NW of New Belgrade.

Part of the Austro-Hungarian Empire from the late 17th century until World War I, Zemun changed hands several times before joining the new Kingdom of Serbs, Croats and Slovenes that later became Yugoslavia.

Today it is a pleasant suburb of cobbled streets and pastel buildings, including the historic Karamata House, which once hosted the Austrian emperor Joseph II. It is centred on Gardoš Hill where the ruins of its medieval fortress are overlooked by the brick **Millennium Tower** (Milenijumska kula). Erected in 1896 to mark the 1,000th year of the Hungarian state, the tower houses an art gallery and an observation platform. At the base of the hill, the **Church of St Nicholas** (Nikolajevska crkva) is Zemun's oldest church. Built in 1731 in Baroque style, it has a superb 18th-century iconostasis and a casket thought to contain the relics of St Andrew. A short, easy walk downhill from here leads to Freedom Quay (Kej oslobođenja), whose bars and cafés attract a lively crowd.

Zemun's park is one of the oldest in Belgrade. It occupies land that was once used as a quarantine zone between the Ottoman and Austro-Hungarian Empires to curb the spread of infectious diseases. The Catholic and Orthodox churches in its grounds were part of the zone where travellers had to spend a three-week quarantine before being permitted to continue.

Millennium Tower
Grobljanska, Zemun. **Open** 10am–9pm daily. **Closed** Public holidays. observation platform (art gallery is free).

Church of St Nicholas
Njegoševa, Zemun. **Open** 7am–7pm daily. 8am & 5pm Mon–Sat; 9am Sun.

⑳ Museum of Contemporary Art

Muzej savremene umetnosti

City Map A2. Ušće 10, Blok 15, New Belgrade. **Tel** (011) 2630940. **Open** 12pm–8pm Wed–Sun. **eng.msub.org.rs**

Set in a park at the confluence of the Danube and the Sava, this distinctive building consists of six elevated angular cubes. Designed in 1965 by renowned Modernist architects Ivanka Raspopović (b. 1930) and Ivan Antić (1923–2005), it is an exemplary model of Serbian modern architecture. Recently reopened after lengthy renovations that began in 2007, the museum has a fine permanent collection of 20th-century modern art from across the world and the former Yugoslavia, and also hosts regular temporary exhibitions.

㉑ House of Flowers

Kuća cveća

Botićeva 6. **Tel** (011) 3671296. No. 41. **Open** 10am–4pm Tue–Sun.

Tito's large white marble tomb lies where flowers once grew in a winter garden within the building where he lived and worked in his final years; his wife Jovanka Broz (1924–2013) is buried in a smaller tomb next to his grave. Built in 1975 in the wooded grounds of his official residence, the edifice became known as the House of Flowers and has received a stream of visitors since Tito's death in 1980 at the age of 88. An exhibition within is devoted to the individually crafted relay batons that were sent to Tito from all over Yugoslavia to celebrate his birthday on 25 May.

The adjacent Old Museum hosts ethnographic displays from the former Yugoslavia. The complex is managed by the **Museum of Yugoslav History** (Muzej istorije Jugoslavije), whose exhibitions about life in pre- and post-war Yugoslavia are housed in the impressive Modernist concrete and glass structure nearby, originally built in 1962 as a home for the 25th May Museum of Tito-related artifacts. Its gift shop sells quirky Socialist-themed souvenirs.

Museum of Yugoslav History
Botićeva 6. **Tel** (011) 3671485. **Open** Summer: 10am–8pm Tue–Sun; winter: 10am–6pm Tue–Sun. **Closed** Public holidays. **mij.rs**

The six angular cubes of the Modernist building of the Museum of Contemporary Art

Serene pond reflecting the beautiful woods, paths and bridges of Topčider Park

㉒ Topčider Park

Topčiderski park

5 km (3 miles) S of the city centre.

Belgrade's first public park was also its most popular until it was eclipsed by Kalemegdan *(see pp52–3)* in the late 19th century, although it has remained a favourite weekend excursion for many locals. This picturesque expanse of woods, parkland and neat stone paths was occupied by Turkish artillery battalions as part of Belgrade's defences until it was acquired by Prince Miloš.

After becoming fearful that his newly completed residence in central Belgrade, the Palace of Princess Ljubica *(see p49)*, was too close to Turkish troops stationed in Kalemegdan Fortress, Miloš set about developing the grounds and constructing a new house here in 1831.

Overshadowed by a colossal plane tree with a girth of 7.4 m (24 ft), the **Mansion of Prince Miloš** (Konak kneza Miloša) features an appealing combination of Oriental and European styles. Many of the mansion's rooms are furnished with the Ottoman-style benches and luxurious Turkish carpets that the prince preferred. Today the mansion is the setting for an interesting exhibition dedicated to the First (1804–13) and Second (1815) Serbian Uprisings.

Mansion of Prince Miloš
Topčider Park. **Tel** (011) 2660442.
Open 10am–5pm Tue–Sun. **Closed** Public holidays.

㉓ Royal Palaces

Kraljevski dvor

Dedinje, 3 km (2 miles) S of the city centre. **Tel** (011) 2635622
Open Apr–Oct: 11am & 2pm Sat & Sun; visits are via guided tours only, which must be pre-booked through the Serbian tourist office centres.
royalfamily.org

Located in the 134-ha (330-acre) Royal Compound in Belgrade's exclusive Dedinje quarter, these two stunning palaces were constructed by King Alexander I Karađorđević (1888–1934) for himself and his family. Clad in white marble, the Serbian-Byzantine Royal Palace was built in 1929 and became the king's residence. Its most striking features are the grand Entrance Hall decorated with copies of medieval frescoes from Dečani and Sopoćani Monasteries, the Baroque Blue Drawing Room and the Renaissance-style Dining Room. Alexander began construction of the nearby Classicist-style White Palace for his three sons in 1934 but he was assassinated the same year. The project was eventually finished in 1937 by his cousin, Prince Regent Paul (1893–1976).

After World War II, the two palaces were taken over by the state and used as official residences by Tito and Milošević. The state still owns and maintains the palaces, but from 2002 the royal family was allowed to start living in them again. King Alexander I's grandson, Crown Prince Alexander II (b. 1945), now lives in the Royal Palace with his sons and his wife Katherine.

㉔ Ada Ciganlija

Ada Ciganlija 2, Čukarica. **Tel** (011) 7857220.
adaciganlija.rs

Also called Belgrade's "seaside", Ada Ciganlija is an island on the Sava that was connected to the mainland in 1967, forming a 4-km (2.5-mile) long artificial lake. Since then its beaches and countless leisure activities have made it the city's top summer attraction, with nearly 300,000 visitors at weekends during the high season. Rollerblading, golf, cycling, tennis, water-skiing and bungee-jumping are among its many activities; less energetic visitors can relax in the restaurants and cafés lining the riverfront or take a stroll through the wooded parkland. The island's eastern tip is bisected by the massive Ada Bridge *(see p27)*.

Deck chairs lined up along the beach on the Sava River

BELGRADE STREET FINDER

Although Serbians use the Cyrillic and Latin alphabets interchangeably, most street signs are written in Cyrillic, as are the destination signs for public transport, so it is useful to have a basic grasp of the alphabet before visiting. Bear in mind that many of Belgrade's streets have been known by different names over the years, so there may be some confusion when locals refer to them by names that don't match those on the latest city maps.

The map references for all Belgrade sights, hotels, restaurants and shops in this guide refer to the Street Finder maps on the following pages. The letter and number in the map reference give the grid reference on the main map. The key map below shows the area covered by the main map. Symbols used on the main map are listed in the key below. The opposite page has an index of street names and places of interest shown on the main map.

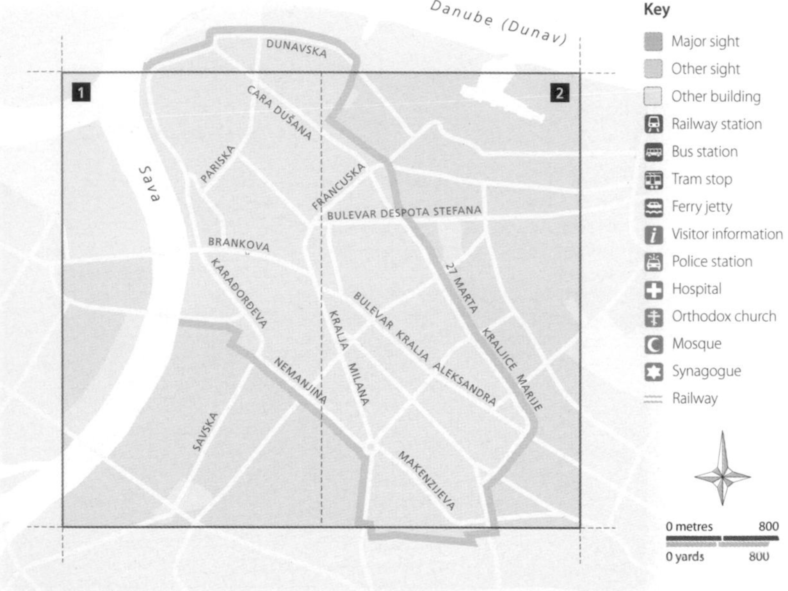

Scale of Maps 1–2

0 metres 500

0 yards 500

Panoramic view of Belgrade at night from the floodlit grounds of Kalemegdan Fortress

Street Finder Index

Sight Index

Ada Ciganlija B5
Automobile Museum D3
Bajrakli Mosque C1
Belgrade Central Bus Station B3
Belgrade Central Railway Station C3
Belgrade Emergency Clinical Centre C5
Belgrade Planetarium B1
Belgrade Zoo B1
Cathedral Church of St Michael B2
Chapel of St Petka B1
Church of St Alexander Nevsky D1
Church of St Mark D3
Church of St Sava D5
Cvijeta Zuzoric Art Pavilion B1
Cultural Centre of Belgrade C2
Despot's Gate B1
Embassy of Canada C5
Embassy of France B2
Embassy of the United Kingdom C4
Ethnographic Museum C2
Faculty of Fine Arts B2
Fresco Gallery C1
Great Ravel B1
Guarnerius Hall D2
House of Flowers D5
Jewish Historical Museum C1
Kafana Question Mark B2
Kalemegdan Fortress B1
Kalemegdan Park B1
Kalenićeva pijaca E5
Kralja Petra School B2
Little Duško Radović Theatre D3
Military Museum B1
Museum of Contemporary Art A2
National Assembly D3
National Library of Serbia D5
National Museum C2
National Theatre C2
Nikola Tesla Museum E4
Palace of Princess Ljubica B2
Palilulska pijaca E3
Royal Palaces D5
Snail Theatre F5
Sukat Šalom Synagogue C2
Tašmajdan Park E3
Temple of St Sava D5
Topčider Park D5
University Children's Hospital D5
The Victor B1
Vukov Spomenik F4
Zindan Gate B1

Street Index

A

27 Marta E3
Aberdareva E3
Admirala Geprata C3
Alekse Nenadovića D5

B

Baba Višnjina E5
Balkanska C4
Beogradska E4
Birčaninova C4
Birjuzova C2
Bistrička F3
Braće Jugovića C2
Braće Krsmanović B3
Brankov most B2
Brankova B2
Brodarska A4
Budimska E2
Bulevar Arsenija Carnojevića A5
Bulevar despota Stefana D2
Bulevar kralja Aleksandra D3
Bulevar Mihajla Pupina A3
Bulevar oslobođenja D5
Bulevar vojvode Bojovića B1

C

Cara Dušana C1
Cara Lazara C2
Cara Nikolaja II E5
Cara Uroša C1
Carice Milice C2
Čarlija Čaplina E2
Čelopečka F4
Cetinjska D2
Čika-Ljubina C2
Crnogorska B3
Čubrina B2
Čumićeva C2
Cvijićeva F3

D

Dalmatinska F4
Dečanska D2
Deligradska D5
Dimitrija Tucovića F4
Dobračina D1
Đorđa Jovanovića D2
Dositejeva D1
Dr Aleksandra Kostića C4
Dragoslava Jovanovića D3
Draže Pavlovića E3
Drinčićeva D2
Dunavska E1
Đure Jakšića C2
Đušina E3
Džordža Vašingtona D2

F

Francuska D2

G

Gavrila Principa C3
Gazela most A5
Golsvordijeva E5
Gospodar Jevremova C1
Gospodar-Jovanova C1
Gračanička B2
Gundulićev venac D1

H

Hadži-Đerina E4
Hercega Stjepana E1
Hilandarska D2

I

Igmanska F4
Illje Garašanina E3
Ivan Begova B2
Ivana Markovića Irca A4
Ivankovačka F4

J

Jaše Prodanovića F2
Jelisavete Načić D2
Jug Bogdanova C3

K

Kamenička C3
Kapetan Mišina C2
Karađorđeva B3
Karnegijeva E4
Katanićeva E5
Kičevska E4
King Alexander Boulevard E4
Kneginje Ljubice D1
Kneginje Zorke D5
Knez Mihailova C2
Knez-Miletina E2
Kneza Danila F4
Kneza Miloša B5
Knićaninova D1
Koče Kapetana E5
Kolarčeva C2
Kondina D3
Kopernikova F3
Kosančićev venac B2
Kosovska D3
Kralja Milana D3
Kralja Milutina D4
Kralja Petra B2
Kraljevića Marka B3
Kraljice Marije E4
Kraljice Natalije C3
Krunska D4
Krušedolska D5
Kursulina E5

L

Ljube Didića F3
Ljube Stojanovića F3
Lomina C3
Loznička F5

M

Mačvanska E5
Majke Jevrosime D3
Makedonska D2
Makenzijeva D5
Mali Tašmajdan E4
Maršala B2
Mihailova C2
Mihizova E1
Milana Tankosića F3
Milеševska F5
Mišarska D4
Mitropolita Petra F3
Mlatišumina F5
Molerova E5
Mutapova E5

N

Nemanjina C4
Nevesinjska E5
Nikodima Milaša F3
Niška F5
Njegoševa D4
Novopazarska E5

O

Obilićev venac C2

P

Palmotićeva D3
Pančićeva D1
Pariska B2
Pasterova C4
Poenkareova F2
Pop Lukina B2
Porečka F2
Požarevačka F5
Preradovićeva F3
Primorska F3
Prince Miloš Street C4
Prizrenska C3
Prote Mateje D5

R

Radivoja Koraća F5
Radoslava Grujića F5
Rajićeva B2
Republic Square C2
Resavska C5
Rige od Fere C1
Ruvarčeva E2
Ruzveltova F4

S

Sadika Ramiza A4
Sajmište A3
Šantićeva E2
Sarajevska B5
Savska B4
Savski trg C4
Simina C2
Sinđelićeva F5
Skadarska D2
Skender-Begova C1
Smitjanićeva E5
Sredačka F5
Stanoja Glavaša E3
Stari savski most B3
Starine Novaka E3
Sterijina F2
Stjepana Ljubiše F4
Strahinjića Bana C1
Studentski trg C2
Svetog Nikole F4
Svetog Save D5
Svetogorska D2
Svetozara Markovića C5

T

Tadeuša Košcuška C1
Takovska E3
Terazije C3
Tomaša Ježa F5
Topličin venac B2
Topolska E5
Trg Nikole Pašića D3
Trg republike C2
Trg Slavija D5
Trnska E5

U

Ušće A2
Uzun Mirkova C1

V

Vase Čarapića C2
Venizelosova E2
Višegradska B5
Višnjićeva C1
Visokog Stevana C1
Vladetina E4
Vladimira Popovića A3
Vojvode Bogdana F4
Vojvode Brane F4
Vojvode Dobrnjca E2
Vojvode Dragomira F5
Vojvode Milenka Tiršova C4
Vojvode Šupljikca F5
Vuka Karadžića C2
Vukice Mitrović F5

Z

Zadarska B2
Zahumska F4
Zarija Vujoševića A3
Zeleni venac C3
Železnička B3
Zemunski put A3
Zetska D2
Zmaj Jovina C2
Zmaja Od Noćaja C1

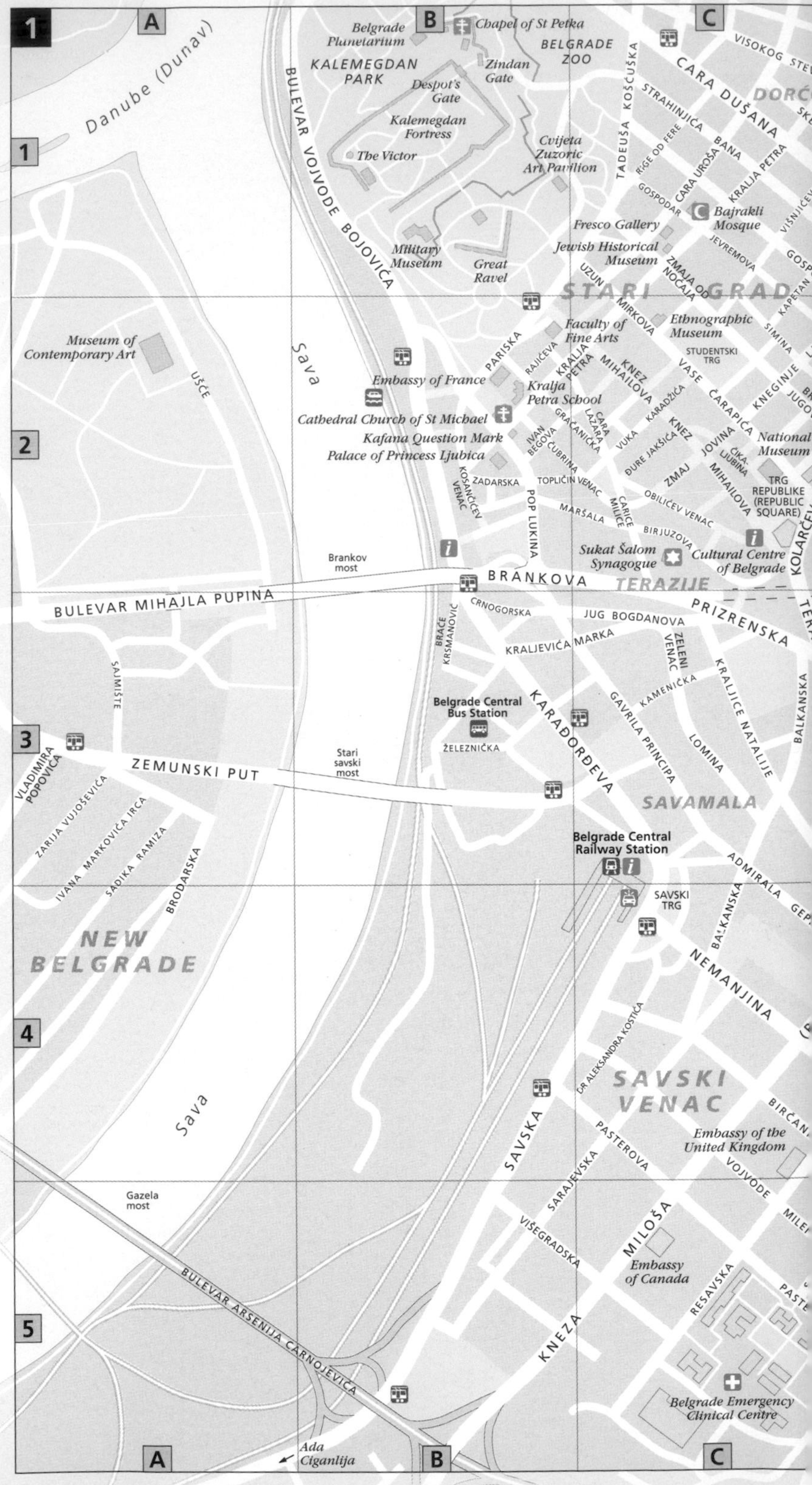

Belgrade Planetarium
Chapel of St Petka
KALEMEGDAN PARK
BELGRADE ZOO
Zindan Gate
Despot's Gate
Kalemegdan Fortress
The Victor
Cvijeta Zuzoric Art Pavilion
Fresco Gallery
Bajrakli Mosque
Jewish Historical Museum
Military Museum
Great Ravel
STARI GRAD
Faculty of Fine Arts
Ethnographic Museum
Museum of Contemporary Art
Embassy of France
Kralja Petra School
Cathedral Church of St Michael
Kafana Question Mark
Palace of Princess Ljubica
National Museum
TRG REPUBLIKE (REPUBLIC SQUARE)
Sukat Šalom Synagogue
Cultural Centre of Belgrade
TERAZIJE
Danube (Dunav)
Sava
BULEVAR VOJVODE BOJOVIĆA
Brankov most
BRANKOVA
BULEVAR MIHAJLA PUPINA
Belgrade Central Bus Station
ZEMUNSKI PUT
Stari savski most
SAVAMALA
Belgrade Central Railway Station
SAVSKI TRG
NEW BELGRADE
SAVSKI VENAC
Embassy of the United Kingdom
Embassy of Canada
Gazela most
BULEVAR ARSENIJA ČARNOJEVIĆA
Belgrade Emergency Clinical Centre
Ada Ciganlija
KARAĐORĐEVA
NEMANJINA
KNEZA MILOŠA
SAVSKA
PRIZRENSKA
KNEZ MIHAILOVA
CARA DUŠANA

D
E
F
2
Belgrade Port
1
DUNAVSKA
GUNDULIĆEV
LJUBICE
DOBRAČINA
KNEGINJE
VENAC
DOSITEJEVA
Church of St Alexander Nevsky
HERCEGA STJEPANA
MIHIZOVA
DUNAVSKA
DOBRAČINA
BANA
FRANCUSKA
DŽORDŽA VAŠINGTONA
ĐORĐA JOVANOVIĆA
VENIZELOSOVA
Beograd Dunav
POENKAREOVA
JELISAVETE NAČIĆ
ŠANTIĆEVA
GUNDULIĆEV VENAC
KNEZ-MILETINA
SKADARSKA
CETINJSKA
SKADARLIJA
BUDIMSKA
VOJVODE
POREČKA
DRINČIĆEVA
ZETSKA
Guarnerius Hall
BULEVAR DESPOTA STEFANA
STERIJINA
ČARLIJA ČAPLINA
DOBRNJCA
HILANDARSKA
SVETOGORSKA
FUVAREVA
JAŠE
PRODANOVIĆA
KONDINA
MAJKE JEVROSIME
Automobile Museum
PALMOTIĆEVA
TAKOVSKA
CVIJIĆEVA
DRAŽE PAVLOVIĆA
LJUBE STOJANOVIĆA
KOPERNIKOVA
MITROPOLITA PETRA
ČARLIJA ČAPLINA
KOSOVSKA
DALMATINSKA
27 MARTA
ĐUŠINA
National Assembly
TAKOVSKA
Palilulska pijaca
PALILULA
PRERADOVIĆEVA
TRG NIKOLE PAŠIĆA
Little Duško Radović Theatre
STANOJA GLAVAŠA
LJUBE DIDIĆA
PRIMORSKA
3
ILIJE GARAŠANINA
KNEZA DANILA
BISTRIČKA
ABERDAREVA
Church of St Mark
MILANA TANKOSIĆA
STARINE NOVAKA
CVIJIĆEVA
DALMATINSKA
NIKODIMA MILAŠA
BULEVAR
TAŠMAJDAN PARK
STREET)
BEOGRADSKA
VLADETINA
KNEZA DANILA
SVETOG NIKOLE
RESAVSKA
KRUNSKA
KRALJA
MALI TAŠMAJDAN
IVANKOVAČKA
STJEPANA LJUBIŠE
DIMITRIJA TUCOVIĆA
MIŠARSKA
SVETOZARA MARKOVIĆA
KARNEGIJEVA
KRALJICE MARIJE
RUZVELTOVA
KRALJA
KRALJA MILUTINA
ALEKSANDRA
DALMATINSKA
Vukov Spomenik
4
BEOGRADSKA
Nikola Tesla Museum
(KING
ČELOPEČKA
VOJVODE BRANE
MILANA
MATEJE
NENADOVIĆA
ZORKE
MOLEROVA
HADŽI-ĐERINA
ALEXANDER
VOJVODE BOGDANA
NJEGOŠEVA
ZAHUMSKA
IGMANSKA
SMILJANIĆEVA
KNEGINJE
KRUNSKA
KIĆEVSKA
BOULEVARD)
PROTE
TRG SLAVIJA
ALEKSE
GOLSVORDIJEVA
TRNSKA
MLATIŠUMINA
SINĐELIĆEVA
MILUTINA
NIŠKA
SREDAČKA
VOJVODE ŠUPLJIKCA
SVETOG SAVE
MAKENZIJEVA
KAPETANA
VIŠNJINA
POŽAREVAČKA
BULEVAR OSLOBOĐENJA
MOLEROVA
KOČE
NJEGOŠEVA
Kalenićeva pijaca
TOMAŠA JEŽA
KNEGINJE ZORKE
BABA
GRUJIĆA
Snail Theatre
LOZNIČKA
5
TIRŠOVA
KURSULINA
NEVESINJSKA
TOPOLSKA
MILEŠEVSKA
Church of St Sava
KATANIĆEVA
MUTAPOVA
VOJVODE DRAGOMIRA
RADOSLAVA
KRUŠEDOLSKA
VRAČAR
RADIVOJA KORAĆA
National Library of Serbia
Temple of St Sava
NOVOPAZARSKA
MAČVANSKA
CARA NIKOLAJA II
VUKICE MITROVIĆ
D
E
F

ΜΡ
ΘΥ
ΙϹ
ΧϹ

CENTRAL SERBIA

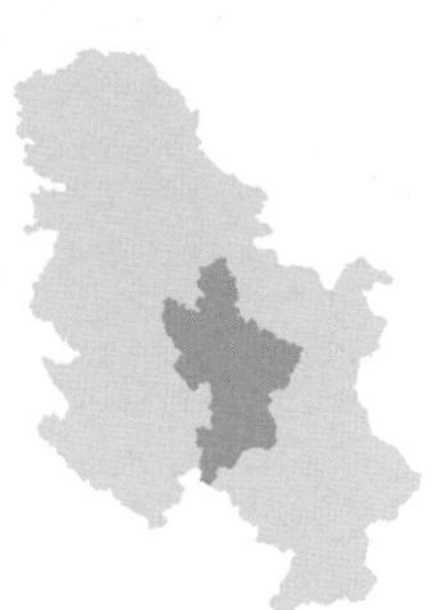

Serbia's historic heartland is home to several of the country's former capitals and many of its finest medieval monasteries. Known as Šumadija, the region takes its name from the forest, or *šuma*, that once covered the area so densely that locals had to climb trees to get their bearings. Today it is still thickly forested in places, but most of the impenetrable foliage has long since been replaced by bucolic villages and a patchwork of cereal crop fields and plum and pear orchards.

Central Serbia's broad plains along the banks of the Great Morava River rise gradually towards the mountains in the east, west and south of Šumadija. When Prince Lazar established his powerful empire here in the 14th century, he chose Kruševac as his capital and ushered in an era of cultural enlightenment. Hidden in secluded valleys and woods, the beautifully frescoed monastery churches of Ljubostinja, Ravanica, Manasija and Kalenić, along with Lazarica Church in Kruševac, were born of this Serbian renaissance. Their distinctive style became known as the Morava School of church architecture and today they attract tourists from all around the world.

After Lazar's death at the decisive Battle of Kosovo in 1389, the Turks pressed in from the south. Lazar's son Stefan was forced to move the capital to Belgrade in 1403, but his successor Đurađ Branković ceded the city to the Hungarians in 1427 and shifted the capital to Smederevo on the Danube. There he built one of Europe's mightiest fortresses, now a popular visitor attraction.

When Smederevo finally fell to the Ottomans in 1459, the medieval state of Serbia was crushed. It wasn't until 1804 that Karađorđe inspired the local Serbs to launch the First Serbian Uprising and drive out the Turks. His tomb and the stunning interior of Topola's Karađorđe Mausoleum Church of St George have since become one of the area's key sights. Prince Miloš, who led the Second Serbian Uprising in 1815, established Kragujevac as his capital, endowing it with splendid 19th-century buildings that are well worth a visit.

The imposing ramparts of the medieval Smederevo Fortress, offering superb views of the Danube

◀ Delicate stonework around the main doorway of Kalenić Monastery

Exploring Central Serbia

Smederevo's proximity to Belgrade makes it the obvious starting point for exploring the region. From here, the route south along the Great Morava River leads to the wooded valleys of the Kučaj Mountains and the fortified monasteries of Manasija and Ravanica. Deeper in the mountains and easily accessible by road are the remarkable karst caverns of Resavska Cave. Further south, at the confluence of the West and South Morava Rivers, lies Kruševac, an excellent base from which to visit the nearby Kalenić and Ljubostinja Monasteries. Northwest of Kruševac, past a valley that runs between the Gledić and Kotlenik Mountains, is the large industrial city of Kragujevac. From here it is an easy day trip west to Borač's hidden church or north to Topola and the pleasant spa town of Aranđelovac.

The Borački krš bluff rising from the rural landscape around Borač

Getting Around

The Belgrade–Niš motorway provides a smooth route between Smederevo and Kruševac. There is also a railway line, but buses are a better option as Serbian trains are not renowned for their speed. Although public transport between towns and cities in the region is reliable, accessing remote monasteries will necessitate hiring either a taxi or a rental car with up-to-date satellite navigation, as some, such as Kalenić, are poorly signposted.

Magnificently decorated interior of the Karađorđe Mausoleum Church of St George, Topola

Sights at a Glance

1. Smederevo
2. *Manasija Monastery pp70–71*
3. Resavska Cave
4. Ravanica Monastery
5. Kruševac
6. Kragujevac
7. Borač
8. Topola
9. Aranđelovac

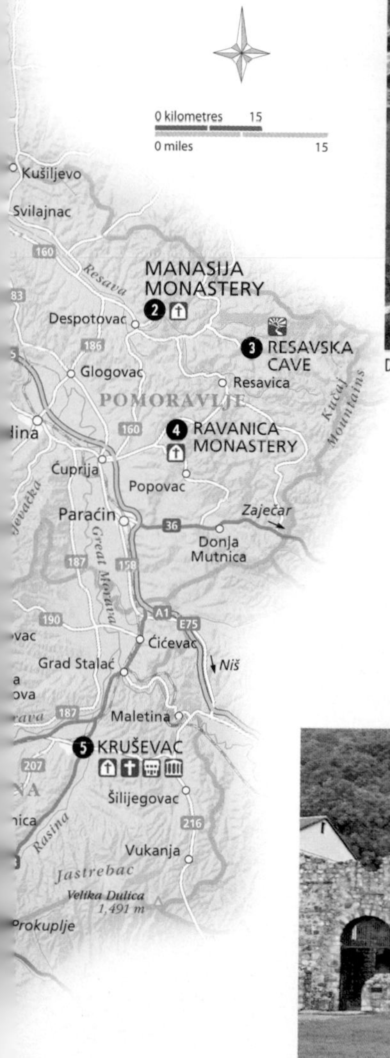

0 kilometres 15

0 miles 15

Detail of St Nicetas from the holy warriors fresco at Manasija Monastery

Key

- Motorway
- Main road
- Other road
- Railway
- Regional border
- Peak

Beautiful 14th-century Church of the Ascension at Ravanica Monastery

For additional map symbols *see back flap*

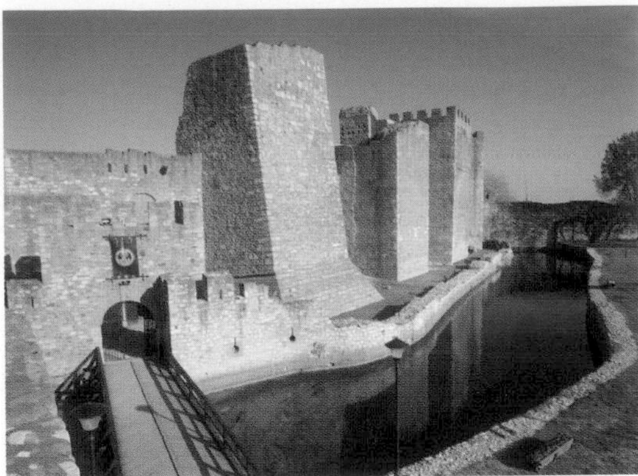

The massive ramparts and towers of Smederevo Fortress on the banks of the Danube

❶ Smederevo

Road Map C3. 54 km (34 miles) SE of Belgrade. 70,000. Belgrade. Kralja Petra 1/8, (026) 615666, 8am–8pm Mon–Fri, 9am–3pm Sat. **toosd.com** Sep: Autumn in Smederevo.

The town began life as a small Roman settlement on the route to Viminacium *(see p104)*. In 1428, after the loss of Belgrade to the Hungarians the previous year and under pressure from the Ottomans, Despot Đurađ Branković selected Smederevo as his new capital and set about constructing a colossal riverside fort to secure himself against attack. **Smederevo Fortress** (Smederevska tvrđava) is now the town's key attraction.

Constructed in the shape of an equilateral triangle with 25 towers linked by 4-m (13-ft) thick walls, it was one of the mightiest medieval fortresses in Europe. Yet within a decade of its completion it had fallen to Sultan Mehmed II despite his marriage to Branković's eldest daughter just a few years earlier. A peace treaty saw Smederevo being handed back to the Serbs in 1444, but Mehmed returned and in 1459, after a three-year siege and heavy bombardment, the fortress was taken for the last time and the medieval Serbian state crushed.

The fort's distinctive Byzantine style of layered red brick and stone is thought to have been chosen by Branković's Greek wife Jerina, who oversaw much of the construction while her husband was preoccupied with running the country. The fort is divided into the Small and Large Towns. It took two years to build the Small Town, an inner citadel and fortified palace for the use of the Branković family, with an elegant Renaissance design, river views and private toilets. The Large Town covers over 10 ha (28 acres) within the fort's main walls; it took several years to complete and was eventually home to around 5,000 people.

Used as a military site by the Ottomans for several centuries, the fort suffered a catastrophic explosion on 5 June 1941, said to have been caused by the blowing up of a German ammunition dump within its walls; much of the southern wall was destroyed and over 2,500 people from Smederevo were killed.

Today the fort's Large Town is popular with locals who promenade here in the evenings; the Small Town is often used for performances and concerts and can be visited for superb views from the ramparts. **Smederevo Museum** (Muzej u Smederevu) is a short walk south of the fort and has an absorbing collection of artifacts on display.

Smederevo Fortress
Tel (026) 222138. **Open** 8am–8pm daily. **smederevskatvrdjava.com**

Smederevo Museum
Omladinska 4. **Tel** (026) 4622138. **Open** 10am–5pm Tue–Fri, 10am–3pm Sat–Sun.

❷ Manasija Monastery

See pp70–71.

❸ Resavska Cave

Resavska pećina

Road Map D3. 20 km (13 miles) E of Despotovac. **Tel** (035) 611110. **Open** Apr–Oct: 9am–5pm daily; Nov–Mar: no fixed hours, the guard at the entrance can arrange limited access. **resavskapecina.rs**

Carved into limestone bedrock by subterranean rivers over 80 million years ago, Resavska Cave lay hidden behind dense undergrowth until its discovery in 1962. Renowned for the striking red (iron oxide), yellow (clay residue) and white (crystallized calcium) colouring of its mesmerizing display of stalactites, stalagmites, columns and stone waterfalls, it has long been considered the country's most impressive cave. Around 3 km (2 miles) of Resavka's tunnels have been explored, of which 800 m (2,625 ft) are open to the public as part of a 45-minute guided tour. Although the cave system consists of three levels, only the upper and middle galleries are open to the public; the lowest is closed due to the presence of an underground stream. With the temperature staying constant at 7° C (45° F), warm clothes are required; those without can rent jackets at the entrance for a small fee.

Ancient limestone stalactite and stalagmite formations at Resavska Cave

Richly decorated iconostasis in Ravanica Monastery's Church of the Ascension

❹ Ravanica Monastery

Manastir Ravanica

Road Map D4. 10 km (6 miles) NE of Ćuprija. **Open** 7am–7pm daily.

With its five domes, intricately decorated stone window and door frames, and thick walls of layered red brick and stone, Ravanica Monastery's Church of the Ascension is one of the earliest examples of the Morava School of church architecture. Ravanica was also the first of Serbia's fortified monasteries to be built. During its construction in the 1370s, its founder, Prince Lazar, had the complex encircled with walls, ramparts and towers, but these were to prove little deterrent to the invading Turks. Successive attacks left the monastery in ruins by the late 17th century after which it was gradually reconstructed.

Today just the fortification foundations remain. The church has lost many of its original frescoes, but among the surviving artworks are bold portraits of holy warriors and of Lazar, his wife Milica, and their two sons. In 1392 Lazar's remains were brought here according to his wishes. They were taken north to Szentendre for safekeeping in 1689, then to Fruška Gora *(see p97)* in 1697 and were only returned to Ravanica in 1989, 600 years after his death.

❺ Kruševac

Road Map C4. 200 km (125 miles) S of Belgrade. 59,000. Belgrade. Majke Jugovića 3, (037) 440332. **turizamkrusevac.com** Sep: International Festival of Orthodox Film.

Founded by Prince Lazar as the Serb capital in 1371, Kruševac was home to his mighty fortress, the spot from where he and his army set out in 1389 for the fateful Battle of Kosovo. In 1403, as the Turks were closing in, Lazar's son Stefan moved the capital north to Belgrade and, in 1454, Kruševac fell to the Turks.

Centred on the black marble Monument to the Kosovo Heroes (1904) on Gazimestanska, modern Kruševac is a pleasant town whose rather drab post-war architecture is relieved by a few 19th-century gems. One of these is the Neo-Classical town hall near the monument. A five-minute walk northwest of the town hall is the Archaeological Park where the city's **National Museum** (Narodni muzej) is set in a beautifully renovated building that first opened in 1863 as one of Serbia's earliest grammar schools. Its exhaustive collection includes a replica of a long Venetian cloak thought to have been worn by Prince Lazar and a rare 15th-century crossbow mechanism. In the park some crumbling walls and a ruined tower are all that remain of the fortress, but the 14th-century St Stephen's Church nearby, better known as **Lazarica Church**, is in remarkably good condition. Its layered brick and stone walls and finely carved stone motifs mark it out as an early instance of the Morava School.

National Museum
Archaeological Park. **Tel** (037) 4291172.
Open 8am–8pm daily.

Lazarica Church
Archaeological Park. **Open** 8am–7pm daily.

Environs

Two monasteries lie within easy reach of Kruševac by car. Built in 1404 by Prince Lazar's widow Milica, **Ljubostinja Monastery** is a wonderful example of the Morava School. It is still a working monastery; the resident nuns produce their own wine and honey. **Kalenić Monastery**, built in 1414, is a masterpiece of the Morava School. Its layered exterior resembles Lazarica Church, while its frescoed interior is graceful and striking.

Ljubostinja Monastery
30 km (19 miles) W of Kruševac.
Open 7am–7pm daily.

Kalenić Monastery
40 km (25 miles) NW of Kruševac.
Open 7am–7pm daily.

The beautifully layered brick and stone façade of Lazarica Church, Kruševac

❷ Manasija Monastery

Manastir Manasija

Nestled deep in the forested Resava Valley, Serbia's most spectacular fortified monastery was founded by Despot Stefan Lazarević in 1418. Wary of the expanding Ottoman Empire, Lazarević took the precaution of encircling his Holy Trinity Church with massive walls punctuated by 11 towers, but in 1438, just 11 years after his death, Manasija fell to the Turks. Major restoration work was carried out in the 18th and 19th centuries; archaeological research and preservation work is still taking place at Manasija, which even today is a working monastery with resident nuns.

15th-Century Tiled Rosette
Part of the original church floor, the rosette was miraculously undamaged when gunpowder kegs stored in the narthex by Austrian troops exploded in 1718.

★ Holy Trinity Church
With its sculpted elements and stylized floral motifs, this is a beautiful early example of the Morava School, built by Lazarević as his burial church, or, as his chronicler Constantine the Philosopher described it, his "silent home". Its façade has been substantially rebuilt and lost much of its original stonework, but the frescoed interior is still stunning.

KEY

① **The monastery kitchen**, next to the refectory, was one of Serbia's largest. Its massive oven was used to prepare meals for up to 300 people.

② **The iconostasis**, a recently installed replica, has been carved from the same Byzantium stone that was used for the original.

③ **A tomb said to be Stefan's** was found beneath the original church floor during restoration. The tomb had been forced open and the grave goods stolen, but the skeleton was intact. DNA analysis shows the man was closely related to Stefan's father Prince Lazar, but the remains could also be those of Stefan's brother Vuk.

④ **The Despot's Keep** was built as a last defence with only one entrance high above the ground. Its granary could hold 20 tonnes of grain to feed 100 beseiged people for a year.

Fortifications and Towers
Each of the monastery's 11 defensive castellated towers had a ground floor and six upper floors. They are distinctive for their machicolations from where stones and hot oil could be dropped onto attacking forces.

For hotels and restaurants in this region see p127 and pp135–6

Old Refectory Ruins
The best preserved of the original monastery structures, the refectory building once had two floors and an interior covered in frescoes.

VISITORS' CHECKLIST

Practical Information
Road Map D3. 150 km (93 miles) SE of Belgrade, 3 km (2 miles) E of Despotovac. **Tel** (035) 611290.
Open May–Oct: 8am–7pm daily; Nov–Apr: 8am–4pm daily. guided tours. 8am Sun.
manasija.rs

Transport
Belgrade. To Despotovac, then a 10-minute taxi ride or a 45-minute walk to Manasija.

Ramparts
The ramparts were 12 m (39 ft) high and 3 m (10 ft) thick. A crenellated wall ran along the top, protecting those defending the monastery.

Stefan Lazarević

A renowned patron of the arts, Lazarević (1377–1427) was also one of Serbia's most accomplished medieval writers. He endowed Manasija Monastery generously and invited monks and scholars here to continue their work of copying and distributing religious texts in a bid to preserve Serbian culture.

Fresco of Despot Stefan Lazarević in monastery church at Manasija

★ Holy Warriors Fresco
The best known of the church's surviving frescoes are the holy warriors Arethas, Nestor and Nicetas in the north choir. They are notable for the volume, shading and vibrancy of their features, which indicate a clear Renaissance influence.

View of the picturesque spa town of Aranđelovac in winter ▶

АПОТЕКА

❻ Kragujevac

Road Map C4. 120 km (75 miles) S of Belgrade. 151,000. Belgrade. Kralja Aleksandra Karađorđevića 44, (034) 332172. **gtokg.org.rs** Jun: Arsenal Fest.

Founded in the mid-15th century, Kragujevac was an unexceptional provincial town until its dramatic rise to prominence in 1818 when Prince Miloš Obrenović established his court here after the Second Serbian Uprising. Its elevated status brought immediate rewards – Serbia's first theatre was built here in 1833 and its first high school followed soon after; both still function and are objects of considerable local pride. Although the capital was moved to Belgrade in 1841, the town continued to prosper thanks largely to the growing Zastava armaments factory which later gained fame for its Yugo and Zastava cars.

Today Kragujevac is Serbia's fourth largest city, with a town centre featuring both modern edifices and a congenial blend of pretty 19th-century buildings and pavement cafés spread out along Kralja Petra street.

A short walk south of the city centre is the Old Church, built by Miloš in 1818. Oddly, all his parliamentary sessions were held outdoors in the church courtyard until 1859 when the adjacent red-brick building was constructed. Behind the church a disused Zastava foundry has been turned into the fascinating **Zastava Industrial Museum** (Muzej stara livnica), and a once heroic statue of a car worker now lingers forlornly outside the defunct Zastava offices.

The route back to the town centre leads past 19th-century buildings that were originally part of the royal compound. The residence of Prince Miloš is now the **National Museum** (Narodni muzej), with an intriguing array of ancient and modern weaponry. The museum's local history exhibition is sited opposite in **Amidža's Mansion** (Amidžin konak). Between these two is the **Small Art Gallery** (Mali likovni salon), holding mostly 20th-century Serbian works.

Within Serbia, Kragujevac is best known for the tragic massacre of over 3,000 of its male inhabitants by the occupying Nazis in October 1941. Executed en masse in retribution for a partisan ambush on German troops, the victims were mainly high school students and their teachers. Kragujevac October Memorial Park (Spomen park Kragujevački oktobar), northwest of the town centre, has scattered sombre monuments that mark mass graves, and the **October 21st Memorial Museum** (Spomen muzej 21. oktobar), which holds moving reminders of the event.

Lake Šumaričko, north of the memorial park, is very good for swimming and boating and is a popular local summer hangout.

Kragujevac's October 21st Memorial Museum with 33 towers of varying heights

Zastava Industrial Museum
Currently closed for renovation.

National Museum, Amidža's Mansion and Small Art Gallery
Vuka Karadžića 1. **Tel** (034) 333302. **Open** 10am–5pm Tue–Fri, 10am–2pm Sat. **muzej.org.rs**

October 21st Memorial Museum
Kragujevac October Memorial Park (Šumarice Memorial Park). **Tel** (034) 335607. **Open** Summer: 8am–6pm daily; winter: 8am–3pm daily. audio guides. **gtokg.org.rs**

Borač's "hidden" church, designed to be concealed from Ottoman invaders

❼ Borač

Road Map C4. 37 km (23 miles) E of Kragujevac. 600.

This sleepy Šumadija village is surrounded by an undulating patchwork of fields and dwarfed by the dark towering rocks of Borački krš, a jagged bluff that rises sharply from the landscape. Borač's main attraction is its small 14th-century "hidden" church, hemmed in by giant boulders at the base of the bluff and partially obscured by trees. Slightly enlarged in the 19th century, the church has been made easily accessible by stone steps and a courtyard, but the original design with its windowless exterior was intended to conceal and defend it from the invading Turks. The overgrown graveyard below is packed with 17th-century peasant gravestones with unusual carvings. Leaning at precarious angles, they feature a multitude of interwoven geometric patterns strongly reminiscent of Celtic symbols and signs.

For hotels and restaurants in this region see p127 and pp135–6

8 Topola

Road Map C3. 39 km (24 miles) N of Kragujevac. 5,000. Kneginje Zorke13, (034) 811172. **topolaoplenac.org.rs**

As the hometown of Karađorđe, the legendary leader of the First Serbian Uprising in 1804, Topola is revered by the Serbs and seen by many as the first capital of modern Serbia. Karađorđe's tomb is located up on Oplenac Hill in the stunning marble **Karađorđe Mausoleum Church of St George** (Crkva svetog Đorđa, Mauzolej Karađorđevića). Founded by his grandson King Peter I in 1912, it was completed in 1930 with a magnificent interior of floor-to-ceiling frescoes copied from medieval Serbian churches and vividly re-created in glittering mosaics. Opposite, **King Peter's House** (Kuća kralja Petra I) was meant to be modest workers' quarters, but the king liked it so much that he spent much of his time there supervising the church's construction. The fortified Karađorđev grad compound lay on the wooded hillside below Oplenac. Today, visitors can explore its ruined walls, a small memorial church Karađorđe built in 1811, and the **Karađorđe House Museum** (Karađorđev konak) set in what was once his residence.

Karađorđe Mausoleum Church of St George
Oplenac Hill. **Open** Apr–Oct: 8am–7pm daily; Nov–Mar: 9am–4pm daily. combined ticket.

Entrance of the Karađorđe Mausoleum Church of St George in Topola

The Romanticist exterior of Prince Mihailo's Staro zdanje in Aranđelovac

King Peter's House
Oplenac Hill. **Open** Apr–Oct: 8am–7pm daily; Nov–Mar: 9am–4pm daily. combined ticket.

Karađorđe House Museum
Karađorđev grad. **Tel** (034) 811280. **Open** Apr–Oct: 8am–7pm daily; Nov–Mar: 9am–4pm daily. combined ticket.

9 Aranđelovac

Road Map C3. 52 km (32 miles) N of Kragujevac. 25,000. Knjaz Miloša 243, (034) 725575, 9am–8pm Mon–Fri, 10am–6pm Sat–Sun.

Founded by Prince Miloš in 1837, modern Aranđelovac is an appealing spa town that lies beneath the densely forested Mount Bukulja (696 m/2,283 ft). Its main draw is the meticulously tended Bukovička Spa Park where 16 ha (40 acres) of lawns and neat flowerbeds are dotted with Modernist white marble sculptures and shaded by a variety of tree species. The frequent visits of Prince Miloš's son Mihailo in the late 19th century did much to promote Aranđelovac's spa credentials; he intended to have a summer residence here, but died before the construction of his fine Romanticist mansion was complete in 1872. Known as Staro zdanje, it was later used as a hotel and then renovated in the 1960s but has since been abandoned and boarded up. Another of the park's notable buildings is the Art Nouveau Knjaz Miloš Pavilion. Built in 1907 on the site of Bukovička's oldest mineral spring, it originally functioned as both a therapeutic spa centre and a mineral water bottling plant for the Knjaz Miloš brand that is still sold throughout Serbia today.

On the outskirts of town is **Risovača Cave** (Risovača pećina). A cave dwelling diorama provides an intriguing glimpse of how life here might once have been. Neanderthal tools and ice age bones of bears and lions from the cave are displayed in the **National Museum** (Narodni muzej).

Risovača Cave
Arandelovac. **Tel** (034) 722883. **Open** 9am–5pm daily.

National Museum
Mišarska 19. **Tel** (034) 712415. **Open** 9am–5pm Mon–Fri, 10am–2pm Sat–Sun.

Karađorđe

Born to a pig farming family in 1768, Đorđe Petrović later became known as Karađorđe (Black George) on account of his violent temper. He fought on the Austro-Hungarian side during their 1789–92 war against Turkey, but when they retreated and allowed the Turks to retake his homeland of Šumadija he joined the *hajduci* (local Serb rebels) in the forests. His combination of military skill and ruthless determination transformed the unruly bunch of guerrillas into a potent army that successfully forced the Turks out of Serbia during the First Serbian Uprising of 1804. Karađorđe established a government and ruled the first modern Serbian state until 1813 when the Turks returned with a vengeance and he escaped into exile.

WESTERN SERBIA

The lush valleys of Western Serbia nurture scattered towns and villages, its highlands teem with hardy cattle and its pristine mountains harbour an abundance of wildlife. It was here amongst the monasteries and hilltop forts of medieval Raška that the Serbian Orthodox conciousness was forged with such vigour that it survived centuries of Turkish domination. Yet, even with the decline of the Ottoman Empire after the Orthodox resurgence, Islamic culture proved equally resilient here, the only part of Serbia where mosques are as common as churches.

The great monasteries of Western Serbia are linked to the golden age of the country's first dynasty. Its founder, Grand Prince Stefan Nemanja, built Studenica; his son Stefan established Žiča; his grandson Stefan Vladislav built Mileševa and another grandson, Stefan Uroš I, founded Sopoćani. Only Studenica and Sopoćani are listed by UNESCO, but all four have sublime medieval frescoes and are outstanding examples of the Raška School of church architecture.

Novi Pazar, with its distinctly Oriental feel, has long dominated the area. Valjevo and Kraljevo boast some fine 19th-century buildings, and the simple dwellings at the open-air village museum of Sirogojno give visitors an idea of how the majority of rural Serbs have lived since medieval times. The Tara Mountains, where some of Europe's last brown bear populations are thriving, have won national park status, as have the Kopaonik Mountains. Kopaonik and Tornik are well-established ski centres, and the Ibar and Lim Rivers provide great rafting. The region also offers good bird-watching, biking, and hiking, while the less energetic can opt for the sedate pace of the Šargan Eight train that heads high into the hills.

Cattle farming has been a part of life here for millennia, with herders migrating between the verdant southern highlands and the northern lowlands. As a result, the area has long been known for its beef and dairy products. Serbia's best beef *ćevapčići* sausages are made in Novi Pazar, while the calorific speciality *lepinja*, a bun stuffed with butter, egg and *kajmak* (salty clotted cream), is found throughout the region.

Traditional wooden buildings of Drvengrad near Mokra Gora, the starting point of the Šargan Eight railway line

◀ *White Angel on the Grave of Christ*, a renowned fresco on the southern wall of Mileševa Monastery

Exploring Western Serbia

Valjevo is a good starting point for exploring Western Serbia, with the town museum providing an excellent overview of the region. From here the road heads south to Kraljevo, which works well as a base for the Ovčar-Kablar Gorge, Maglič Fortress and Studenica Monastery. The route continues south through the Ibar River valley past Kopaonik to Novi Pazar, home to ancient monasteries and mosques, then west through the verdant Pešter highlands to Mileševa Monastery and Prijepolje. Crossing the Zlatibor Mountains brings visitors to Zlatibor, the hopping-off point for Tara National Park, the Sirogojno open-air museum, the Šargan Eight railway and Tornik Ski Centre. From here, the road north to Valjevo follows the Dinaric Alps, which stretch out along the Adriatic coast from Slovenia to Albania.

Getting Around

Although railway lines connect Valjevo, Užice and Kraljevo to Belgrade, services are likely to be slow and uncomfortable. Buses are a more attractive option. Local buses link smaller towns and villages, but as schedules are not always strictly adhered to it is important to allow plenty of time for your journey. The best option is to rent a car in Belgrade and explore the region at your own pace.

Snow-covered hotel in Kopaonik, a popular ski centre in Western Serbia

Key

- Motorway
- Main road
- Other road
- Railway
- International border
- Regional border
- Peak

For hotels and restaurants in this region see pp127–8 and pp136–7

The 13th century Maglič Fortress near Kraljevo, one of Serbia's most dramatic and best-preserved hilltop fortresses

0 kilometres 25

0 miles 25

Sights at a Glance

1 Valjevo
2 Ovčar-Kablar Gorge
3 Kraljevo
4 Maglič Fortress
5 Studenica Monastery
6 Kopaonik
7 Novi Pazar
8 Sopoćani Monastery
9 Crna Reka Monastery
10 Prijepolje
11 Mileševa Monastery
12 Zlatibor
13 Sirogojno
14 Šargan Eight
15 Tara National Park
16 Užice

Brightly painted wooden windows in Drvengrad village near Mokra Gora

For additional map symbols *see back flap*

Colourful houses and pleasant pavement cafés lining the cobbled main street of Valjevo's historic Tešnjar quarter

❶ Valjevo

Road Map B3. 90 km (56 miles) SW of Belgrade. 60,000. Belgrade. Birčaninova 42, (014) 221138, 7.30am–3.30pm Mon–Sat. **tov.rs** May: Jazz Fest Valjevo; Oct: Pork Crackling Festival.

Snug beneath the forested Valjevo Mountains, this pleasant town has an appealing historic centre that is split in two by the Kolubara River. The northern half, developed in the early 19th century after Serbs liberated the town from the Turks, is focused on pedestrianized Kneza Miloša.

At the street's eastern end is the award-winning **National Museum** (Narodni muzej), with a series of superbly presented exhibitions, including a section dedicated to World War I when Valjevo was a military hospital town treating typhus patients from all over Serbia; American and British volunteer nurses were among the heroic medical staff. Just behind the museum is the town's oldest building, the 18th-century Turkish Governor's house known as the **Muselim's Residence** (Muselimov konak) that today houses an exhibition about the First and Second Serbian Uprisings. A 20-minute walk north of the museum along Vojvode Mišića is the sturdy **Nenadović Tower** (Kula Nenadovića), built during the First Serbian Uprising by local rebel leader Jakov Nenadović (1765–1836) to protect the town from the invading Turks.

Near the museum, a stone bridge links Kneza Miloša to the Tešnjar quarter on the opposite side, once occupied by Turkish traders and craftsmen during Ottoman rule. In recent years the houses lining its cobbled main street have been turned into characterful bars and restaurants with a lively nightlife.

National Museum and Muselim's Residence
Trg vojvode Mišića 3. **Tel** (014) 221041. **Open** 9am–6pm Tue–Sat (to 9pm Fri & to 3pm Sun). **museum.org.rs**

Nenadović Tower
Kula Nenadovića. **Open** Currently closed to the public.

Environs

Tucked away in a hidden valley is the small **Pustinja Monastery**, which is famed for the marvellously vivid and well-preserved 17th-century frescoes of Serbian saints and Biblical characters on its façade and interior walls.

Pustinja Monastery
Poćuta, 25 km (15 miles) SW of Valjevo. **Open** 7am–7pm daily.

❷ Ovčar-Kablar Gorge

Ovčarsko-kablarska klisura

Road Map C4. 100 km (62 miles) S of Belgrade.

Carved out by the West Morava River, this densely wooded gorge meanders between the steep cliffs of the Ovčar and Kablar mountain ranges for 20 km (12 miles). It is an ornithologist's paradise with over 100 bird species – including golden eagles and peregrine falcons – nesting in its oak and birch forests. Serbian Orthodox monks escaping tyranny during the Byzantine and Ottoman eras found refuge here as early as the 14th century; at one point over 300 monasteries were scattered throughout the gorge. Today only 10 remain, linked by a network of roads and hiking paths with spectacular views. The Ovčar Banja spa, set midway through the gorge, has a 38° C (100° F) mineral water pool and good access to the hiking routes; hotel staff can organize boat trips on the nearby Lake Međuvršje.

Isposnica svetog Save, hidden away in the ruggedly beautiful Ovčar-Kablar Gorge

❸ Kraljevo

Road Map C4. 140 km (87 miles) SW of Belgrade. 69,000. Belgrade. Trg srpskih ratnika 25, (036) 316000. **jutok.org.rs** Jul: Merry Downriver Ride, Jazzibar Festival; Sep: Kraljevski Filmski Festival.

Spread across a shallow valley at the heart of the Raška region, Kraljevo is an attractive city with some fine buildings and a good

For hotels and restaurants in this region see pp127–8 and pp136–7

choice of recreational activities. It owes much to the Obrenović dynasty – King Milan I (1854–1901) changed its name from Karanovac to Kraljevo ("king's town") after his coronation at nearby Žiča Monastery in 1882; Milan's granduncle Prince Miloš (1780–1860) sketched out the town plan in 1832. The circular central hub that he envisaged became the nucleus of Kraljevo. Named Trg srpskih ratnika or Serbian Warriors' Square, it is dominated by a monument to the soldiers killed in the Balkan Wars (1912–13) and World War I. The city's experience of World War II was less heroic – the Nazis shot over 2,000 local men and boys in October 1941 in retaliation for partisan attacks on the occupying German forces. The execution site to the north of town is marked by a memorial of broken marble columns.

The main sights are clustered around the city park where the fascinating collection of the **National Museum** (Narodni muzej) includes Neolithic cult objects, fragments of original frescoes from Žiča Monastery, a 14th-century German sword and the jagged shell of a NATO cluster bomb from 1999. Just behind the museum is the Orthodox **Holy Trinity Church** (Crkva svete Trojice), endowed by Prince Miloš in 1824; opposite is the Ottoman-style **Vasa's Residence** (Gospodar Vasin konak) dating from 1830 and today occupied by a religious bookshop and a craft workshop.

During the summer months locals flock to the city beach on the riverfront; the riverboat bars moored upstream are also popular. Mountain biking in the vicinity can be arranged by the tourist office on Trg srpskih ratnika, as can rafting on the Ibar River along with a variety of other adventure sports.

National Museum
Trg svetog Save 2. **Tel** (036) 333004. **Open** 9am–8pm Mon–Fri, 9am–1pm Sat–Sun. **nmkv.rs**

Holy Trinity Church
Trg svetog Save. **Open** 7am–7pm daily. 8am Sat & Sun.

Vasa's Residence
Trg svetog Save.

Kraljevo's circular Serbian Warriors' Square centred on the war monument

4 Maglič Fortress

Tvrđava Maglič

Road Map C4. 26 km (16 miles) SW of Kraljevo.

One of Serbia's most imposing and best-preserved hilltop forts, Maglič was built in the 13th century to guard the Ibar Valley pass. Serbian archbishop Danilo II built St George's Church, cells and a palace here in the 14th century. The remains of these structures can be seen today, encircled by seven towers and a great keep, linked by the fort's 2-m (7-ft) thick walls. The Turks occupied the fortress from 1459, and it was last used defensively during the 1815 Second Serbian Uprising when Serbian rebels attacked the Turks garrisoned in the fort. Substantial repairs carried out during the 1980s included the replacement of the wooden walkways along the battlements, which visitors can climb for breathtaking views.

The exquisite marble-clad Church of the Virgin Mary at Studenica Monastery

5 Studenica Monastery

Manastir Studenica

Road Map C4. 60 km (37 miles) SW of Kraljevo. **Tel** (036) 5436050. **Open** 5am–8pm daily. 5am & 7pm Mon–Fri, 6am Sat–Sun. **manastirstudenica.rs**

Considered by many to be the most beautiful monastery in Serbia, Studenica is renowned for its wonderful 13th- and 14th-century frescoes. Set on a picturesque spot chosen by Stefan Nemanja (1113–99), this UNESCO World Heritage Site takes its name from the nearby Studenica River.

Of its three churches, the oldest and most important is the Church of the Virgin Mary (Crkva svete Bogorodice), founded by Stefan Nemanja in 1191 and containing his tomb. The church façade is clad in white marble with elaborately sculpted mythical beasts and floral motifs adorning the stone door and window frames in an elegant blend of Byzantine and Romanesque that became known as the Raška School of church architecture. The interior frescoes were completed in 1209; the best known of them is the monumental image of Christ on the western wall *(see p24)*. During the Ottoman era the monastery was repeatedly ransacked and set on fire by the Turks when they reoccupied Serbia in 1813. The frescoes were so badly damaged that an amateur restoration team painted over them in 1846 and it wasn't until the 1950s that they were properly restored.

Skiers taking to the slopes at Kopaonik ski resort

6 Kopaonik

Road Map C5. 275 km (171 miles) S of Belgrade. **skijalistasrbije.rs**

Along with Zlatibor *(see p86)* and Stara planina *(see p121)*, Kopaonik is best known for its international ski resort. It is the country's largest mountain range and has had national park status since 1981. The main ski centre at Ravni Kopaonik is set around the two highest peaks – Gobelja (1,934 m/6,345 ft) and Pančićev vrh (2,016 m/6,614 ft) – and has 12 km (7 miles) of cross-country ski tracks, over 55 km (34 miles) of downhill ski runs, and several resort hotels. More accommodation is available in nearby Brzeće village, linked to Ravni Kopaonik by a 3-km (2-mile) cable car. Outside the ski season the region is perfect for hiking and bird-watching.

7 Novi Pazar

Road Map C5. 300 km (186 miles) S of Belgrade. 69,000. Belgrade. 28. novembra 27, (020) 338030. **tonp.rs** **novipazar.rs** Aug: Old City Music Festival.

With its mosques, tea houses and Eastern-influenced architecture, Novi Pazar oozes Oriental charm and is the cultural heart of the country's Bosniak population. Yet it is also the site of Serbia's oldest Orthodox church.

In 1455 the region fell to the Turks under Ottoman general Isa-beg Isaković, who founded Novi Pazar in 1461 and Bosnia's capital, Sarajevo, a year later. The walls and several towers of the military fortress Isaković built in Novi Pazar have long since been incorporated into the town's central park.

The main draw is Prvog maja or 1st May Street, located in the old town. Known locally as Istanbul Street, it is lined with characterful family-run jewellery shops, bakeries and coffee and tea houses. Just off the pedestrianized street are the crumbling walls of the **Isa-beg Hammam**, a bathhouse that was commissioned by Novi Pazar's Turkish founder. Partially renovated, it is now a small café, with a shaded courtyard that is a great spot for a glass of Turkish tea. At the far end of 1st May Street, where the town's first residential quarter was located, is the 16th-century Altun-alem Mosque with its 25-m (82-ft) high minaret, visible from afar and audible five times a day *(see p23)*.

The **Ras Museum** (Muzej Ras), set in an attractive 19th-century Ottoman-style building across the Raška River, contains an intriguing collection, including fossils and fine weapons such as several 18th-century *yataghans*, long curved Turkish knives.

Isa-beg Hammam
Prvog maja. **Open** 8am–10pm daily.

Ras Museum
Stevana Nemanje 20. **Tel** (020) 331681. **Open** 8am–3pm Mon–Fri, 9am–3pm Sat. **muzejras.org**

Environs

The **Sts Peter and Paul Church** (Crkva svetog Petra i Pavla) was built around the 9th century on the site of a 4th-century Roman church. The founder of the powerful Nemanjić dynasty, Stefan Nemanja, was baptized and married here. The simple stone structure has three layers of battered frescoes dating back to the 11th century, and is notable for its circular foundation and an unusual balcony in the cupola reserved for royal worshippers.

The overgrown ruins of Stari Ras Fortress, on a hilltop west of Novi Pazar, have not yet been fully excavated and are only accessible by a rough track. The fort served as capital of the Serbian state of Raška between the 8th and 13th centuries. Both Stari Ras and Sts Peter and Paul Church have been added to the UNESCO World Heritage Site list alongside Sopoćani Monastery.

Sts Peter and Paul Church
Open Irregular hours (key available from the nearby house or ask at the visitor information centre in town).

The Raška River flowing through the city of Novi Pazar

Sopoćani Monastery, built by Stefan Uroš near the source of the Raška River

8 Sopoćani Monastery

Manastir Sopoćani

Road Map C5. 12 km (8 miles) W of Novi Pazar. **Open** 6am–7pm daily. 6am daily.

Taking its name from the nearby source of the Raška River – *sopot* means "spring" – Sopoćani was built in the late 13th century by King Stefan Uroš I (1223–77) and dedicated to the Holy Trinity. Using the formidable wealth he had accrued from his gold and silver mines, Uroš constructed a larger church than any that had come before; he also employed the finest fresco painters from Constantinople. The monastery prospered for several centuries until it was destroyed by the Turks in 1689 during the Great Migration. For over 200 years the remnants of its sublime frescoes were exposed to the elements. Restoration work began in 1926 and a notable number of frescoes were saved. Their monumental size and visionary quality have earned Sopoćani a place on UNESCO's World Heritage Site list.

9 Crna Reka Monastery

Manastir Crna Reka

Road Map C5. 30 km (18 miles) S of Novi Pazar. **Open** 5am–7pm daily. 5am daily.

Set high in the hills of the Crna Reka ("black river") valley, this extraordinary monastery built into the face of a steep cliff is accessible only by a rickety wooden bridge. The natural caves within the cliff face were occupied by monks as early as the 13th century, but the tiny barrel-vaulted church wasn't established until the 16th century. Its frescoed interior holds the miracle-working relics of St Peter of Koriša. The rest of the monastery's fascinating interior comprises a warren of odd-shaped rooms and staircases, a tiny healing spring, and a small cave where a hermit lived 300 years ago. The current small community of monks follow a strict routine of intensive prayer, meditation and work comparable to the austere regimes of the Mount Athos monasteries.

10 Prijepolje

Road Map B4. 270 km (168 miles) SW of Belgrade. 13,500. Trg Bratstva i jedinstva 1, (033) 710140, 7am–3pm Mon–Fri. **turizamprijepolje.org.rs**

Sprawled along the Lim River amidst forested hills, this attractive town was founded in the 14th century as a staging post on the Dubrovnik–Constantinople trade route. Its prosperity waned as the Ottoman Empire declined, and today it has few sights of interest, but is a great base for bird-watching, rafting and hiking trips. It is only a short drive from Mileševa Monastery and the ruins of Mileševac Fortress. **Prijepolje Museum** (Muzej u Prijepolju) has a well-presented collection covering the region's Roman past and featuring an engaging ethnographic section.

Prijepolje Museum
Valterova 35. **Tel** (033) 715185. **Open** 9am–4.30pm Mon–Fri; 9am–3pm Sat. **muzejuprijepolju.org.rs**

Environs

Built in the 14th century to protect Mileševa Monastery and later developed into a Turkish outpost, Mileševac Fortress perches dramatically on a hill high above the town. It is in need of restoration and there are plans to make it more easily accessible to the public.

11 Mileševa Monastery

Manastir Mileševa

Road Map B4. 6 km (4 miles) SE of Prijepolje. **Open** 6am–8pm daily. 6am & 5pm Mon–Sat; 8am Sun.

This striking monastery was built between 1219 and 1235 by King Stefan Vladislav (c. 1198–1264). St Sava's remains were kept here until 1594 when the Turks burnt them on Belgrade's Vračar Hill, where the Temple of St Sava now stands. Despite being torched by the Turks in 1459, most of the monastery church's glorious frescoes are in remarkably good condition. An image of the *White Angel on the Grave of Christ* fresco *(see p76)* on the southern wall was sent as a symbol of peace in the first satellite broadcast signal from Europe to America in 1962, and was later broadcast into space in an attempt to communicate with alien life forms.

Mileševa Monastery, an important Serbian Orthodox spiritual centre

The traditional wooden buildings of Drvengrad, located above Mokra Gora village ▶

Snowy landscape around Zlatibor, one of Serbia's top centres for winter sports

⓬ Zlatibor

Road Map B4. 200 km (125 miles) SW of Belgrade. Belgrade. Miladina Pećinara 2 (031) 841646, 8am–10pm daily. **zlatibor.org.rs** Jul: Hillsup Festival.

One of Serbia's top destinations, Zlatibor is packed with families during the summer and sports fans in the winter. Set in the picturesque Zlatibor range at an altitude of around 1,000 m (3,280 ft), it has exceptionally clean air, which first attracted health-conscious visitors in the 18th century. The resort, centred on a lake that is surrounded by rides and food stalls, offers a range of adventure activities from zorbing to off-roading.

Environs

Along with Stara planina *(see p121)* and Kopaonik *(see p82)*, **Tornik Ski Centre** is one of the country's three main ski resorts. It is named after the highest peak in Zlatibor, Tornik (1,496 m/ 4,908 ft), which can be reached throughout the year by ski lift. Tornik has 8 km (5 miles) of ski runs, downhill mountain biking and carting tracks, cross-country ski routes, an aerial adventure playground and a year-round bobsleigh track. A 9-km (6-mile) cable car link to Zlatibor is currently under construction.

Tornik Ski Centre
Tel (031) 3150004. **Open** Ski lift and bobsleigh summer: 11am–5.30pm Wed–Sun; winter: 9am–4pm daily.
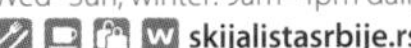 **skijalistasrbije.rs**

⓭ Sirogojno

Road Map B4. 24 km (15 miles) E of Zlatibor. **Tel** (031) 3802291. **Open** Apr–Oct: 9am–7pm daily, Nov–Mar: 9am–4pm daily. Aug: World Music Festival. **sirogojno.rs**

Known as the Old Village, this charming collection of 19th- and early 20th-century rural dwellings in Sirogojno offers a fascinating glimpse of Serbian village life before the advent of electricity and modern farming techniques. Since its founding in 1980 as the country's only open-air museum, around 55 buildings from the Zlatibor area have been dismantled and painstakingly reassembled here.

The main exhibits, dating to around 1881, are a pair of wooden family homes built on stone foundations. Both have two rooms with earthen floors and open fireplaces; the entire family slept in one room, using the second for cooking, eating and relaxing. There are also raised corn barns, underground stores for root vegetables, a dairy, a cask-making workshop and a forge. The oldest exhibit is an 1845 cottage with wooden tiles pegged to its roof.

Museum visitors can sample an excellent selection of traditional dishes in the authentic museum restaurant and can sleep in comfortable period cottages within the complex.

A 10-minute drive away is **Stopića Cave** (Stopića pećina), a limestone river cave with a stunning entrance 18-m (59-ft) high and 35-m (115-ft) wide, massive halls and a series of spectacular cascading travertine terraces that were formed from limestone deposits, similar to those at Pamukkale in Turkey.

Stopića Cave
5 km (3 miles) from Sirogojno.
Tel (031) 583377. **Open** 9.30am–4pm daily.

Traditional wooden huts at the Old Village open-air museum in Sirogojno

A Šargan Eight steam locomotive on its journey from Mokra Gora station

⑭ Šargan Eight

Šarganska osmica

Road Map B4. 225 km (140 miles) SW of Belgrade. **Tel** Mokra Gora station: (031) 800003. **Open** Apr–Oct: trains depart daily from Mokra Gora at 10.30am & 1.30pm; there may also be services at 8am & 4.10pm; in Jul & Aug the 4.10pm train runs daily. **zeleznicesrbije.com**

Originally built in 1925 as part of the Užice to Sarajevo narrow gauge railway, the Šargan Eight line is named after a complex engineering feat that used a figure-of-eight loop with 10 bridges and 22 tunnels to allow steam trains to negotiate the steep 300-m (985-ft) height difference between Mokra Gora and Šargan-Vitasi. The line was closed in 1974, but determined locals battled to reopen it and, with the help of famous Serbian film director Emir Kusturica, they eventually succeeded. The line has been fully operational since 2003, with steam trains pulling old-fashioned wood-panelled carriages up the mountain for a two-hour round trip.

Environs

Drvengrad ("timber town"), above Mokra Gora, is a village of traditional wooden buildings built from scratch as a set for Kusturica's 2004 film *Life is a Miracle*. Today it functions as a hotel, with quirky rooms in houses that stand on streets named after figures Kusturica admires, including Tesla and Fellini. There is also a restaurant, a gallery and a bookshop.

Drvengrad
Mokra Gora. **Tel** (031) 800686. for non-guests only. Jan: Küstendorf International Film and Music Festival. **mecavnik.info**

⑮ Tara National Park

Nacionalni park Tara

Road Map B4. 160 km (100 miles) SW of Belgrade. Milenka Topalovića 3, Bajina Bašta, (031) 863644. **nptara.rs**

Named after Mount Tara (1,591 m/5,219 ft), the national park is a sparsely populated wilderness on the Bosnian border. Densely forested with birch, pine, juniper and endemic Serbian spruce, it is a haven for brown bears, wild cats, chamois, golden eagles and countless other species. Over 200 km (125 miles) of well-marked cycling and hiking paths crisscross the park; maps are available at the information centres in Bajina Bašta and Mitrovac, which also rent out bikes. Due to the very real danger posed by bears, visitors are advised to always walk or cycle in groups, especially in winter.

The beautiful mountainous landscape of Western Serbia's Tara National Park

⑯ Užice

Road Map B4. 170 km (105 miles) SW of Belgrade. 60,000. Belgrade. Jul: ParkFest.

The city began life in the 14th century as a small market town set beneath a hilltop fortress. Its location in a valley encircled by mountains meant that centuries later, after World War II, the only way to accommodate the city's rapidly expanding population was to build the many high-rise concrete blocks that typify its appearance today.

The fort was taken by the Turks in 1456 and the town prospered under its new rulers until the Serbs regained control after the First Serbian Uprising. During World War II it was heroically liberated from Nazi control by Tito's partisans and existed as the Republic of Užice for 67 days before the Nazis returned with a vengeance. The expansive collection of the **National Museum** (Narodni muzej) gives visitors a thorough overview of the region's complex history. It is housed in the building that briefly served as the partisans' headquarters; to the rear is a rare statue of Tito and several vast halls that were tunnelled deep into the hillside and used for ammunition and armament production during the partisan occupation.

Daily life in Užice revolves around the wide Partisan Square (Trg partizana) that is overlooked by the monolithic Hotel Zlatibor and the theatre; both date from the Communist era and are in urgent need of renovation. During the summer months, locals usually head for the nearby riverside beaches where daredevils will sometimes jump from the railway bridge. The panoramic views from the fort's ruins are superb.

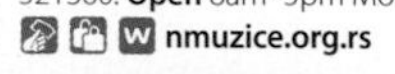

National Museum
Dimitrija Tucovića 18. **Tel** (031) 521360. **Open** 8am–5pm Mon–Sat. **nmuzice.org.rs**

Modern concrete high-rises amidst traditional red-roofed houses in Užice

NORTHERN SERBIA

Watered by the Danube, Sava and Tisa Rivers and covered with golden fields stretching to the horizon, Vojvodina's endless flat expanses are the bread basket of Serbia. Its six official languages and 26 ethnic groups reveal a cultural complexity that has long been sustained by the region's fertile soil, while its rich heritage of ancient ruins, dramatic fortresses and fine buildings is a testament to both the misfortunes and the achievements of migrant communities past and present.

The great plains north of Belgrade, formed 10 million years ago by the Pannonian Sea, were inhabited by successive waves of Indo-European tribes before the Romans arrived in the 1st century BC. The fascinating remains of Sirmium, one of the Roman Tetrarchy's four capitals, can be seen under the city of Sremska Mitrovica, and are an unmissable sight for history enthusiasts.

Marauding Huns, Goths and Avars ended Roman rule. The Slavic tribes that followed were displaced by Hungarians in the 10th century, who built a mighty fortress at Bač; its evocative ruins are now a local attraction. The Turks ruled the region until they in turn were ousted in the 17th century by the Habsburgs, who encouraged Serbs to settle in the region in return for protecting its southern borders. The Habsburgs also reinforced their defences by building Petrovaradin Fortress, today one of the top sights in Vojvodina. Across the Danube, Novi Sad was founded by Serb merchants who gifted it the marvellous edifices that set it apart from other towns; the Bačka Bishop's Palace and the buildings around Freedom Square are especially striking.

Of the Christian architecture created by the region's German migrants, the splendid Catholic cathedrals of Novi Sad and Vršac are well worth a visit, while the folk-influenced Naïve art of Kovačica's Slovaks and the sublime Art Nouveau structures of Subotica will appeal to art lovers.

No visit to this beautiful region would be complete without a walking or driving tour through the forested hills of Fruška Gora to explore the serenely graceful Orthodox monasteries that are scattered across these gentle slopes.

The elegant Neo-Gothic Church of the Name of Mary in Freedom Square, the pedestrianized hub of Novi Sad

◀ Subotica's Art Nouveau Raichle Mansion, built by architect Ferenc Raichle in 1904

Exploring Northern Serbia

Novi Sad, northwest of Belgrade on the A1/E75 motorway, makes an excellent jumping-off point from which to explore central Vojvodina. The city is packed with fine architecture and has the added bonus of Petrovaradin Fortress on the Danube's opposite bank. The wineries and historic buildings of Sremski Karlovci are a day trip away, as are the ruins of the fortress at Bač and Roman Sirmium at Sremska Mitrovica. The Fruška Gora monasteries are within easy reach, and it is worth allowing an extra day or so to explore them more thoroughly. Novi Sad is also a good base for Vršac, where a medieval fortress towers over the city and the surrounding vineyards. The A1/E75 continues north from Novi Sad past wheat, maize and soya fields to the marvellous Art Nouveau city of Subotica.

Subotica's Art Nouveau synagogue, now used for concerts and cultural events

Sights at a Glance

1. *Novi Sad pp92–5*
2. Sremski Karlovci
3. *Fruška Gora Monastery Tour p97*
4. Sremska Mitrovica
5. Bač
6. Subotica
7. Kovačica
8. Vršac
9. Bela Crkva

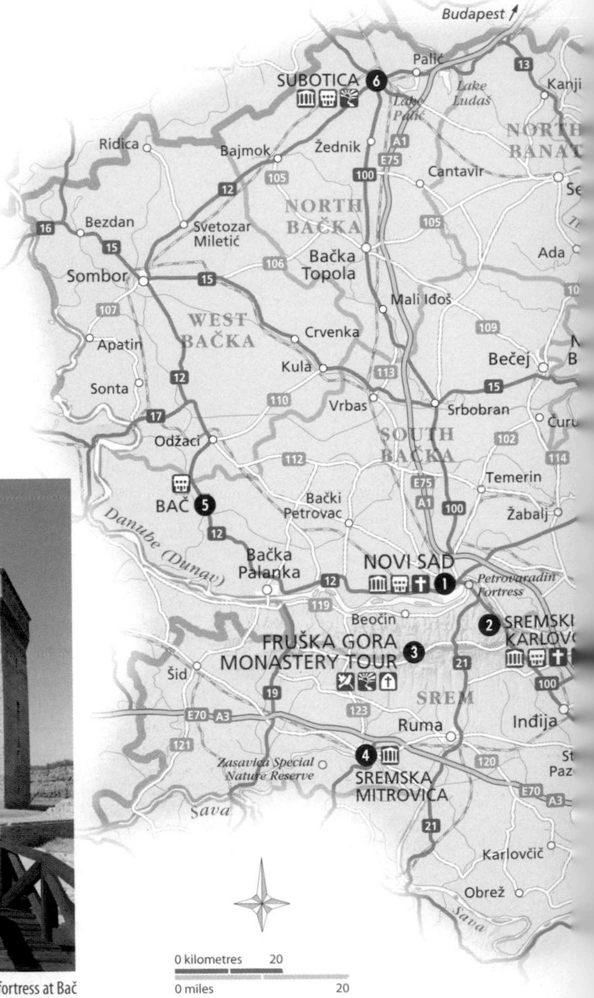

The restored keep of the 14th-century fortress at Bač

The twin towers of the Cathedral of St Nicholas and the grey spire of the Church of the Holy Trinity rising above the roofline of Sremski Karlovci

Getting Around

Railway lines link Belgrade with Novi Sad, Sremska Mitrovica, Subotica and Vršac, but Serbian trains are not the most comfortable or punctual, so travelling by bus or car is a better option. The A1/E75 motorway that runs between Belgrade, Novi Sad and Subotica is excellent, but as the local roads are poorly signed car drivers will need a satellite navigation system or a good road map.

Vase decorated in the folk-influenced Naïve art tradition of Kovačica

Key

- Motorway
- Main road
- Other road
- Railway
- International border
- Regional border

For additional map symbols *see back flap*

❶ Novi Sad

The core of Serbia's second city boasts broad pedestrianized streets lined with delightful Neo-Classical buildings and outdoor cafés. Serbian merchants established Novi Sad as a trading town in 1694, shortly after the construction of Petrovaradin Fortress had begun across the Danube, and the town matured into a "Serbian Athens" where Serbian culture flourished. In 1849 Hungarian troops in Petrovaradin shelled the city, razing most of it. It escaped major damage during the World Wars, but NATO's 1999 bombing destoyed all three of its bridges and much of its infrastructure. Novi Sad has since undergone a transformation – the bridges have been rebuilt and the damage repaired, there is a thriving social scene and the EXIT festival has become an internationally acclaimed event.

The yellow-brick Church of the Name of Mary opposite City Hall on Freedom Square

Museum of Vojvodina

Dunavska 35–37. **Tel** (021) 420566. **Open** 9am–7pm Tue–Fri, 10am–6pm Sat–Sun. free on Sun.
muzejvojvodine.org.rs

The incredibly broad collection of the Museum of Vojvodina (Muzej Vojvodine) covers the region's complex history in exhaustive detail. Accompanied by English-language handouts, the neatly arranged exhibitions document Vojvodina during the Roman Empire and the medieval Hungarian Empire, the Ottoman and Habsburg Empires, then as part of Yugoslavia and, more recently, Serbia. Highlights of the collection include a pair of splendid bejewelled Roman helmets from the 4th century, a fine 18th-century carriage and a mock-up of Dunavska street as it looked a century ago.

Bejewelled Roman helmet, Museum of Vojvodina

Dunavska

Lined with charming pastel buildings constructed after the 1849 bombardment, the cafés and ice cream parlours of this pleasant pedestrianized street attract both locals and visitors as they make their way between the centre of town and the Danube Park. It is one of Novi Sad's oldest streets and was originally used to transport goods to and from the river.

Bačka Bishop's Palace

Junction of Zmaj Jovina & Dunavska.

One of the architectural gems of Novi Sad, the Bačka Bishop's Palace (Vladičanski dvor) is a marvellous fusion of Romantic and Secessionist styles. The building features beautiful bifora and trifora windows framed by decorative stonework against walls clad in warm brick-red tiles. The original palace was destroyed by heavy shelling from Petrovaradin Fortress across the river during the Hungarian Revolution of 1849 and was replaced by the current building in 1901. When Prince Regent Alexander I Karađorđević paid a visit to Novi Sad in 1919, he chose to make his address to the people from the balcony of the Bačka Bishop's Palace.

Cathedral of St George

Nikole Pašića. **Open** 7am–8pm daily. 9am Sun.

The old 1740 building was destroyed during the 1849 bombardment. Rebuilt in 1853, the Saborna crkva svetog Đorđa has a barrel-vaulted interior with a Neo-Baroque belfry, superb stained-glass windows, stunning frescoes and a fine iconostasis by Paja Jovanović (1859–1957).

Stained-glass church window

St Nicholas Church

Nikolajevska porta. **Open** 7am–7pm daily.

The Russian-influenced, onion-domed Nikolajevska crkva was built in 1730 and is the city's oldest church. Damage from the bombardment of 1849 was set right soon after and the striking iconostasis added in 1862.

Bifora windows surrounded by decorative stonework, Bačka Bishop's Palace

For hotels and restaurants in this region see p128 and pp137–8

Novi Sad's magnificent City Hall, built in 1895 on Freedom Square in the heart of town

Einstein's sons were baptized here in 1913 as his first wife, the Serbian Mileva Marić (1875–1948), had family in the town.

Freedom Square

Church: **Open** 8am–1pm daily.

Encircled by splendid buildings, Freedom Square (Trg slobode) has been the city's focal point since it was laid out in the 18th century and used as a market-place. Today celebrations and exhibitions are held here. In the centre stands a statue of Novi Sad mayor, politician and writer Svetozar Miletić (1826–1901). The square's southwestern side is dominated by the striking Neo-Classical City Hall (Gradska kuća), topped by a tower that once held "Matilda", a bell that was melted down during World War II. Opposite is the Roman Catholic Church of the Name of Mary (Crkva imena Marijinog). Built in 1895 on the site of Novi Sad's first Catholic place of worship from 1702, this tremendous church is the city's largest, yet its Neo-Gothic design, high narrow windows and slender 72-m (236-ft) spire lend it a graceful air of weightlessness. Its cavernous interior, illuminated by several Hungarian stained-glass windows, is lined with columns supporting the vaulted ceiling.

Synagogue

Jevrejska.

One of over 20 designed by the Hungarian architect Lipot Baumhorn (1860–1932), the Synagogue (Sinagoga) is distinctive for its Art Nouveau-influenced façade. It was built in 1909 on Jevrejska (Jewish street) on the site of four earlier synagogues to serve the city's growing Jewish community. By World War II about 4,000 Jews lived in Novi Sad, but only 1,000 survived the Nazi occupation; most of these later emigrated to Israel. State-owned since 1991, the Synagogue is now used for concerts and cultural events.

VISITORS' CHECKLIST

Practical Information

Road Map B2. 94 km (58 miles) NW of Belgrade. 222,000. Trg slobode 3/3, (021) 421811, 6617343. **novisad.travel** Jul: EXIT Music Festival.

Transport

Belgrade.

The Strand

Štrand. **Open** Summer: 8am–10pm Mon–Fri, 8am–12am Sat–Sun.

Hugely popular throughout the summer, this riverside beach below Freedom Bridge (Most slobode) has a wide stretch of sand with deckchairs, umbrellas and beach bars. There are also shaded grassy areas and plenty of activities for kids. It can get crowded, especially at weekends, and the bars pump out dance tunes all day. A 2-km (1.5-mile) cycle lane and footpath runs next to the river between the town centre and the beach, which is also accessible by bus.

Petrovaradin Fortress

See pp94–5.

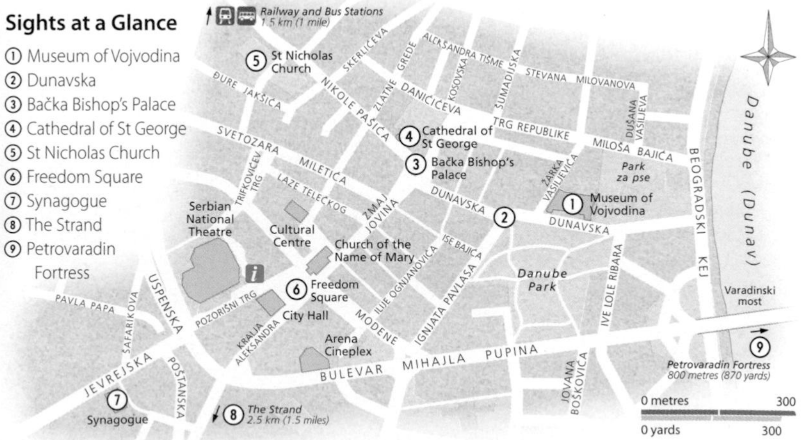

Petrovaradin Fortress

Petrovaradinska tvrđava

Dominating the high ground of the Danube's eastern bank, this formidable fortress was built by the Habsburgs after they wrested Petrovaradin from the Ottomans in 1687. Designed by French military architect Sebastian Vauban, it could shelter 30,000 men in 16 km (10 miles) of labyrinthine subterranean tunnels and was fitted with 18,000 defensive loopholes. The fort proved its worth even before completion when the Turks were defeated at the Battle of Petrovaradin in 1716. A section of the defensive tunnels can now be visited as part of a tour. The highly acclaimed EXIT music festival is held within the fortress every July.

The Gates of Petrovaradin
Leopold's Gate is the fort's main entrance; its numerous other gates include Carl VI's, Ludwig's, Molinari's, Kamenica and Communication Gates.

Lower Town and St George
The star-shaped fort complex was split into upper and lower parts. The Lower Town was home to officers and the Roman Catholic St George's Church (Crkva sveti Đurađ), built in Baroque style in the early 18th century.

KEY

① **Leopold's Gate**, the main gate of the fortress, is adorned with the Austrian Empire's coat of arms.

② **The Cavalier**, built in 1711, was the highest and most important wall of the inner defences.

③ **The Royal Gate**, fronted by a massive arch, is a 50-m (164-ft) long passage into the Upper Fortress.

④ **The Long Barracks** was the main building used to accommodate soldiers and officers.

⑤ **Ludwig's Bastion** is part of the pedestrian entrance to the fortress.

⑥ **St George's Church** features a statue of St Ignatius on its façade and has a large crypt where local nobles were buried.

⑦ **The Belgrade Gate**, a massive 10-m (33-ft) high entryway, was an essential part of the defence system of Petrovaradin Fortress.

Fortified Upper Town
Soldiers' barracks and the arsenal were located in the Upper Town. During the 1849 Hungarian Revolution, the Hungarian garrison stationed in the fortress refused to surrender to Austrian forces and instead bombarded Novi Sad across the Danube, destroying most of the town in the process.

For hotels and restaurants in this region see p128 and pp137–8

★ City Museum
Housed in the former Gunners' Barracks, the museum's impressive exhibitions are dedicated to Petrovaradin's history and 18th- and 19th-century Novi Sad city life.

VISITORS' CHECKLIST

Practical Information
Road Map B2. Petrovaradin Fortress: Novi Sad. **Open** 8am–5pm Tue–Sun. Jul: EXIT Music Festival. **novisad.travel**. City Museum: Tvrdava 4, Petrovaradin. **Tel** (021) 6433145. **Open** 9am–5pm Tue–Sun. **museumns.rs**

Transport
No. 3 from Novi Sad. Taxis are also available, or visitors can walk across the Varadin Bridge.

0 metres 100
0 yards 100

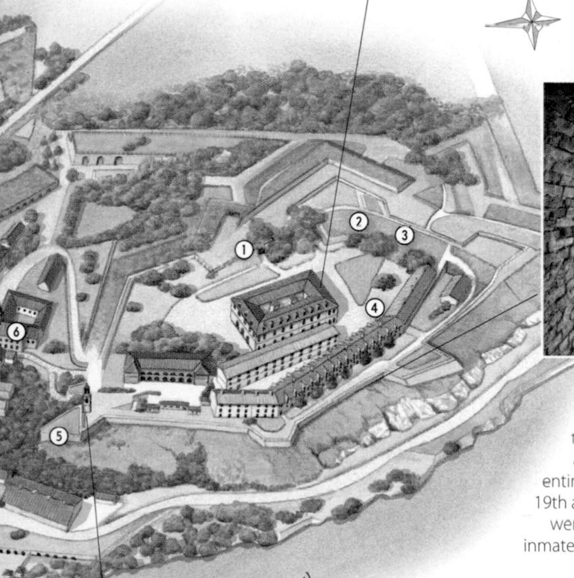

★ Underground Galleries
For extra security, officers would be familiar only with their allotted section of tunnel, and very few people knew the entire layout of the network. In the 19th and 20th centuries the tunnels were used as dungeons – famous inmates included Karađorđe and Tito.

★ Clock Tower
One of the main attractions of Petrovaradin, the 18th-century clock tower is famous for having a short hand indicating minutes and a long hand showing the hours so that the time could be read from a distance.

EXIT Music Festival

This music festival began in 2000 as a student protest against the Milošević regime under the slogan "EXIT 10 years of madness". Milošević was ousted in October 2000 and the following year the festival moved to Petrovaradin. Since then it has been held here every July, steadily gaining in reputation and size – it routinely attracts over 150,000 visitors – and featuring major international acts such as the Sex Pistols, Lily Allen, the Arctic Monkeys and Kraftwerk.

Revellers at the award-winning EXIT, one of Europe's top festivals

Sremski Karlovci's tent-shaped Chapel of Peace (Kapela mira), dating to 1817

❷ Sremski Karlovci

Road Map B2. 80 km (50 miles) NW of Belgrade. 8,700. Patrijaha Rajačića 1; 9am–6pm Mon–Fri, 10am–6pm Sat–Sun; (021) 882127. **karlovci.org.rs** Sep: Sremski Karlovci Wine Festival.

The town came into its own under Habsburg rule after the end of the Austro-Ottoman War in 1699. It was the seat of the Metropolitan Bishop of the Serbian Orthodox Church, and a great cultural centre for Serbs.

The main square's marble Four Lions Fountain (1799) is a local icon. It is said that those who drink from it will return to the town. The **Patriarch's Palace** (Patrijaršijski dvor), modelled on 19th-century Classicist Italian mansions, dominates the square. Next to it, the 1762 Orthodox **Cathedral of St Nicholas** (Saborna crkva svetog Nikole) has a magnificent iconostasis by Jakov Orfelin (d. 1803) and Teodor Kračun (1732–81). The adjacent 1768 Roman Catholic **Church of the Holy Trinity** (Crkva svetog Trojstva) is famed for its Baroque wooden doors. Further south is Serbia's oldest grammar school, founded in 1791. Its current Art Nouveau-influenced structure was built in 1891. There is also an excellent **City Museum** (Gradski muzej) and wineries producing the town's famous wines.

Patriarch's Palace
Trg Branka Radičevića. **Open** 8am–2pm Mon–Fri, 8am–noon Sat–Sun.

Cathedral of St Nicholas
Trg Branka Radičevića. **Open** 7am–7pm daily. 7 or 8am & 6 or 7pm Sun.

Church of the Holy Trinity
Trg Branka Radičevića. **Open** for service. 8am–noon Sun.

City Museum
Patrijarha Rajačića 16. **Tel** (021) 881637. **Open** 9am–5pm Mon–Sat.

❸ Fruška Gora Monastery Tour

See p97.

❹ Sremska Mitrovica

Road Map B2. 75 km (47 miles) W of Belgrade. 37,600. Svetog Dimitrija 10, (022) 618275. **tosmomi.rs** Aug: Srem Folk Fest. **sremfolkfest.org.rs**

This pleasant town on the Sava has attractive buildings of the 18th and 19th centuries, but most visitors are riveted by what lies beneath. This was the site of the powerful Sirmium, ruled by Galerius as one of the Roman Tetrarchy's four capitals. It is also said to be the birthplace of six Roman emperors. Sirmium has been buried since its destruction by the Avars in 582, but key sites have been excavated. The **Imperial Palace** (Carska palata) ruins are a top attraction; the massive stone walls, complex underfloor heating system and mosaics, enclosed within a purpose-built structure, offer a fascinating glimpse of the past.

The vast collection of the **Museum of Srem** (Muzej Srema) has altars to Jupiter, huge stone sarcophagi belonging to Roman centurions and a sundial with what is said to be the world's only example of a sculpture of Heracles's twin brother Iphicles. A large floor mosaic from the 4th-century villa of a wealthy Roman family is also on display.

Imperial Palace
Pivarska 2. **Tel** (022) 621568. **Open** 9am–6pm daily.
carskapalata.rs

Museum of Srem
Trg Svetog Stefana 15. **Open** 8am–3pm Mon, 8am–6pm Tue–Fri, 10am–4pm Sat–Sun.

❺ Bač

Road Map B2. 46 km (28 miles) W of Novi Sad. 5,400. Trg Zorana Đinđića 4, (021) 772222.

The ruined fortress of one of Vojvodina's oldest towns lies on the outskirts of Bač. First mentioned in Byzantine Emperor Justinian's correspondence in 535, Bač was a fortified settlement that Mongolian invaders sacked in 1241. The current fort dates back to the 14th century when Hungarian King Charles I (1288–1342) built it on what was then an island. The Turks conquered Bač in 1529 and held it until 1699. It was then given to the Habsburgs, who deliberately destroyed the fort in 1704 to prevent the Hungarian rebels under Rákóczi (1676–1735) from taking control. The towers and walls are in ruins but the central keep has been fully restored.

The Wineries of Sremski Karlovci

The town's winemaking reputation goes back to the Ottoman era, when many citizens were involved in its production and often paid their taxes in wine. The dessert wine Bermet originates from here; its secret recipe of fruit and spices is said to have been created by monks who were trying to preserve the wines they produced. There are more than 20 wineries around town, each with its own specialities. Wine tastings can be arranged through the visitor information office.

❸ Fruška Gora Monastery Tour

Forced out of Southern Serbia by the Ottomans in the 16th and 17th centuries, Orthodox monks settled in Fruška Gora. The 35 monasteries they built here played a vital role in preserving Serbian Orthodox culture during Ottoman rule by becoming repositories for religious artwork and holy relics, and fostering the copying and distribution of religious manuscripts. Only 15 communities remain, and although smaller and less majestic than the great medieval monasteries to the south, they are attractive and make for an enjoyable tour.

⑤ Fruška Gora National Park
The densely forested Fruška Gora mountain became a national park in 1960. A thin strip of land 80 km (50 miles) long and 539 m (1,768 ft) at its highest point, the park hosts pine martens, eastern imperial eagles, boar and deer *(see p21)*.

① Krušedol Monastery
Founded in 1516, Krušedol has a splendid iconostasis *(see p25)* in its Church of the Annunciation, as well as a few fragments of original 16th-century frescoes.

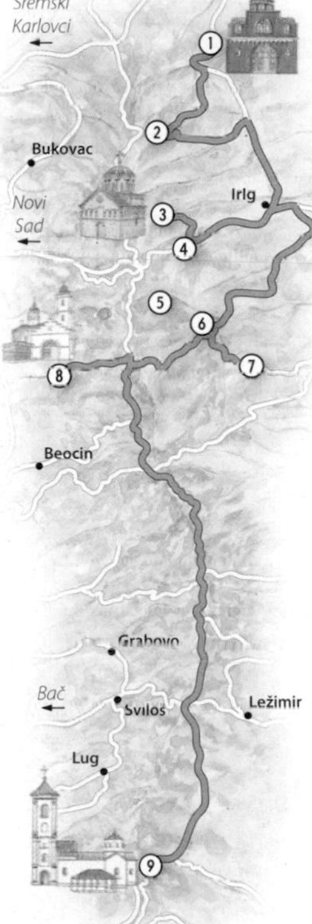

Key

Tour route

Other road

0 kilometres 10

0 miles 5

② Grgeteg Monastery
Restored in the 19th century, Grgeteg's St Nicholas Church has a stunning marble iconostasis which replaced Jakov Orfelin's older version in 1899.

③ Staro Hopovo Monastery
This tiny stone monastery was rebuilt in 1752 after the original 16th-century wooden building was destroyed by an earthquake.

Tips for Drivers

Length: 85 km (53 miles). This can be driven in a day, but it is worth spending two or three days here. A satellite navigation device is recommended.
Places to stay: Vrdnik village has several decent dining and accommodation options.

④ Novo Hopovo Monastery
Known for its 17th-century frescoes and a fine iconostasis by Baroque master Teodor Kračun, St Nicholas Church shows Byzantine influence.

⑥ Vrdnik Monastery
The Classical-style church at "Little Ravanica" is famed for having held the relics of Prince Lazar between 1697 and 1941.

⑦ Jazak Monastery
Built in Morava School style with a trefoil base, Jazak's church has an opulent Baroque iconostasis dating to 1769.

⑧ Rakovac Monastery
The church has fragments of 16th-century frescoes as well as a 1763 Baroque iconostasis.

⑨ Đipša (Divša) Monastery
This 16th-century monastery was rebuilt in 1744, and again in 1980 to repair World War II damage. It is an active nunnery.

The colossal, richly decorated Art Nouveau City Hall on Subotica's central square

❻ Subotica

Road Map B1. 190 km (118 miles) N of Belgrade. 96,500. Trg slobode 1; (024) 670350; 8am–6pm Mon–Fri, 9am–1pm Sat. **visitsubotica.rs** May: International Festival of Children's Theatres; Jul: Palić European Film Festival; Aug: Dužijanca, Interetno Festival. **interetno.net**

Defined by its fabulous Art Nouveau architecture, Subotica is an appealing city shared by Hungarians, Serbs, Croats and Bunjevci; until World War II it also had a sizable Jewish community that contributed greatly to its development. The city began life in the 14th century as a staging post on the salt trade route between Vienna and the Carpathians. It spent time under Ottoman rule before becoming part of the Habsburg Empire, but didn't take off until the railway arrived in 1869, bringing a swift upturn in its fortunes and population. The city's Art Nouveau buildings, known locally as Secessionist, were built to emphasize its elevated status, yet were inspired by an artistic protest against rapid urbanization. Architects chose to source their ideas from nature, hence the asymmetry, odd colour combinations, floral motifs and organic lines.

Subotica's central Freedom Square (Trg slobode) is dominated by the large 1910 Art Nouveau **City Hall** (Gradska kuća), with a glorious interior and soaring tower *(see p27)*. It was designed by Hungarian architects Marcell Komor (1868–1944) and Dezső Jakab (1864–1932). The duo also built the 1902 **Synagogue** (Sinagoga), a short walk away. One of the largest in Europe, it is unique for its Hungarian Art Nouveau style. It fell into disrepair after World War II, but has recently been restored and is used for cultural events. The **City Museum** (Gradski muzej) opposite the synagogue offers a good overview of the city's history.

A 10-minute walk east, the **Raichle Mansion** (Palata Ferenca Rajhla), another fine Art Nouveau building, houses the Modern Art Gallery. Built by Ferenc Raichle (1869–1960) in 1904, it is a breathtaking concoction of colour and organic motifs and heart shapes.

City Hall
Trg slobode. **Open** For guided tours only. 12pm daily (book through the tourist office).

Synagogue
Trg sinagoge 2. **Tel** (024) 533797. **Open** 10am–4pm Tue–Sat.

City Museum
Trg sinagoge 3. **Tel** (024) 555128. **Open** 10am–6pm Tue–Sat. **gradskimuzej.subotica.rs**

Raichle Mansion
Park Ferenca Rajhla 5. **Tel** (024) 553725. **Open** 8am–7pm Mon–Fri, 8am–1pm Sat. **likovnisusret.rs**

Environs

Palić is an atmospheric lakeside health resort that had its heyday in the late 19th century when Komor and Jakab built its striking Art Nouveau buildings. This haven of tranquillity is perfect for bird-watching trips, cycling, walking or just enjoying the wooded gardens and lake views.

Palić
7 km (4.5 miles) E of Subotica. Trg slobode 1, Subotica, (024) 670350, 8am–6pm Mon–Fri, 9am–1pm Sat. **palic.rs**

❼ Kovačica

Road Map C2. 50 km (31 miles) NE of Belgrade. 6,300. Masarikova 69, (013) 660460. **took.org.rs**

Famed for the Naïve art of its Slovak residents, Kovačica is also home to Serbs, Romanians and Hungarians. The Slovaks, who arrived in the late 18th century, formed a close-knit community that still maintains its old customs. As with other isolated rural groups, Naïve art developed as a colourful expressive style for untaught artists influenced by agrarian life and folk myth.

The **Gallery of Naïve Art** (Galerija naivne umetnosti) holds the works of the town's best-known artists, Jan Sokol (1909–82), Mihal Bireš (1912–81) and Martin Jonaš (1924–96). The **Martin Jonaš Memorial House** (Spomen kuća Martina Jonaša), with a charming blue tiled façade, is a repository of Jonaš's art.

Straw doll, Naïve art

Gallery of Naïve Art
Masarikova 65. **Open** 8am–4pm Mon–Fri, 10am–3pm Sat–Sun. **naivnaumetnost.com**

Martin Jonaš Memorial House
Čaplovičova 25. **Tel** (013) 661157. **Open** 8am–4pm Mon–Fri, 10am–3pm Sat–Sun.

For hotels and restaurants in this region see p128 and pp137–8

The splendid Roman Catholic St Gerhard's Church, built by German settlers in Vršac

8 Vršac

Road Map C2. 80 km (50 miles) NE of Belgrade. 35,700. Trg pobede 1, (013) 831055, 8am–4pm Mon–Fri. **to.vrsac.com** Jul: Wreath of Vršac; Sep: Grape and Wine Festival. **vrsackivenac.org.rs**

The complex history of Vršac is reflected in its diverse architectural heritage. The town lies beneath Vršac Hill, the westernmost point of the Carpathians, upon which Despot Đurađ Branković's **Vršac Castle** (Vršački zamak) has stood ever since he downsized from his fortress at Smederevo in the 15th century. The recently reconstructed castle has fine views of the area.

In 1594, shortly after the Turks took control, the Serbs of Vršac and the Banat region rose up against them and fought under the banner of St Sava. Their rebellion was unsuccessful but the Ottoman commander, Sinan Paša, was so unnerved that he had St Sava's relics taken from Mileševa Monastery to Belgrade and publicly burnt on Vračar Hill, where the Temple of St Sava now stands. The leader of the revolt, Bishop Teodor Nestrović, was canonized as St Teodor of Vršac in 1994.

The town's substantial Muslim community left in 1716 when it fell to the Habsburg Empire; they were gradually replaced by ethnic Germans whose winemaking expertise revived the region's ancient wineries. They also built the magnificent Neo-Gothic St Gerhard's Church (Rimokatolička crkva Svetog Gerharda) on Vuka Karadžića in 1863, but it has been neglected since they were forced to leave the town after World War II.

Other sights include the 1785 Orthodox **Cathedral of St Nicholas** (Saborna crkva Svetog Nikole), standing opposite the stately Baroque **Palace of the Bishop of Banat** (Vladičanski dvor). The fascinating **Pharmacy on the Steps** (Apoteka na stepenicama) holds the entire contents of the town's first pharmacy, which operated from 1784 to 1971. For an overview of the area's history visit the **City Museum** (Gradski muzej), and to learn about Vršac's centuries-old winemaking traditions book a tasting tour of one of the local wineries at the visitor information centre at Trg pobede.

Vršac Castle
Vršac Hill. **Tel** (013) 838053. **Open** 11am–6pm Tue–Sun. **muzejvrsac.org.rs**

Cathedral of St Nicholas
Jaše Tomića. **Open** 7am–7pm daily.

Palace of the Bishop of Banat
Jaše Tomića. **Open** Currently undergoing restoration and closed to the public; expected to reopen in late 2016/early 2017; check before visiting.

Pharmacy on the Steps
Stevana Nemanje. **Tel** (013) 831899. **Open** 10am–5pm Mon–Fri, 10am–4pm Sat, 10am–2pm Sun. **muzejvrsac.org.rs**

City Museum
Bulevar Žarka Zrenjanina 20. **Tel** (013) 838053. **Open** 10am–5pm Mon–Fri, 10am–4pm Sat, 10am–2pm Sun. **muzejvrsac.org.rs**

9 Bela Crkva

Road Map D2. 95 km (59 miles) E of Belgrade. 9,000. 1. oktobra 49, (013) 852354, 7.30am–2.30pm Mon–Fri. Jun: Flower Carnival.

An attractive little town on the Romanian border, Bela Crkva is best known for its 150-year-old Flower Carnival held every year in July. The festival has its roots in the town's horticultural past when ethnic German settlers in the 18th and 19th centuries developed vineyards and flower farms across the region. After World War II the Germans either left voluntarily or were forcibly evicted and as a result the agronomical prowess of Bela Crkva declined. Today the flower festival is smaller than it used to be, but still attracts large numbers of visitors. The beaches around the lakes just outside town are another popular local attraction during the summer.

A beautiful, serene lake in the countryside around Bela Crkva, a popular spot during the summer

EASTERN SERBIA

As a frequently volatile border zone during the Roman, Byzantine and Ottoman eras, Eastern Serbia was where monarchs built military camps and mighty fortresses rather than splendid monasteries or proud cities. Although it has remained less developed and less visited than other parts of the country ever since, the east boasts archaeological gems and stunning landscapes where little has changed for centuries and isolated communities still believe in pagan magic.

The Danube has been the setting for much of the region's history, and provides a glorious backdrop to many of its sights today. The Lepenski Vir archaeological site offers an insight into the lives of the Mesolithic and Neolithic settlers who carved fish-like faces from sandstone pebbles in recognition of the river's abundant food supply, while the Viminacium Roman military camp and the Diana Roman fort emphasize the Danube's early strategic importance.

The UNESCO World Heritage Site Felix Romuliana, built by Emperor Galerius, is another Roman landmark in the region. It is also a reminder of the Romans' pagan beliefs – Galerius was a keen persecutor of Christians and the last Roman ruler to be deified. After his death, Christianity spread across the region and flourished in the medieval Serbian kingdoms, but was soon overwhelmed by the Islamic culture of the expanding Ottoman Empire. The Serb fortress at Golubac, which guarded the entrance to the spectacular Iron Gates gorge, eventually fell to the Turks who then erected Ram Fortress upstream to strengthen their river defences. They also built several hammams (baths) across the region; some, like the one at Sokobanja, have developed into popular spa resorts.

Of the many ethnic groups that migrated here over the years, Wallachian Vlachs were among the most common. They brought with them distinct traditions and magical pagan rituals that are still practised by their isolated communities. The best-known Vlach witches can be found near Negotin, which also has a reputation for fine wines from riverside vineyards, a perfect accompaniment to local fish soup or bean stew.

Colourful Roman mosaic depicting a bird at Viminacium, founded as a Roman military camp in the 1st century AD

◀ The Danube River flowing through the imposing cliffs of the Iron Gates gorge

Exploring Eastern Serbia

The road hugs the Danube from Golubac to Kladovo, making it perfect for admiring the dramatic scenery of the Iron Gates and Đerdap National Park. The caves near Kučevo are best reached by taking the road south from Golubac; for Rajkova turn off the Danube road just before or after Lepenski Vir. From Kladovo the road follows the river south to Negotin and its vineyards. Zaječar is best base from which to explore Felix Romuliana; both lie south of Negotin via a picturesque valley framed by forested hills. From Zaječar the road follows the Beli Timok River through another scenic valley to the pretty, historic town of Knjaževac. The spa baths at Sokobanja are a short drive away, and from there it is easy to join the A1/E75 to Belgrade or Niš.

Leopard detail from a mosaic of Dionysus from Felix Romuliana, Gamzigrad

Getting Around

While it is theoretically possible to travel by train between Belgrade, Kučevo, Zaječar and Knjaževac, the journey is likely to be slow and uncomfortable. Local buses cover the whole area but are rarely punctual, and services are less frequent in more remote areas. A hire car is the preferable and most practical option for touring this part of the country.

Sokograd Fortress amidst the autumn foliage above the town of Sokobanja

Sights at a Glance

1. *Along the Danube pp104–5*
2. Kučevo
3. Negotin
4. Zaječar
5. *Felix Romuliana, Gamzigrad pp110–11*
6. Knjaževac
7. Sokobanja

Key

- Motorway
- Main road
- Other road
- Railway
- International border
- Regional border
- Peak

The mighty Danube River, with Golubac Fortress guarding the entrance to the Iron Gates gorge

0 kilometres 20

0 miles 20

Tombstones at the Old Church in Negotin

For additional map symbols *see back flap*

❶ Along the Danube

The Danube's route through Serbia is at its most dramatic at the lofty limestone cliffs of the 100-km (62-mile) long Iron Gates gorge. The Roman Emperor Trajan (AD 53–117) was the first to build a road here, leaving behind the Tablet of Trajan to mark the feat. Medieval empires on opposite banks once fought over the great riverside forts at Golubac and Ram, and the river functions as a border even today. Although Trajan's route and many other historic sites were submerged when the colossal Đerdap Dam raised the water level, a modern road weaves through the gorge today, allowing cyclists to follow the Danube Cycling Route, and the mighty river itself remains a highway linking the furthest points of Europe.

② Ram Fortress
This 15th-century Ottoman fortress (Tvrđava Ram), an example of a defensive structure designed to withstand artillery fire, played a crucial role during the 1787–91 Austro-Turkish War.

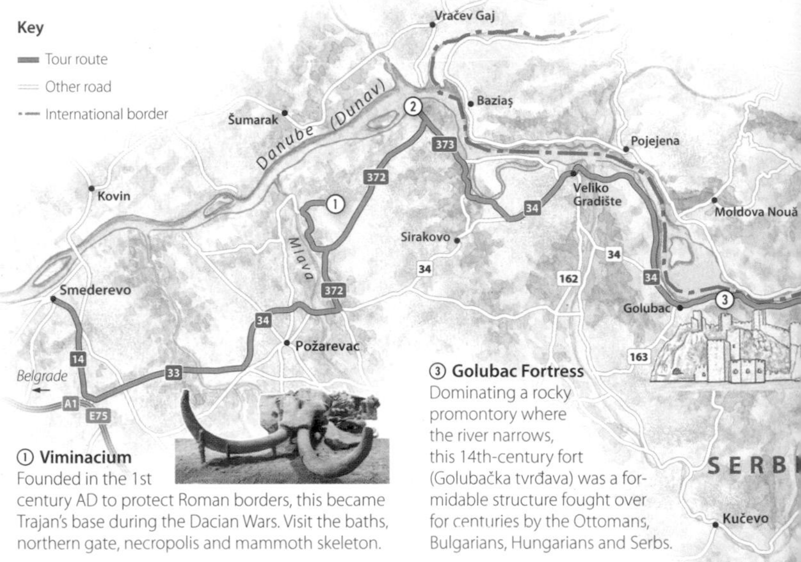

① Viminacium
Founded in the 1st century AD to protect Roman borders, this became Trajan's base during the Dacian Wars. Visit the baths, northern gate, necropolis and mammoth skeleton.

③ Golubac Fortress
Dominating a rocky promontory where the river narrows, this 14th-century fort (Golubačka tvrđava) was a formidable structure fought over for centuries by the Ottomans, Bulgarians, Hungarians and Serbs.

Tips for Visitors

Starting points: Smederevo or Kladovo.
Length: 350 km (217 miles).
Danube Cycling Route: W **dunav-info.org**
Đerdap National Park: Kralja Petra I 14a, Donji Milanovac (park HQ). W **npdjerdap.org**
Golubac: (012) 638613. W **tvrdjavagolubacki grad.rs/en**
Lepenski Vir: (030) 501501. Mar–Jan: 9am–8pm daily (Feb closed). W **lepenski-vir.rs**
Viminacium: Summer: 9am–7pm daily (to 4pm in winter). W **viminacium.org.rs/en**

0 kilometres 10
0 miles 10

⑤ Rajkova Cave
Named after the outlaw Rajko, who used it as a hiding place, Rajkova Cave (Rajkova pécina) has two caverns and an underground river. About half of its 2.3-km (1.5-mile) length is open to visitors *(see p108)*.

⑥ The Iron Gates and Đerdap National Park

Europe's largest river gorge, the Iron Gates (Đerdapska klisura) is actually four interconnecting gorges that cut through the Carpathians in Đerdap National Park (Nacionalni park Derdap). The canyon is just 150 m (492 ft) wide at points, with cliffs up to 500 m (1,640 ft) high.

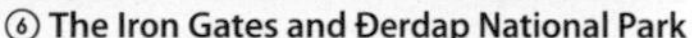

④ Lepenski Vir

Archaeologists discovered seven layers of civilizations at this settlement, which saw continuous human inhabitation for 2,000 years from the Mesolithic era (c. 7,000 BC onwards). Some of Europe's oldest stone idols were found here and are now displayed in the site museum.

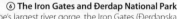

⑦ Tablet of Trajan

Visible only by boat, the monumental Tablet of Trajan (Tabula Traiana) was carved in AD 103 to commemorate the completion of Trajan's road. It was moved here from its original position when the river level rose in 1972.

⑧ Đerdap Dam

One of Europe's biggest hydroelectric power plants and the largest on the Danube, Đerdap Dam (Đerdapska brana) generates more than 10 billion kW/year. When it was built in 1972 it made the river rise 35 m (115 ft) and fatally blocked the migration route of the Beluga sturgeon *(see p21)*.

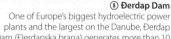

⑨ Diana Roman Fort

First built during Trajan's reign as a military camp, the fort (Rimsko utvrđenje Diana) was destroyed by Huns in the 4th century and rebuilt by Justinian in AD 530. There is little information available on site, but the ruined walls and foundations are clearly visible.

Massive ramparts and octagonal tower of Golubac Fortress on the banks of the Danube River ▶

The 19th-century house of composer Stevan Stojanović Mokranjac, now a museum

❷ Kučevo

Road Map D3. 130 km (81 miles) SE of Belgrade. 4,000.

This small town is best known for its Vlach heritage and for the caves nearby. **Ceremošnja** has a stunning 20-m (66-ft) high cavern adorned with stalactites, waterfalls and an underground stream. **Ravništarka**'s longer passage draws visitors to the Black Hall, a cavern of black rock streaked with white calcite; it also has an underground river. **Rajkova** *(see p105)* is named for Rajko Vojvoda, said to have been an innkeeper by day and a bandit by night, who robbed Turkish caravans and hid the spoils here.

Ceremošnja Cave (pećina)
Ceremošnja, 18 km (11 miles) S of Kučevo. **Tel** (012) 855039. **Open** Apr–Oct: 10am–7pm daily; Nov–Mar: 10am–4pm.

Ravništarka Cave (pećina)
Ravnište, 13 km (8 miles) S of Kučevo. **Tel** (012) 855039. **Open** Apr–Oct: 10am–7pm daily; Nov–Mar: by appointment only.

Rajkova Cave (pećina)
Majdanpek, 51.5 km (32 miles) E of Kučevo. **Tel** (030) 584204. **Open** Apr–Oct: 9am–5pm; Nov–Mar: by appointment only.

❸ Negotin

Road Map E3. 250 km (155 miles) SE of Belgrade. 17,000. Kraljevića Marka 6, (019) 547555, 7am–4pm Mon–Fri. **toon.org.rs** Sep: Days of Mokranjac. **mokranjcevi-dani.com**

This animated provincial town has long had a reputation for good wine, but has only lately begun to be recognized for the ancient tradition of witchcraft practised by the region's small Vlach community. Despite the church's attempts to suppress it, Serbs frequently visit seeking supernatural answers to their problems. Baba Jovanka, a famous local witch, is said to be able to predict the future.

The town is proud of its two notable sons: Hajduk Veljko (1780–1830), hero of the First Serbian Uprising whose statue dominates the town square, and Stevan Mokranjac (1856–1914), composer and pedagogue. The town's oldest house holds the **Hajduk Veljko Museum** (Muzej Hajduk Veljka), and Mokranjac's 19th-century home is now the **Mokranjac House Museum** (Mokranjčeva kuća). Both are part of the **Krajina Museum** (Muzej Krajine), which offers an overview of the region's history. Veljko was buried at the **Old Church** (Stara crkva), built below ground level in 1803 to obey the Ottoman rule that a church should be lower than a man on horseback. The 18th- and 19th-century tombstones with mysterious symbols are thought to have been found locally and brought here in the 19th century. Winery tours can be organized by the visitor centre.

Set on a wooded hillside just outside Negotin, **Bukovo Monastery** has a simple church founded in the 14th century by the powerful Serb king Stefan Milutin; the adjacent bell tower was a later addition.

Mokranjac House Museum
Vojvode Mišića 8. **Tel** (019) 543341. **Open** 8am–6pm Mon–Fri.

Hajduk Veljko Museum
Stanka Paunovića 17. **Tel** (019) 543341. **Open** 8am–6pm Mon–Fri.

Old Church
Profesora Kostića ul. **Open** 8am–2pm daily. 8am Sun.

Krajina Museum
Vera Radosavljević 1. **Tel** (019) 543341. **Open** 8am–6pm Mon–Fri.

Bukovo Monastery
Tel (019) 543460. **Open** 7am–6pm daily. 8am Sun. **manastirbukovo.org**

❹ Zaječar

Road Map D4. 244 km (152 miles) SE of Belgrade. 44,000. Svetozara Markovića 2, (019) 421521. **tozajecar.co.rs** Jul: Gitarijada. **gitarijada.org**

Although this is a pleasant town with attractive 19th-century architecture, the main focus for most visitors is the **National Museum** (Narodni muzej) on the town square. It holds many of the artifacts found at nearby Felix Romuliana *(see p110–11)*. The highlights include several well-preserved mosaics from the palace of Emperor Galerius, gold coins, a fragment of an arch with the inscription "Felix Romvliana" and the only marble head of Galerius in existence.

National Museum
Dragoslava Srejovića br. 2. **Tel** (019) 422930. **Open** 8am–6pm Mon–Fri, 9am–6pm Sat–Sun, 9am–1pm on public holidays. **muzejzajecar.org**

Zaječar's National Museum, housed in a Classical-style building dating to 1927

❺ Felix Romuliana, Gamzigrad

See pp110–11.

Brightly coloured houses in Stara čarsija, the charming old town quarter of Knjaževac

6 Knjaževac

Road Map D4. 263 km (163 miles) SE of Belgrade. 18,000. Knjaza Miloša 37, (019) 735230. **toknjazevac.org.rs** Aug: Serbian Youth Culture Festival **www.festivalkulture.com**

Surrounded by forested hills, farmland and scenic valleys, Knjaževac is a peaceful provincial town on the Svrljiški Timok River with a delightful old quarter known as Stara čarsija. Meticulously restored and painted in pretty pastel colours, its 19th-century buildings line the river between two bridges that complete the picture postcard appeal. The **City Museum** (Muzej grada) is devoted to 19th-century interior decor but also has a section dedicated to prominent 19th-century politician Aca Stanojević, who once owned the house in which the museum is based. The **Heritage Museum** (Zavičajni muzej) on the opposite bank is set in the Art Nouveau mansion of a rich mining family. Its artifacts outline the region's history and include the wonderful Popović collection of several hundred 19th- and 20th-century double-knitted socks collected from over 200 regional hamlets and villages by local couple Svetozar and Vidosava Popović.

City Museum
Njegoševa 6. **Tel** (019) 732228. **Open** 8am–4pm Mon–Fri.

Heritage Museum
Karađorđeva 15. **Tel** (019) 731407. **Open** 8am–4pm Mon–Fri.

7 Sokobanja

Road Map D4. 236 km (147 miles) SE of Belgrade. 8,000. Trg oslobođenja 2, (018) 830271. Aug: Sokobanja Accordion Festival.

"You arrive old, you leave young" is the catchy slogan used to advertise one of Serbia's most popular spa towns. Visited by thousands every year, the town is often fully booked during the summer. The Romans were the first to appreciate its air quality and curative springs, and later the Ottomans built baths here, but it wasn't until Prince Miloš began visiting in the 19th century that it became fashionable.

Named after Sokograd, the ruined 7th-century clifftop fortress nearby, the town lies on the Moravica River between the Ozren and Rtanj Mountains of the Carpathians. It benefits from natural 28–45° C (82–113° F) springs and several mountain air currents thought to be curative for lung diseases. Its main sights are near its pleasant central square where the restored 15th-century Turkish baths can be accessed via the **Specijalna bolnica** health centre. Opposite the baths is an 1884 Orthodox church and Miloš's19th-century residence, now hosting shops and a café.

Find out about the plentiful walking, cycling and picnicking in the surrounding hills at the visitor information centre.

Specijalna bolnica
Vojvode Mišića 48. **Tel** (018) 830914, 830144. **soko-banja.rs**

Vlach Magic

The Vlach minority of Serbia are descendants of migrants from the Wallachia region of western Romania. This borders Serbia's Timočka Krajina region, home to a large number of the country's Vlachs. While most are members of the Romanian Orthodox Church, many still believe in the pagan practice of witchcraft and magic. This remains cloaked in mystery for the outside world as Vlachs have always lived in closed communities. What is known is that certain families have magic powers that are kept secret and passed down through females. Each Vlach village relies upon one or more local witches to counter black magic or to cast white magic spells. Vlach and non-Vlach Serbs from across the country come to consult well-known witches such as Baba Jovanka about problems regarding their health or personal lives.

The restored 15th-century Turkish baths in Sokobanja's town square

❺ Felix Romuliana, Gamzigrad

Protected by 20 massive towers, this UNESCO World Heritage Site would have served as Galerius's retirement palace had he not died two years before its completion in AD 313. One of at least 17 Roman emperors born on what is now Serbian territory, Galerius was the last to be deified. He and his influential pagan mother were buried on nearby Magura Hill where their tumuli can still be seen. Named after Galerius's mother, the complex was damaged by Huns in the 5th century and by Slavs and Avars in the 7th century, after which it was abandoned. Although most of the objects found here are now in the Zaječar museum, the foundations, pillars, mosaics and grassy mounds that remain give visitors a sense of the grandeur of a Roman palace.

Head of Galerius
The bust of Galerius found at the site is now on display at the National Museum in Zaječar *(see p108)*.

★ Western Gate
Flanked by two mighty outer towers and two inner towers from the earlier fortifications, the Western Gate is today used as the front entrance. It would originally have been the complex's back door as the Eastern Gate was designed to be the main entrance.

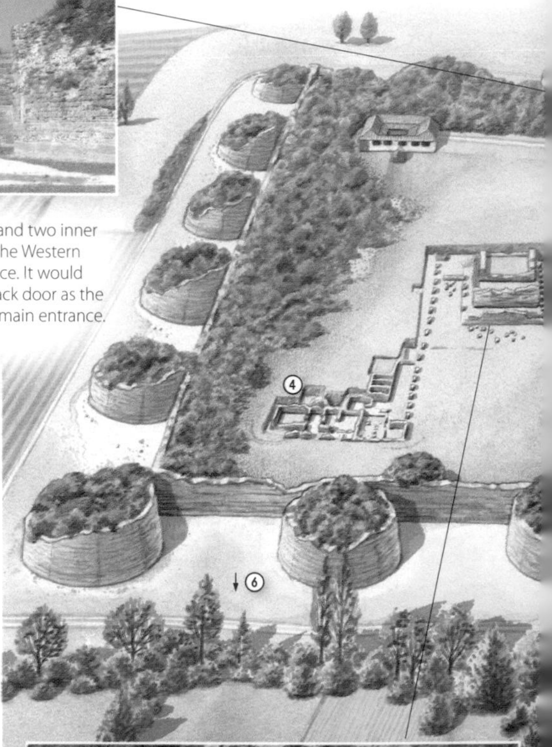

④

↓ ⑥

KEY

① **The original defensive towers** of the complex were superseded by far more massive structures.

② **The palace of Galerius** occupied the northern part of the complex. In its heyday, it had a pagan temple, a dining area, a private bathing room, an ornamental garden and floors covered with elaborate mosaics.

③ **A large Christian basilica** was built over the ruined southern wing of the palace in the 4th century by missionaries, an ironic twist considering the emperor's passion for persecuting Christians. The complex was ravaged soon after by the Huns.

④ **The public baths**, situated in the southeastern corner of the complex, would have been accessed via a gate between two defensive towers.

⑤ **The Eastern Gate's** two smaller towers were part of the original defences of the complex.

⑥ **The tumuli and mausolea** on Magura Hill (1 km/0.5 mile east) are where Galerius was deified before being buried alongside his mother.

★ Temple of Jupiter
Only the lower foundations of this massive structure have survived. As a successful military leader, Galerius venerated Jupiter who was commonly worshipped by Roman soldiers.

★ Roman Mosaics
Corridors and rooms were paved with intricate mosaics, mostly geometric in design. One showing the solar system was found where Galerius had his stibadium (semicircular dining seat), and another of Dionysus, the god of wine, was uncovered in the triclinium, the emperor's dining and entertaining room.

VISITORS' CHECKLIST

Practical Information
Road Map D4. 1 km (0.5 mile) SE of Gamzigrad, 11 km (7 miles) W of Zaječar. **Tel** (019) 422930.
Open Apr–Oct: 8am–8pm daily; Nov–Mar: 8am–4pm daily.
muzejzajecar.org

Transport
Hourly buses from Zaječar to Gamzigrad take 15 minutes, then Felix Romuliana is a 15-minute walk away; taxis from Zaječar to Felix Romuliana take 15 minutes.

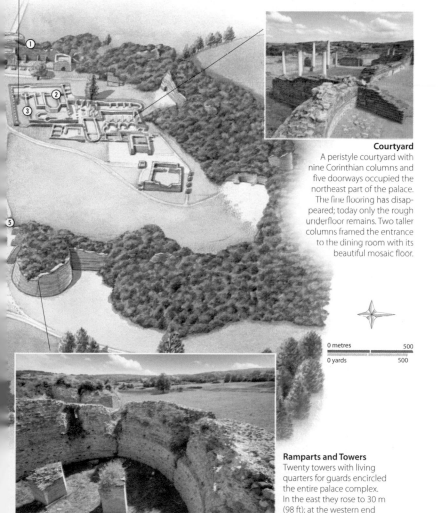

Courtyard
A peristyle courtyard with nine Corinthian columns and five doorways occupied the northeast part of the palace. The fine flooring has disappeared; today only the rough underfloor remains. Two taller columns framed the entrance to the dining room with its beautiful mosaic floor.

0 metres 500
0 yards 500

Ramparts and Towers
Twenty towers with living quarters for guards encircled the entire palace complex. In the east they rose to 30 m (98 ft); at the western end they were 20 m (66 ft) high.

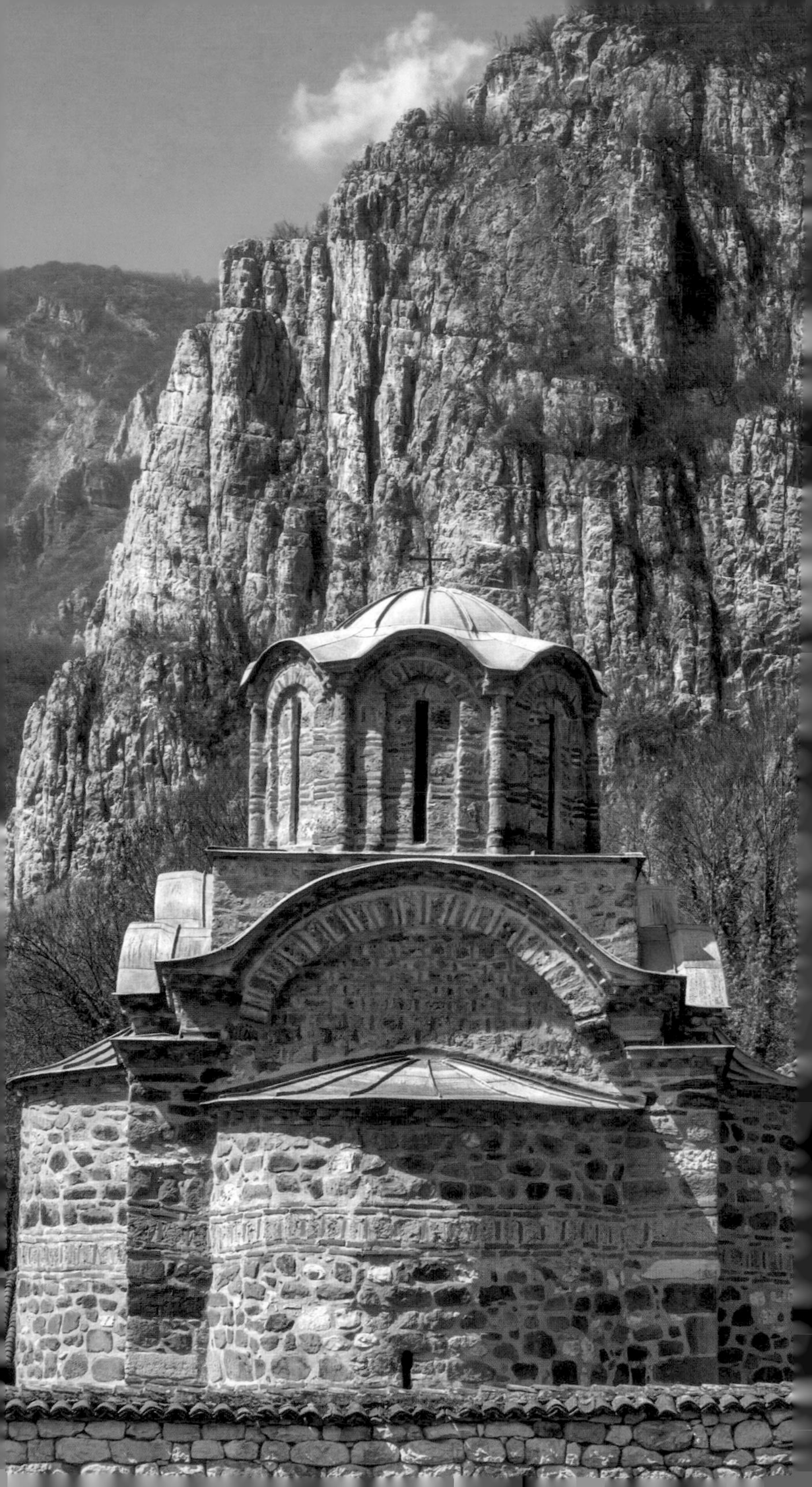

SOUTHERN SERBIA

Fought over for centuries by successive empires, this strategic region was coveted for its natural corridors to Bulgaria and Greece through mountainous river valleys that sheltered scattered settlements and blocked access to intruders. Those turbulent years have faded into history, leaving behind a legacy of legends and picturesque ruins; these once indomitable mountains have long since been conquered by keen hikers, cyclists and nature lovers.

Niš has dominated the region since the Roman era, when a military camp was established close to the confluence of the Nišava and South Morava Rivers. The immense Ottoman fortress built on the same site is now a popular attraction and symbol of the city. The legendary Roman emperor Constantine the Great was born here and some of the country's most remarkable Roman mosaics can be seen within the ruins of his summer villa in Mediana, outside Niš. Another of southern Serbia's famous sons, Emperor Justinian, had a fine Byzantine city built from scratch at Caričin Grad; its evocative overgrown foundations are all that remain today.

Of the medieval Christian architecture that sprung up before the arrival of the Turks, Kuršumlija's St Nicholas Church, Vranje's St Petka's Church and the isolated Poganovo Monastery are worth a visit. Niš, Vranje and Pirot developed into Ottoman towns and, despite their preponderance of modern architecture, have several attractive museums between them.

Wherever you go in this picturesque region, the mountains follow; many are in the Stara planina Nature Park, highly rated by bird-watchers and crisscrossed with well-marked paths. Mountain huts offer simple accommodation while spa resorts at Prolom Banja and Lukovska Banja provide more comfortable facilities.

No trip to the south would be complete without visiting the otherworldly stone columns that rise mysteriously from the ground at Devil's Town and are considered to be Serbia's most unusual natural sight.

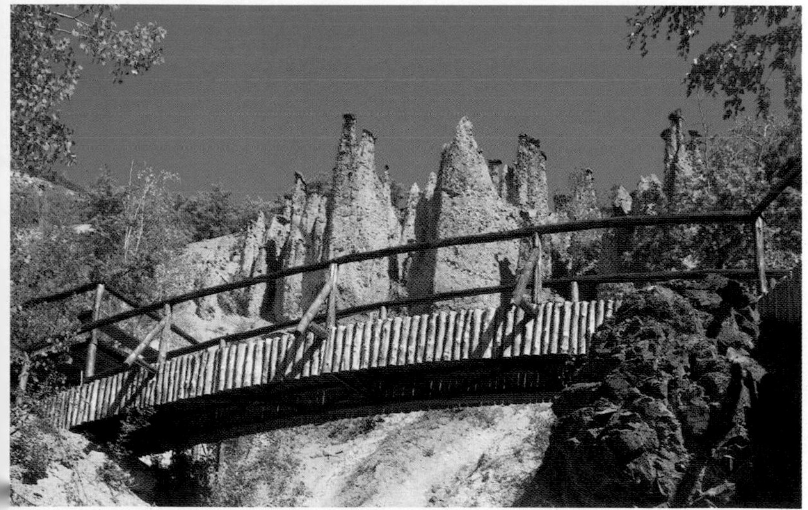

The unique, naturally formed stone columns of Devil's Town near Kuršumilija

◀ Picturesque 14th-century Poganovo Monastery standing at the base of steep cliffs near Pirot

Exploring Southern Serbia

Niš makes an excellent base from which to explore Southern Serbia. The road east to Pirot follows the Roman Via Militaris that once linked Belgrade with Serdica (Sofia) and Constantinople (Istanbul). Although still a busy road often clogged with trucks, it passes through picturesque landscapes. A motorway linking Niš and Sofia has been under construction for many years and is likely to be open in the near future. From Pirot a delightful road winds through craggy gorges to the isolated Poganovo Monastery in the Stara planina Mountains. Visitor information centres at Niš and Pirot have hiking maps and links to agencies running tours and activities in the mountains. Caričin Grad, off the A1/E75 from Niš, can be visited en route to Vranje. Kuršumlija, Devil's Town, Prolom Banja and Lukovska Banja are easily accessible via Prokuplje.

Detail, Monument to the Liberators of Niš, Niš

Getting Around

Niš is connected by rail to Kuršumlija, Vranje and Pirot, but buses are likely to be more comfortable. The Prolom Banja and Lukovska Banja resorts can both arrange transport from Niš or Belgrade, but visitors planning to visit out of the way sights such as Poganovo Monastery or Caričin Grad will either need to engage a local taxi or consider hiring a car from Niš. Allow plenty of time for the trip as the mountain roads are narrow and slow in places.

Sights at a Glance

1 *Niš pp116–17*
2 Kuršumlija
3 Devil's Town
4 Caričin Grad
5 Pirot
6 Stara planina Nature Park
7 Vranje

Gravestones from the Roman era found within Niš Fortress

For hotels and restaurants in this region see p129 and p139

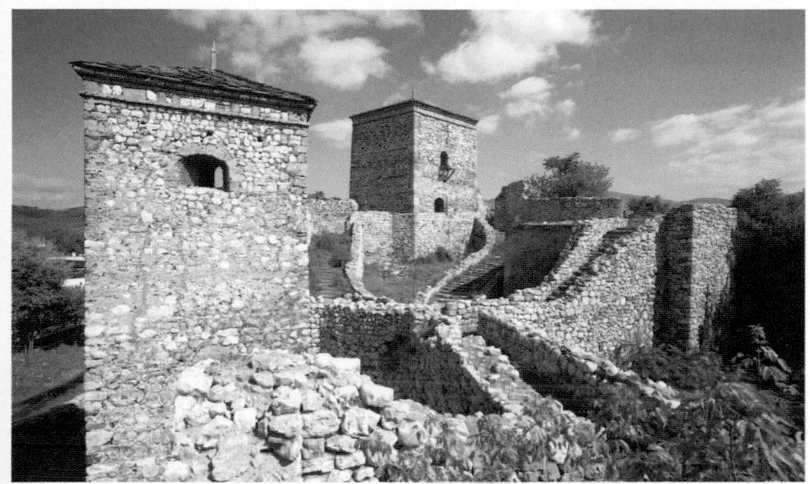

Momčilov Grad fortress, built in the 14th century at Pirot by Bulgarian ruler Momčilo

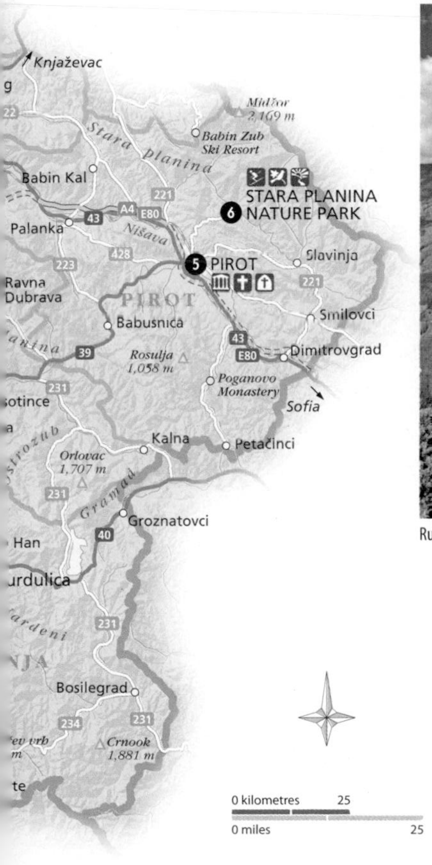

Knjaževac
Midžor
2,169 m
Babin Zub
Ski Resort
Stara planina
Babin Kal
221
STARA PLANINA
6 NATURE PARK
43
A4
E80
Palanka
Nišava
428
223
5 PIROT
Slavinja
221
Ravna
Dubrava
PIROT
Babusnica
Smilovci
43
39
Rosulja
1,058 m
E80
Dimitrovgrad
Poganovo
Monastery
231
Sofia
Kalna
Petačinci
Orlovac
1,707 m
231
Gramad
Groznatovci
40
231
Bosilegrad
234
231
Crnook
1,881 m
0 kilometres 25
0 miles 25

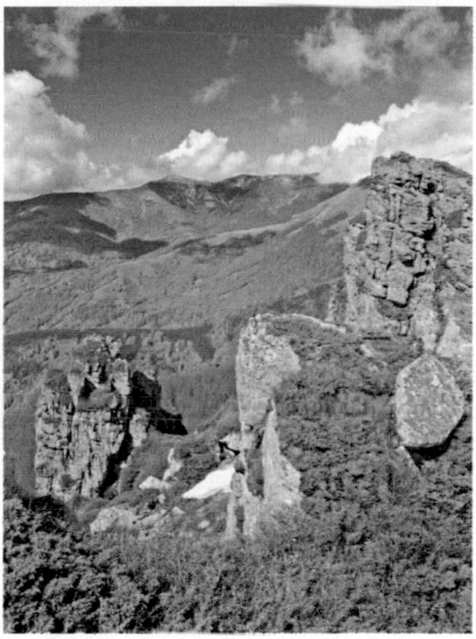

Rugged landscape of the Stara planina Nature Park

Key

- Motorway
- Motorway under construction
- Main road
- Other road
- Railway
- International border
- Regional border
- Peak

For additional map symbols *see back flap*

❶ Niš

Niš lost much of its fine 19th-century architecture to Allied bombing raids during World War II, but its massive Ottoman fortress escaped relatively unscathed. It remains the city's key attraction along with the lively pedestrianized town centre and historic sights. Although the city has been occupied since Neolithic times, it developed most rapidly during the Roman era when it was the hometown of Constantine the Great and an important stage of the Roman Via Militaris route between Belgrade and Constantinople. The best examples of Roman remains can be seen at Mediana, just outside the centre. Held by Bulgarians, Byzantines and Serbs before falling to the Turks in the 15th century, Niš was eventually liberated in 1878.

The graceful three-domed Bali-beg Mosque, with Roman ruins beside it

Grim structures at the concentration camp built by the Nazis, now a museum

Red Cross Camp Museum

Bulevar 12. februara. **Tel** (018) 25678. **Open** 9am–4pm Tue–Fri, 10am–3pm Sat–Sun.

This Nazi concentration camp set up in 1941 is now a grim museum (Muzej logor Crveni krst) with rusting barbed wire fences, signs in German and a bullet-scarred execution wall. It was used to hold Jews, Serbs and Roma during the Nazi occupation of Serbia. Of the estimated 35,000 people that passed through it, 10,000 are thought to have been killed. While some executions were carried out within the camp, most took place on Mount Bubanj, 4 km (2.5 miles) south, where three concrete fists now dominate the Bubanj Memorial Park. The museum's collections of documents and personal possessions are displayed in bleak rooms where up to 250 prisoners slept on concrete floors covered only with straw. The camp was liberated by Tito's partisans in 1944 and was subsequently used to hold Stalinist sympathizers before becoming a museum in 1967.

Niš Fortress

Niška tvrđava.
niskatvrdjava.com

Built by the Ottomans in 1723 upon the foundations of its Roman, Byzantine and medieval predecessors, the fortress (Niška tvrđava) has 2 km (1.5 miles) of 8-m (26-ft) high walls. Today these enclose the city park where locals gather and cultural events are held throughout the year. The fort's colossal Istanbul Gate *(see p26)* faces the city centre across the Nišava River. The oldest structure within the fort is the 15th-century Turkish hammam, which lies to the left of the main gate and is now a café. To the right of the gate is the old Turkish arsenal, today occupied by souvenir shops. The open-air amphitheatre beyond it was fashioned from the crater left behind after an ammunition dump was hit by Allied bombs during World War II. Further into the park lies the 16th-century Bali-beg Mosque, which lost its minaret after the city was liberated from Ottoman rule. Just behind it are the foundations of the central square of Byzantine Niš, the ruins of a grand Roman villa and a few Roman gravestones.

Obrenovićeva

From the central King Milan Square (Trg kralja Milana), with its equestrian Monument to the Liberators of Niš, Obrenovićeva runs south away from the fort. Niš's main street and covered market during the Ottoman era, it is now a pedestrianized zone of shops and small malls with a mix of architectural styles. The only reminder of its Turkish heritage is Kopitareva, a narrow street off Obrenovićeva that is crammed with popular cafés and Oriental-style buildings.

Malls and shops lining the sides of pedestrianized Obrenovićeva street

National Museum

Nikole Pašića 59. **Tel** (018) 248189. **Open** 9am–7pm Tue–Fri, 9am–5pm Sat–Sun.
narodnimuzejnis.rs

The museum (Narodni muzej), despite its small size, conveys an intriguing impression of the city's multiple layers of civilization through a series of excellent displays. Artifacts include prehistoric finds, Celtic jewellery, a bronze retirement diploma awarded to a Roman soldier and a 6th-century Christian sarcophagus. There is also a section devoted to Constantine's summer residence at Mediana.

The Cathedral of the Holy Trinity, consecrated after the liberation of Niš

Cathedral of the Holy Trinity

Prijezdina 7. **Open** 8am–7pm daily. 8.30am Sun.

The second largest cathedral in Serbia after the Temple of St Sava in Belgrade *(see p55)*, this impressive church (Crkva svete Trojice) was built between 1856 and 1872 towards the end of Ottoman rule when the Turks were under pressure from Western Europe to grant the Serbs greater religious freedom. Despite allowing the building to go ahead, the Turks were so outraged when the completed cathedral's domes rose higher than their mosques that they refused to give permission for religious services to be conducted. Much of the interior was destroyed by fire in 2003 and has since been restored.

Skull Tower

Ćele kula, Bulevar Zorana Đinđića. **Open** 9am–7pm Tue–Fri, 9am–5pm Sat–Sun.

Described by 19th-century French traveller Alphonse de Lamartine as "...a white tower... gleaming like marble...", this infamous landmark (Ćele kula) has since been enclosed within a chapel. Originally 5 m (16 ft) high and constructed from 952 human skulls, the macabre tower dates to 1809 when Serb rebels took on the Turkish garrison stationed at Niš during the First Serbian Uprising. The Serbs eventually lost and, when rebels led by Stevan Sinđelić found themselves surrounded, they blew themselves up along with several of their enemies by detonating a pile of gunpowder kegs. Huršid Paša, the city's Turkish commander, had the heads of the Serb rebels stuffed and sent to Istanbul; their skulls were built into this grisly tower at the entrance to Niš to serve as a grim warning to other rebels. Just a few original skulls now remain; the rest were either taken as ghoulish souvenirs or buried by locals over the years.

Remains at the Skull Tower

VISITORS' CHECKLIST

Practical Information

Road Map D4. 240 km (150 miles) SW of Belgrade. 183,000. Fortress main gate, (018) 250222, 8am–7pm Mon–Fri, Sat closed, 9am–2pm Sun; Vožda Karađorđa 7, (018) 521321. **visitnis.com** Aug: Nišville International Jazz Festival; Sep: Burek Days. **nisville.com**

Transport

Niš.

Mediana

Bulevar Cara Konstantina, 5 km (3 miles) east of the town centre. **Tel** (018) 550433. Vožda Karađorđa 7, (018) 521321. **Open** The site is currently under construction and entry is by appointment with the visitor information centre.

Roman Emperor Constantine the Great (280–337) built himself a grand summer villa in the wealthy Niš suburb of Mediana. Archaeologists' excavations of the villa's ruins have revealed a remarkable 1,000 sq m (1,200 sq yd) of mosaics along with frescoes and many artifacts that will be displayed in a new site museum. The mosaics have recently been protected by a purpose-built shelter and archaeological explorations continue; it is estimated that only 3 per cent of the site has been unearthed to date.

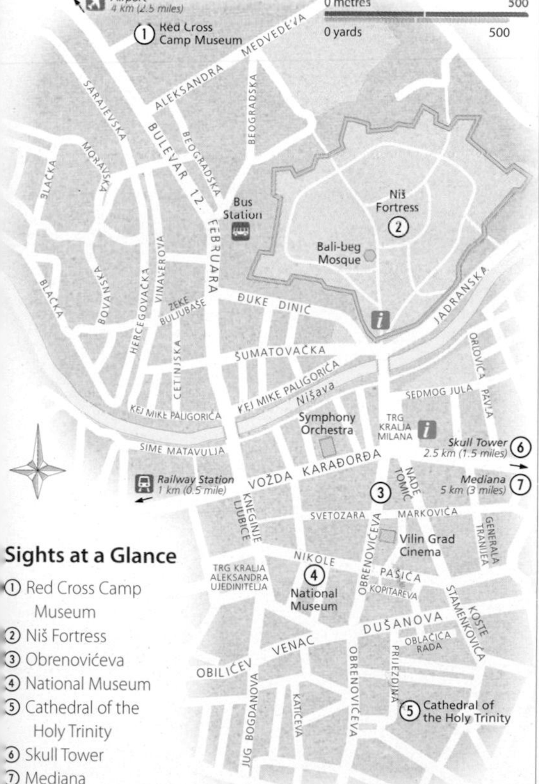

Sights at a Glance

1. Red Cross Camp Museum
2. Niš Fortress
3. Obrenovićeva
4. National Museum
5. Cathedral of the Holy Trinity
6. Skull Tower
7. Mediana

The remains of the Mother of God nunnery at Kuršumlija

❷ Kuršumlija

Road Map C5. 64 km (40 miles) W of Niš. 13,000. Palih Boraca 15, (027) 380963. **tokursumlija.rs**

Once the site of a Roman military outpost called Ad Fines ("on the borders") after its location on the boundaries of two Roman provinces, Kuršumlija has found itself "ad fines" once again, ever since neighbouring Kosovo declared itself independent in 2008.

The town is unremarkable, but its historic significance is embodied by the Church of St Nicholas (Crkva svetog Nikole). An early example of the layered red-brick and stone structures typical of the Raška School of church architecture, it was built in 1168 by Grand Prince Stefan Nemanja (1113–99), the founder of the powerful medieval Serbian Nemanjić dynasty. Destroyed during the 17th-century Austro-Ottoman War, the church was substantially restored during the 19th century. Nemanja's wife Ana founded the nearby Mother of God nunnery (Manastir svete Bogorodice) of which only the ruined foundation walls remain.

Kuršumlija is also well known for its proximity to the intriguing rock formations at Devil's Town and the popular **Prolom Banja** and **Lukovska Banja** spa resorts in the nearby mountains.

Prolom Banja
26.5 km (16.5 miles) S of Kuršumlija.
Tel (027) 8388111.
prolombanja.com

Lukovska Banja
35 km (22 miles) W of Kuršumlija.
Tel (027) 385999.
lukovskabanja.com

❸ Devil's Town

Đavolja varoš

Road Map D5. 30 km (19 miles) SE of Kuršumlija. **Tel** (027) 381344. djavoljavaros.com

The rock towers at Devil's Town gained international fame when they made it onto the 2010 shortlist for new wonders of the world. Accessed via the wooded slopes of Mount Radan, past some mineral springs and the entrance to a 13th-century gold mine, the 202 towers can be viewed from wooden platforms. These unusual formations are the result of natural erosion that has left groups of towers measuring up to 20 m (66 ft) high and capped with chunks of stone. Of the many legends associated with them, the most popular says they were created when the devil appeared at an incestuous marriage of siblings and turned them and their wedding party to stone.

❹ Caričin Grad

Road Map D5. 62 km (39 miles) S of Niš.

Discovered in the early 20th century, the monumental ruins of this remote hilltop site are thought to have belonged to Justiniana Prima, a splendid 6th-century city built by the Byzantine Emperor Justinian (482–565) close to his birthplace. Despite its massive gates and fortified walls, the city was overrun by Avars and abandoned within a century of its construction. It was supplied with water by a 20-km (13-mile) aqueduct, and foundations of no fewer than nine basilicas have been unearthed at the site, along with several residences and palaces. The mosaics found within these have been covered with protective layers of sand. The remains of a cathedral and bishop's palace lie within the acropolis at the heart of the complex, which had fine views of the region. Much of the site is overgrown and there is little infrastructure, but multilingual information boards help visitors navigate their way around the sprawling ruins.

❺ Pirot

Road Map E5. 72 km (45 miles) E of Niš. 39,000. Srpskih vladara br. 82, (010) 320838, 8am–4pm Mon–Fri, 8am–1pm Sat. **topirot.com** Aug: International Folk Festival.

Surrounded by the Stara planina Mountains, this pleasant town lies on the old road between Belgrade and Constantinople and was a staging post during the Roman period. Its earliest remains are that of the small Byzantine fortress rebuilt by the Bulgarian ruler Momčilo (1305–45) and later occupied by the Ottomans. Known as Momčilov Grad, the substantial walls and towers of the stone fort stand

The great ruins and foundations at Caričin Grad (Justiniana Prima)

For hotels and restaurants in this region see p129 and p139

Museum of Ponišavlje set in a 19th-century house in Pirot

just outside the town, but are currently closed to the public. Pirot is known for its tradition of making cheese, *kilims* (rugs) and ceramics. Some lovely examples of the latter two, along with an original carpet loom and traditional 19th-century furniture, are on display at the Museum of Ponišavlje (Muzej Ponišavlja), which is set in a characterful 19th-century home that was once owned by a wealthy local merchant. Also worth a quick visit is the Old Church (Stara crkva), built below ground level in 1834 to obey the Turkish rule that Christian churches could not be higher than mosques.

Environs

Poganovo Monastery lies in a gloriously isolated spot beneath steep cliffs, accessed by a narrow road that winds its way through the spectacular Jerma Gorge. Built in the late 14th century, the monastery was restored in the 19th. Its well-preserved frescoes were added by Greek painters in the 16th century.

Poganovo Monastery
31 km (19 miles) S of Pirot.
Open 8am–7pm daily.

6 Stara planina Nature Park

Park prirode Stara planina

Road Map E5. 29 km (18 miles) NE of Pirot. Srpskih vladara br. 82, Pirot, (010) 320838, 8am–4pm Mon–Fri (to 1pm Sat). **topirot.com** **srbijasume.rs**

Running from the eastern edge of Serbia right across Bulgaria to the Black Sea, the picturesque Stara planina (Old Mountains) boast myriad waterfalls, lakes, gorges and canyons. Home to over 200 bird species, the park is listed on the international IBA (Important Bird and Biodiversity Area) register; it also shelters 147 endangered plant species as well as bears, snow voles and ground squirrels. Detailed information about hiking routes and mountain accommodation can be found at the excellent visitor information centre in Pirot.

The Stara planina also contain the highest peaks in Serbia – Babin Zub at 1,758 m (5,768 ft) and Midžor at 2,169 m (7,116 ft). The **Babin Zub Ski Resort** has 13 km (8 miles) of runs and is one of Serbia's three main ski centres along with Kopaonik *(see p82)* and Zlatibor *(see p86)*.

Babin Zub Ski Resort
50 km (31 miles) N of Pirot.
Tel (011) 2223986. **Open** Dec–Apr: 9am–3.30pm daily. **skijalistasrbije.rs**

Skiers making their way to the slopes at the Babin Zub Ski Resort in Stara planina

7 Vranje

Road Map D5. 125 km (78 miles) S of Niš. 55,000. 29. novembra 2, (017) 417545.

Overshadowed by mountains that form a natural border with Kosovo, Vranje lies in a densely cultivated valley beside the South Morava River. This is the southernmost city in Serbia and most of its sights come from the time it spent under Ottoman rule from 1455 to 1878.

The **Holy Trinity Cathedral** (Crkva svete Trojice), built below ground level in 1841 to be less prominent than local mosques, dominates the city centre. From the centre, the pedestrianized Kralja Stefana Prvovenčanog, with lively pavement cafés, leads uphill towards Staniše Stošića Square and the **Pasha's Residence** (Pašin konak). Built in 1756, this was once the residence of the pasha (Turkish governor) and now houses the city museum. It consists of two buildings linked by a hidden bridge; the main building facing the square was for the pasha while the rear building was for his harem. Further up the hill is a 17th-century Turkish hammam, restored in 2003 although not open to the public. Beyond this lies the Roma quarter, Gornja Čaršija, famous for its folk musicians. According to legend, the White Bridge nearby was built in 1844 by a distraught local Turk who shot his daughter by mistake while trying to kill her illicit Serbian lover. Another legend asserts that each time the Turks tried to add a minaret to the pretty 14th-century **St Petka's Church** (Crkva svete Petke) next door, the minaret collapsed so they eventually gave up trying. The church is very popular for christenings.

Holy Trinity Cathedral
Dositejeva. **Open** 7.30am–8pm daily. 8am Sun.

Pasha's Residence
Pionirska 1. **Tel** (017) 423875. **Open** 8am–3pm Mon, 8am–8pm Tue–Fri, 9am–1pm Sat–Sun.

St Petka's Church
Devet Jugovića. **Open** Opening times not fixed, enquire at the tourist office.

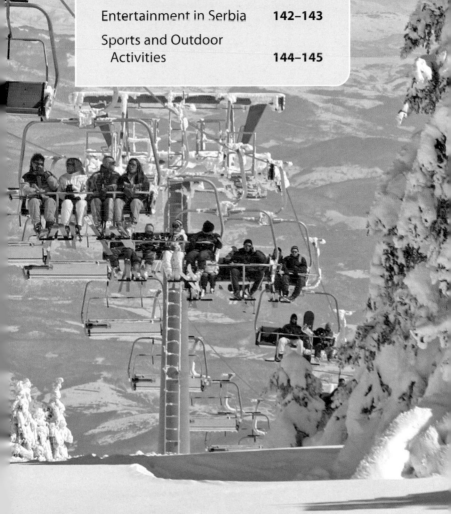

TRAVELLERS' NEEDS

Where to Stay 124–129

Where to Eat and Drink 130–139

Shopping in Serbia 140–141

Entertainment in Serbia 142–143

Sports and Outdoor Activities 144–145

WHERE TO STAY

From mountainous spa hotels and rooms within medieval monasteries to luxurious hotels in cities and rural farmsteads, Serbia offers an ever-expanding choice of places to stay to suit most tastes. Until recently, the accommodation situation in Serbia was much the same as that of any other Eastern European nation emerging from decades of state control, but over the last few years much of the country's ageing hotel stock has been refurbished to international standards. To cope with increasing tourist numbers, new facilities are being built to suit all budgets. Even the more remote parts of Serbia have cottoned on to the trend by promoting village and rural tourism and giving visitors the chance to experience traditional ways of life that are rapidly fading into history.

Valjevo's Hotel Grand, set in a 19th-century building on Trg Živojina Mišića

How to Book

Most of the hotels listed in this guide can be reserved online through their own websites. Bookings can also be made through intermediary apps and sites such as **Booking.com**, **Hotels.com** and **Hostelbookers**, which frequently have prices that are discounted well below the establishment's standard rates; hotel owners are kept on their toes by these booking sites as positive user reviews have become vital to their marketing strategy. For the few hotels that don't have websites, an email or phone call will usually suffice. Smaller hotels are unlikely to accept debit or credit cards, so carry enough cash to cover your bill just in case. **Couchsurfing**, which allows travellers to book to stay with a local family for a short period, is also popular.

Facilities

Unlike many of their European counterparts, Serbian hotel rooms rarely provide kettles to make tea and coffee, although most have fridges and mini-bars. The Serbian summer can be stiflingly hot, so air conditioning is a must unless you are up in the mountains. Rooms usually have flatscreen TVs with various international cable channels. Nearly all hotels offer Wi-Fi throughout the property, although the signal strength will depend on your proximity to the nearest router.

Disabled Travellers

Budget and mid-range hotels tend not to cater for disabled travellers and only a handful of Serbia's high-end hotels do. Plan well ahead and speak to the hotels directly before you book to check the range of facilities they have in place.

Children and Family-friendly Hotels

Serbians love children and hotel staff are happy to welcome families, but it is important to book cots and extra beds you may require well in advance, especially during high season when demand can easily outstrip supply.

Small family-friendly hotels are the most common accommodation option found away from Serbia's major towns and cities. They tend to be family-owned and consequently well-run and welcoming, but usually don't have restaurants, so eat out if you are likely to be arriving late. Hotel sizes vary from about five to 15 rooms and prices are generally between 3,500–6,000 dinars (€30–50). They are more likely than larger hotels to accept pets, but check in advance.

Apartment Hotels

Less common outside Belgrade, apartment hotels offer great value, particularly for families or groups travelling together, and are the only self-catering option available apart from hostels.

Spa Hotels

The Romans built baths, the Turks built hammams and in more recent years the Serbians have built spa hotels all over the country to exploit its multitude of natural hot springs. Most have a local source of natural mineral water, but some are just equipped with spa centres. The best ones offer a range of treatments and have qualified medical staff on site to assess guests' individual needs; casual visitors can just relax in the hot pools, saunas and steam rooms. Many high-end spa hotels have their own replica hammams, but Serbia's only functioning original Turkish bath is the 15th-century one in the spa town of Sokobanja *(see p109)*.

◀ Skiers taking the ski lift up to the top of the run at Kopaonik

Drvengrad's boutique Hotel Mećavnik, set in a complex of traditional wooden houses

Boutique Hotels

Belgrade has many imaginative boutique hotels whose quirky charm sets them apart from functional modern hotels or lavishly appointed luxury hotels. Those outside the capital sometimes miss the mark by opting for tastelessly bright colour schemes, but there are nonetheless a number of characterful gems to be found in Serbia.

Budget Accommodation

Hostels are an attractive budget option in Serbia's largest cities, but a rarity elsewhere. They are a great way to socialize with other travellers and will often organize cheap city tours and group trips to nearby sights.

An increasingly popular alternative is staying in Serbian homes via Couchsurfing and rural or village tourism. You can register on the Couchsurfing website to stay with locals, reducing your accommodation bill to nothing and gaining an invaluable opportunity to learn more about the country and its people through your hosts.

Rural and village tourism offers private accommodation in villages or *salaši* (farmsteads) via the local tourist office. The **National Tourism Organisation of Serbia** website has a list of farmsteads and local tourist offices, and the website of the government-supported **Seoski turizam Srbije** (Serbian Rural Tourism) is also an excellent resource for planning a stay in Serbia's rural areas *(see p144)*.

Recommended Hotels

Hotels in this guide have been selected across a wide price range and represent the most commendable options in their location and category. Value for money, quality of furnishings, facilities, the overall setting and atmosphere and the warmth of the welcome have been taken into consideration. The best are highlighted as DK Choice.

Belgrade has its fair share of splendid hotels and the historic **Hotel Moskva** *(see p126)*, with its Art Nouveau façade and sumptuous interior, is among the finest. Many Central Serbian hotels are pleasant family-run affairs, but few are as unique and enjoyable as **Smederevo Stasea Apartments** *(see p127)*, styled on the town's great fort. Western Serbia's most appealing accommodation is at Sirogojno's museum village where the cozy **Lodging Cabins** *(see p127)* have been modelled on traditional rural dwellings, while in Eastern Serbia Negotin's **Villa Delux** *(see p129)* lives up to its name. In the south the **Grand Hotel** *(see p129)* in Niš is recommended for its sleek modern comfort and service, and in the north the enormously atmospheric **Hotel Leopold I** *(see p128)* in Novi Sad's Petrovaradin Fortress stands out as one of Serbia's most impressive historic hotels.

The prices listed are charged by the hotel during high season (June–September) for a double room, inclusive of taxes. Hotels are listed by regions that are further divided into towns, then by price range and finally by name.

DIRECTORY

How to Book

Booking.com
booking.com

Couchsurfing
couchsurfing.com

Hostelbookers
hostelbookers.com

Hotels.com
hotels.com

Budget Accommodation

National Tourism Organisation of Serbia
serbia.travel

Seoski turizam Srbije
selo.rs

The historic Hotel Moskva, a luxury hotel in Belgrade's Old Town

Where to Stay

Belgrade

Bed and Breakfast Zemun (RSD)
Family
Gundulićeva 21, Zemun
Tel *(0) 603456116*
Exceptionally well-run family hotel in historic Zemun with small but cozy and clean rooms.

Downtown Central Hostel (RSD)
Hostel **City Map** C2
Kolarčeva 7, Stari grad
Tel *(011) 4073861*
W dchostel.rs
Superb central hostel with an attractive modern interior, pleasant communal areas, spacious doubles and shared bathrooms.

Basco Silicon Valley Apartments (RSD)(RSD)
Apartment **City Map** C1
Strahinjića bana 20, Stari grad
Tel *(0) 646476991*
W bascoagency.com
Modern central apartment for up to four guests, with large kitchen and living area. They have more apartments in other locations.

Belgrade Boutique Hotel (RSD)(RSD)
Boutique
Miloja Đaka 32, Savski venac
Tel *(011) 3677888*
W bbh.rs
Spacious and elegantly furnished rooms overlooking a courtyard with a small outdoor pool. The junior suite boasts a spa bath.

Boutique Rooms (RSD)(RSD)
Boutique **City Map** C2
Trg republike 3/VI, Stari grad
Tel *(011) 4088182*
W boutiquerooms.rs
Small, fashionable boutique hotel with bold colours, quirky design and the Boutique café *(see p134)*.

Central Park Residence (RSD)(RSD)
Apartment **City Map** C1
Gospodar Jevremova 3, Stari grad
Tel *(0) 63229761*
W centralparkresidence.rs
Comfortable hotel with doubles and large apartments. Located conveniently close to the Old Town and Kalemegdan Fortress.

Crystal Villa Kalemegdan (RSD)(RSD)
Boutique/Modern **City Map** C1
Strahinjića bana 7, Stari grad
Tel *(011) 2637856*
W villakalemegdan.com
Appealing, small hotel next to Kalemegdan Park with good city views from the rooftop terrace bar. Generous buffet breakfast.

Feel Belgrade Downtown Apartments (RSD)(RSD)
Apartment **City Map** D1
Kneginje Ljubice 11, Stari grad
Tel *(0) 63242422*
W feelbelgrade.com
Roomy apartments for up to four people, with living area, modern kitchen and balcony with views of the Old Town. Great value.

Hotel Argo (RSD)(RSD)
Modern **City Map** D4
Kralja Milana 25, Vračar
Tel *(011) 3640425*
W argohotelbelgrade.com
Located on the main street into the Old Town, this small hotel has bright modern rooms and exceptionally helpful staff.

Hotel Le Petit Piaf (RSD)(RSD)
Historic **City Map** D2
Skadarska 34, Stari grad
Tel *(011) 3035252*
W petitpiaf.com
Fabulous location in the heart of historic Skadarska with comfortably furnished rooms, attentive service and generous breakfasts.

Konak Dedinje Beograd (RSD)(RSD)
Family
Vladimira Gaćinovića 2, Savski venac
Tel *(011) 4066244*
W konakdedinje.com
This decent family-run hotel is a 10-minute drive from the centre, with small, comfortable rooms, a restaurant opposite and attentive owners who are eager to help.

Prince Hall (RSD)(RSD)
Boutique/Modern **City Map** C2
Knez Mihailova 25, Stari grad
Tel *(011) 4070443*
W princehallpalace.com
Smart hotel at a great location with tastefully furnished rooms that are adorned with original artworks by local artists.

Villa Skadarlija (RSD)(RSD)
Historic **City Map** D2
Zetska 10, Stari grad
Tel *(011) 7245128*
W villaskadarlija.rs
Delightful place in the city's old bohemian quarter. Large comfortable rooms with parquet floors and plush furnishings.

ZigZag Belgrade (RSD)(RSD)
Apartment **City Map** C2
Maršala Birjuzova 50, Stari grad
Tel *(0) 652352455*
W zigzag.rs
Remarkably cool apartments and rooms with bags of style, plenty of space, a sauna and a gym.

Price Guide
Prices are based on one night's stay in high season for a standard double room, inclusive of service charges and taxes.

(RSD)	under 4,500 dinars
(RSD)(RSD)	4,500 to 10,000 dinars
(RSD)(RSD)(RSD)	over 10,000 dinars

Courtyard Marriott (RSD)(RSD)(RSD)
Boutique **City Map** C2
Vase Čarapića 2–4, Stari grad
Tel *(011) 4003000*
W marriott.co.uk
Although the modern building is out of keeping with its historic neighbours, it is hard to find fault with its slick, ultramodern interior.

Hotel Evropa (RSD)(RSD)(RSD)
Historic **City Map** C2
Sremska 1, Stari grad
Tel *(011) 3626017*
W hotelevropa.rs
Set in a 19th-century building refurbished to a high standard with marble, leather and wood.

Hotel Metropol Palace (RSD)(RSD)(RSD)
Luxury **City Map** E4
Bulevar kralja Aleksandra 69, Palilula
Tel *(011) 3333100*
W metropolpalace.com
Massive luxury hotel with a state-of-the-art spa centre and an opulent designer interior.

DK Choice

Hotel Moskva (RSD)(RSD)(RSD)
Historic/Luxury **City Map** C3
Terazije 20, Terazije
Tel *(011) 3642069*
W hotelmoskva.rs
A prominent city landmark, this striking 1908 Art Nouveau building has been lavishly restored. It boasts a hammam, sauna, spa and the excellent Tchaikovsky restaurant *(see p135)*. Its guests have included Albert Einstein, Robert De Niro and Brad Pitt.

Café Moskva in the luxury Hotel Moskva, a popular Belgrade meeting place since 1908

Pleasant rooftop terrace of the Square Nine Hotel with good city views

Square Nine Hotel RSD RSD RSD
Luxury/Boutique **City Map** C2
Studentski trg 9, Stari grad
Tel *(011) 3333500*
W squarenine.rs
Elegant high-end hotel with a spa, hammam, indoor pool and a classy Japanese restaurant, Ebisu *(see p135)*, on the roof terrace.

Central Serbia

ARANĐELOVAC: Hotel Izvor RSD RSD RSD
Luxury **Road Map** C3
Mišarska bb
Tel *(034) 700400*
W a-hotel-izvor.com
All-inclusive five-star spa hotel with a huge indoor pool, aqua park and a choice of therapies.

ĆUPRIJA: Plava Laguna RSD
Family **Road Map** D4
Ravanička 4a
Tel *(035) 8470958*
W plavalagunacuprija.rs
Delightful place that is a good base for trips to Manasija, 23 km (14 miles) away, and Ravanica, 12 km (7 miles) away.

KRAGUJEVAC: Hotel Kragujevac RSD RSD
Modern **Road Map** C4
Kralja Petra I 21
Tel *(034) 335811*
W hotelkragujevac.com
Fine, recently modernized central hotel. The rooftop restaurant, Panorama *(see p136)*, has a terrace with impressive views.

KRAGUJEVAC: Hotel President de Luxe RSD RSD
Boutique **Road Map** C4
Janka Veselinovića 52
Tel *(034) 6305935*
W hotelpresident.rs
Characterful hotel with a classic style that is a refreshing alternative to modern decor.

KRUŠEVAC: Hotel Golf Luxury RSD RSD
Modern **Road Map** C4
Gavrila Principa 74
Tel *(037) 3462820*
W hotelgolf.co.rs
There are no golfing facilities, but the hotel has an attractive indoor pool and wellness centre.

SMEDEREVO: Royal Apartments RSD RSD
Family **Road Map** C3
Gorička 23 AB
Tel *(026) 4632550*
W royalapartments.rs
Bright and airy one- and two-bedroom apartments with fully equipped kitchens.

DK Choice

Smederevo Stasea Apartments RSD RSD
Boutique **Road Map** C3
Goranska 165
Tel *(026) 670270*
W apartmanistasea.com
Castle-themed, castle-shaped hotel bursting with character. Its generously sized rooms and apartments are characterfully furnished with quirky decorative features and original wall murals; some have balconies with delightful Danube views.

TOPOLA: Motel Jezero RSD RSD
Family **Road Map** C3
Beogradski put bb
Tel *(018) 526208*
W moteljezero.com
Simple hotel on the Belgrade road with a good traditional style restaurant and rooms that are clean and simply furnished.

Western Serbia

DRVENGRAD: Hotel Mećavnik RSD RSD
Boutique **Road Map** B4
Mokra Gora
Tel *(031) 800686*
W mecavnik.info
Rooms in the traditional wooden houses of Drvengrad are uniquely designed and decorated with Serbian art. The Lotika restaurant *(see p136)* is in the same complex.

KRALJEVO: Turist RSD RSD
Modern **Road Map** C4
Trg srpskih ratnika 1
Tel *(036) 322366*
W hotel-turist.net
Facing the circular central square, Turist has well-appointed rooms and Panorama *(see p136)*, a rooftop eatery with great views.

MOKRA GORA: Konačište Osmica RSD
Family **Road Map** B4
Mokra Gora bb
Tel *(031) 800505*
W sarganskaosmica.rs
En suite rooms in a fantastic spot at Mokra Gora station with views of the Šargan Eight trains.

NOVI PAZAR: Hotel Vrbak RSD RSD
Boutique **Road Map** C5
37. Sandžačke divizije 2
Tel *(020) 314844*
W hotelvrbak.com
Distinctive circular hotel that combines a Soviet-era concrete building with Oriental influences.

OVČAR-KABLAR GORGE: Wellness Centar Kablar RSD RSD
Spa **Road Map** C4
Ovčar Banja, Čačak
Tel *(032) 5596102, 5596106*
W wellnesscentar-kablar.com
Lovely hotel in the Ovčar-Kablar Gorge. Its indoor pool has water from the mineral hot springs.

PRIJEPOLJE: Mileševa Monastery RSD
Family **Road Map** B4
Manastir Mileševa
Tel *(033) 710540*
W turizamprijepolje.org.rs
Atmospheric place with bright rooms and polished wood floors. Book at Prijepolje's tourist office.

RUDNO: Vila Selena RSD
Family **Road Map** C4
Konačište "Vila Selena" Rudno
Tel *(0) 653518644*
W vilaselena.com
Cozy wooden bungalows in a mountain village 25 km (15 miles) from Studenica Monastery.

DK Choice

SIROGOJNO: Lodging Cabins RSD
Family **Road Map** B4
Old Village (Staro selo)
Tel *(031) 3802291*
W sirogojno.rs
Set on a wooded hillside, the seven traditional-style houses have incredibly cozy wood-panelled interiors *(see p86)*. The Krčma tavern *(see p137)* serves classic Serbian dishes.

STUDENICA: Studenica Monastery RSD
Family **Road Map** C4
Konak Manastir Studenica
Tel *(064) 6467492*
W manastirstudenica.rs
This traditional *konak* (residence) in the monastery grounds has airy rooms and mountain views.

For more information on types of hotels *see pages 124–5*

Eco Hostel Republic in Užice, decorated in Soviet military style

UŽICE: Eco Hostel Republik RSD
Hostel **Road Map** B4
Zelje Đurića 34
Tel *(031) 510087*
W republik.rs
Well-run hostel with doubles, a triple and dorms. Currently Užice's only decent accommodation.

VALJEVO: Hotel Grand RSD
Historic **Road Map** B3
Trg Živojina Mišića 1
Tel *(014) 227133*
Central hotel set in a historic building with an overwhelming sense of faded grandeur.

ZLATIBOR: Konačište RSD
Family **Road Map** B4
Miladina Pećinara 2
Tel *(031) 845103*
W zlatibor.org.rs
Pleasant rooms above the tourist information office a five-minute walk from the resort's centre.

ZLATIBOR: Hotel Mir RSD RSD RSD
Family **Road Map** B4
Jovanke Jeftanović 125
Tel *(031) 845151*
W hotelmirzlatibor.com
Smart new hotel with sauna, hot tub and spacious rooms boasting fine mountain views.

Northern Serbia

BELA CRKVA: Villa Oaza RSD
Family **Road Map** D2
Zelengorska 3
Tel *(0) 658233390*
W vilaoaza.com
Agreeable family-run guesthouse with consistently high standards. Great value. Pets are welcome.

FRUŠKA GORA: Borove Noći RSD
Family **Road Map** B2
Laze Gojkovica 58
Tel *(0) 62620530*
Wonderful rural cottages in the woods for up to six people. They make a great base for visiting the Fruška Gora monasteries.

KOVAČICA: Resort Relax RSD RSD
Spa **Road Map** C2
Vinogradska 2
Tel *(013) 660480*
W relax-kovacica.com
Large modern spa hotel with indoor and outdoor pools, sauna and spa centre. All rooms are en suite and have a kitchenette.

NOVI SAD: Varad Inn RSD
Hostel **Road Map** B2
Štrosmajerova 16
Tel *(021) 431400*
W varadinn.com
This superb hostel occupies a renovated 18th-century Baroque building in Petrovaradin's Lower Town. The characterful interior has a choice of doubles, dorms and family rooms, each with air conditioning and private bathroom. There is a shared kitchen.

NOVI SAD: Hotel Veliki RSD RSD
Family **Road Map** B2
Nikole Pašića 24
Tel *(0) 631835454*
W hotelvelikinovisad.com
Centrally located hotel featuring spacious rooms and the good Café Veliki *(see p138)*.

NOVI SAD: Vojvodina RSD RSD
Historic **Road Map** B2
Trg slobode 2
Tel *(021) 6622122*
W hotelvojvodina.rs
The façade of this handsome 19th-century building belies its dated interior, but its unbeatable location makes up for it.

DK Choice

NOVI SAD: Hotel Leopold I RSD RSD RSD
Luxury **Road Map** B2
Petrovaradinska tvrđava
Tel *(021) 4887878*
W leopoldns.com
Set in a stunning Renaissance building within Petrovaradin Fortress, this sumptuous hotel oozes period charm. The rooms are lavishly furnished and most have magnificent views of the Danube and Novi Sad. Nearby, the highly regarded Osam tamburaša *(see p138)* serves traditional Serbian cuisine.

PALIĆ: Hotel Park RSD RSD
Historic **Road Map** B1
Park heroja 15
Tel *(024) 753245*
W elittepalic.rs
Elegant 19th-century hotel with vast rooms, some with lake views, set back from the lake in wooded gardens. The Mala gostiona restaurant serves good fish *(see p138)*.

SREMSKA MITROVICA: B&B Atrium RSD RSD
Family **Road Map** B2
Kralja Petra I 5
Tel *(022) 612613*
Modern hotel in the town centre with marble and parquet floors, stylishly furnished en suite rooms and professional staff.

SREMSKI KARLOVCI: Premier Prezident Hotel RSD RSD RSD
Luxury **Road Map** B2
Karađorđeva 2
Tel *(021) 884111*
W premierprezidenthotel.com
Splendid five-star hotel with Baroque interior decor. Central location and great facilities.

SUBOTICA: Pansion Mali Hotel RSD
Family **Road Map** B1
Harambašićeva 25
Tel *(024) 552977*
W malihotelsubotica.com
Highly rated guesthouse offering value for money a 10-minute walk from the city centre.

SUBOTICA: Hotel Best Western Gloria RSD RSD RSD
Family **Road Map** B1
Dimitrija Tucovića br. 2
Tel *(024) 672010*
W hotelgloriasubotica.com
Great central option with double rooms and apartments, some overlooking the striking City Hall.

VRŠAC: Hotel Srbija RSD RSD
Modern **Road Map** C2
Svetosavski trg 12
Tel *(013) 834170*
W hotelsrbija.rs
Gracefully refurbished rooms that are a bit on the small side but offer guests sweeping city views.

VRŠAC: Villa Breg RSD RSD RSD
Luxury **Road Map** C2
Goranska bb
Tel *(013) 831000*
W villabreg.com
Five-star spa hotel with outdoor infinity pool, indoor pool, tennis courts, a fine restaurant and spacious, well-appointed rooms.

Eastern Serbia

DONJI MILANOVAC: Hotel Lepenski Vir RSD RSD
Spa **Road Map** D3
Radnička bb
Tel *(030) 590210*
W hotellepenskivir.co.rs/index.asp
Huge spa hotel on the Danube that is the nearest good accommodation to the Lepenski Vir archaeological site.

KLADOVO: Aquastar Danube (RSD)(RSD)(RSD)
Family **Road Map** E3
Dunavski kej 1
Tel *(019) 810810*
W hotelkladovo.rs
Upmarket hotel by the Danube with indoor and outdoor pools, the pleasant Imperator restaurant *(see p138)* and great river views.

KNJAŽEVAC: Konak Barka (RSD)
Family **Road Map** D4
Kadijski krst bb
Tel *(019) 731222*
Appealing place set in gardens just outside the town centre. Popular with hunters planning trips into the nearby mountains.

NEGOTIN: Hotel Beograd (RSD)(RSD)
Luxury **Road Map** E3
Trg Stevana Mokranjca 2
Tel *(019) 547000*
W hotelbeograd.rs
This elegant hotel is set in a renovated 19th-century building in the very heart of Negotin.

DK Choice

NEGOTIN: Villa Delux (RSD)(RSD)
Luxury **Road Map** E3
Naselje gradište bb
Tel *(019) 548885*
W vila-delux.eu
This delightful family-run hotel, a 15-minute walk from the town centre, offers guests large, luxuriously appointed rooms. The buffet breakfast has a staggering array of options, including Turkish Delight, Serbian *burek* and chocolate doughnuts.

Comfortable double room at Negotin's family-run Villa Delux hotel

SOKOBANJA: Hotel Soko Terme (RSD)(RSD)
Spa **Road Map** D4
Wellness and Spa Centar SokoTerme
Tel *(018) 884856*
W sokoterme.net
This popular castle-shaped hotel just outside the centre is booked to capacity throughout the summer. It boasts three pools and a wide range of spa treatments.

VIMINACIUM: Viminacium Archaeological Park (RSD)
Family **Road Map** C3
Archaeological Park Viminacium, Stari Kostolac bb
Tel *(0) 62669013*
W viminacium.org.rs
Simple accommodation in single, double and triple en suite rooms within the archaeological park. The restaurant serves authentic Roman meals made from 3rd-century recipes.

VINCI: Guesthouse Bajka (RSD)
Family **Road Map** D3
3. ulica 7
Tel *(0) 652224190*
W guesthousebajka.com
Charming accommodation in a tranquil forest a short walk from the Danube. Golubac Fortress is just 9 km (5 miles) away.

ZAJEČAR: Srbija Tis Hotel (RSD)(RSD)
Modern **Road Map** D4
Nikole Pašića bb
Tel *(019) 422540*
W srbijatis.co.rs
Atmospheric concrete relic of the Communist era with decor from its Yugoslavian heyday, an antiquated lift and a decent traditional-style restaurant.

ZAJEČAR: Vila Tamaris (RSD)(RSD)
Boutique **Road Map** D4
Ljube Nešića 58
Tel *(019) 428781*
W vilatamaris.co.rs
Although the garish red neon sign outside isn't very inviting, Vila Tamaris is in fact a smart, well-run hotel with some very bold colour schemes.

Southern Serbia

LESKOVAC: Hotel ABC (RSD)(RSD)
Modern **Road Map** D5
Moše Pijade bb
Tel *(016) 234040*
W hotel.abcleskovac.com
Ultramodern central hotel that is a good base for a trip to Caričin Grad (15 km/9 miles away) or to experience the annual grilled meat festival held in September.

LUKOVSKA BANJA: Jelak Hotel (RSD)(RSD)
Spa **Road Map** C5
Lukovska Banja
Tel *(027) 385999*
W lukovskabanja.com
Nestling within a wooded valley, this peaceful place is one of two modern spa hotels in Lukovska Banja. It offers well-furnished en suite rooms and plenty of water-based therapies.

NIŠ: Etno Konak Tašana (RSD)
Family **Road Map** D4
Prijezdina 8a
Tel *(0) 642023200*
W prenocistetasana.freshcreator.com
Wonderful small hotel with bags of character and artfully decorated rooms overlooking the central courtyard. Free bike hire.

NIŠ: Artloft Hotel (RSD)(RSD)
Boutique **Road Map** D4
Oblačića Rada 8A/7
Tel *(018) 305800*
W artloft.rs
Stylish central hotel offering contemporary rooms featuring abstract art by local artists. Great breakfast and exceptional service.

DK Choice

NIŠ: Grand Hotel (RSD)(RSD)(RSD)
Luxury **Road Map** D4
Vožda Karađorđa 12
Tel *(018) 505700*
W grandhotelnis.com
The largest hotel in Niš is a modern, upmarket affair in an enviable central location with spacious and comfortably furnished rooms. There is an excellent restaurant, and business facilities include two large conference rooms. Staff provide a very high standard of service.

PIROT: Hotel Sin-Kom (RSD)
Family **Road Map** E5
Nikole Pašića bb
Tel *(010) 322505*
W hotel-sinkom.com
This is a highly rated modern hotel just five minutes from the town centre. The spotless rooms have parquet floors and slightly dated furniture. It is a popular location for local weddings.

PROLOM BANJA: Radan Hotel (RSD)(RSD)
Spa **Road Map** D5
Prolom Banja
Tel *(027) 8388111*
W prolombanja.com
Situated high in the mountains and offering wonderful views, this recently renovated popular spa hotel has two pools and a vast choice of treatments offered by qualified medical staff.

VRANJE: Ponte Bianco (RSD)(RSD)
Modern **Road Map** D6
Branislava Nušića 2
Tel *(017) 399990*
W pontebianco.rs
Vranje's best hotel combines an outstanding pizza restaurant with spotless modern rooms. Friendly staff provide a warm welcome.

For more information on types of hotels *see pages 124–5*

WHERE TO EAT AND DRINK

With tourist numbers on the increase and living standards on the rise in Serbia, new restaurants are constantly opening and old establishments are being refurbished and updated. Service standards are generally high. Typical Serbian food still dominates, with an array of grilled meat dishes the staple of most restaurant menus, although foreign influences are gradually creeping in – pizza parlours are becoming a common sight in regional towns, vegetarianism is emerging and the range of good quality international cuisine available in large cities such as Novi Sad, Niš and Belgrade is steadily expanding.

One of the charming cafés in Belgrade's bohemian Skadarlija neighbourhood

Choosing a Restaurant

Restaurants can be easily found all over Serbia. Those outside the major cities are most likely to be traditional *etno* eateries serving "national" cuisine – fish, grilled meat and salads. Some *etno* places are simple affairs but others offer rustic decor, open fires and pleasant gardens. For quick snacks most small towns have bakeries selling *burek* and kiosks serving grilled meat to take away. The popularity of Italian food means pizza is included on several menus, but don't expect them to live up to your expectations of their American or Italian equivalents. Several vegetarian, vegan and organic restaurants have sprung up in Belgrade, and many places also either specialize in or serve a good standard of Asian, Italian, Mediterranean, French, South American and Middle Eastern cuisine. Non-smokers should opt for places that either have outdoor seating or a separate non-smoking section.

When to Eat

Most restaurants open between 10am and noon until around midnight, although some open earlier to catch the breakfast crowd. The same dishes are offered throughout the day and last orders for dinner *(večera)* are usually taken an hour before closing. Some places offer excellent value lunch *(ručak)* menus that change every day and are served between noon and 5pm as long as there is availability.

Reservations

Outside the capital, there is little need to make reservations – just turn up and if a table is not marked as reserved you may sit at it. Belgrade's best restaurants can get very busy, especially at weekends, so it is a good idea to book ahead. If possible, consider making your reservation by email via the establishment's own website rather than by telephone as staff do not always speak fluent English.

Reading the Menu

Most restaurants in Serbia's larger towns and cities will offer customers an *engleski jelovnik* or English menu with descriptions of meals and their ingredients. Establishments that are located further afield and see fewer foreign diners are unlikely to be as well prepared, so it is usually worth remembering or writing down a list of the names of some of your favourite Serbian dishes to ask for. Some of the common menu categories you should look out for include *jela sa roštilja* (grilled dishes), *salate* (salads), *supe i čorbe* (soups), *riba* (fish dishes), *prilozi* (side dishes) and *poslastice* (desserts).

Children

It is not unusual to see young children out late with their families at restaurants across Serbia, and they are generally most welcome so long as they don't misbehave. High chairs are sometimes available and although it is fairly rare to find children's menus, it is never a problem to request extra plates so that dishes can be shared.

High chairs for seating young children, sometimes available in Serbian restaurants

Šopska salata, a cold vegetarian salad popular throughout the Balkans

Vegetarians and Vegans

Despite the obvious dominance of meat in Serbian cuisine, vegetarians need not despair. Cafés and restaurants generally have a reasonable selection of salads and meat-free dishes made with fresh local ingredients. Women can tell their waiter *"ja sam vegetarijanka"*, men can say *"ja sam vegetarijanac"* or both can simply use *"ne jedem meso"* ("I don't eat meat"). Vegans and vegetarians benefit from the Serbian Orthodox tradition of fasting at Christmas and Easter because during this time only *posno*, fasting food that doesn't contain animal-related products, is eaten. This means that throughout the year it is possible to ask *"da li je posno?"* ("Is it fasting food?") about any food product you're about to buy or consume. *Šopska salata*, a salad with tomato, cucumber, onion, pepper, parsley and cheese, is a staple of most restaurant menus. Vegans should order it *bez sira* (without cheese).

Smoking

Smoking is something of a national hobby in Serbia. Old legislation stipulated that restaurants should have separate non-smoking and smoking sections, but in practice this meant that an establishment's few tables with no-smoking signs were vastly outnumbered by tables where diners smoked freely. New laws banning smoking in restaurants, cafés, bars and hotels were passed at the end of 2015, but as no deadline was set it remains to be seen if such a radical cultural change will be readily implemented.

Bills and Tipping

Many large or well-established restaurants will take payment by card, but always carry cash just in case. A service charge is never included in the bill, but it is customary to leave a tip of 10 per cent if you are satisfied with the meal and service. When paying by card you can request that this be added to the bill.

Recommended Restaurants

The restaurants and cafés in this guide vary in style from cutting-edge designer decor to palatial mansions and bohemian bare-brick interiors. They have been chosen from all over Serbia across a wide price range and variety of cuisines. Those places highlighted as DK Choice are exceptional in some way, either because they offer great value for money or because their food stands out from the crowd.

The legendary *kafana* **Dva jelena** *(see p134)* on Belgrade's historic Skadarska street is notable as a traditional eatery that embodies the country's true flavour. **Kanjon** *(see p137)* in Western Serbia's Prijepolje and **Stara vodenica** *(see p139)* in Eastern Serbia's Sokobanja are both delightful examples of idyllic "national" restaurants with superb local cuisine and bags of character. In Central Serbia, Kragujevac's **Panorama** *(see p136)* is a smart modern eatery with a great international menu, several local rakias (fruit brandies) and a sleek designer interior, while Northern Serbia's **Project 72** *(see p138)* in Novi Sad is highly recommended for its innovative approach to fine dining and excellent service.

High-end places in Serbia are often sited in smart city hotels, where the price the customer pays is as much for the classy service and ambience as it is for the quality of the cuisine. The guide's restaurants and cafés are listed by regions that are further divided into towns, then by price range and finally by name.

Chef preparing an Italian meal at the stunning Comunale restaurant in Belgrade's riverside Beton Hala development

The Flavours of Serbia

Serbian cuisine is a rich blend of Turkish, Mediterranean, Austrian and Hungarian influences made with fresh local ingredients and accompanied by a diverse choice of drinks. Predominantly meat based, it is heavy and calorific, so the main meal of the day tends to be lunch, with *burek* (pastry) for breakfast and a light snack for dinner. Fish dishes are also popular and salads and meat-free options are available too. The wonderful range of delicious fresh breads includes ceremonial breads for Christmas and *slavas*.

Raspberries, produced primarily in Western Serbia and exported worldwide

Burek, a popular pastry snack often filled with cheese, minced meat or spinach

Southern Serbia

Pirot's famous yellow cheese, *pirotski kačkavalj*, is produced with milk from sheep grazed on the slopes of the Stara planina. The town's cheese-making prowess is so highly regarded that it was recently awarded an EU-wide patent to protect its name from misuse by rogue manufacturers.

Savoury *burek* made from thin layers of pastry filled with cheese, spinach or minced beef is a cheap takeaway snack all over Serbia, but proud locals like to claim that it originates from the south; the city of Niš even holds an annual Burek Days festival *(see p30)*.

Northern Serbia

Doughy foods such as bread and pasta are typical of Northern Serbia's tantalizing blend of Hungarian, Austrian and Turkish cuisine. Cabbage is a commonly used ingredient – *podvarak* is a baked dish of pork and pickled cabbage while *sarma* are small parcels of minced beef and rice wrapped in pickled cabbage leaves. *Gulaš* (goulash), a meat and vegetable stew, is on every restaurant menu and Turkish baklava and Viennese cakes are usually available as desserts.

Selection of typical Serbian breads and pastries

Grilled Meat Dishes

Serbia remains best known for the grilled meat dishes that dominate menus throughout the country. Paired with a wide range of delicious, freshly baked breads, they have been an essential part of the national diet since they were introduced by the Turks. Traditionally barbecued over charcoal and eaten for lunch, popular dishes include *ćevapčići, kobasice, pljeskavice* and *ražnjići*. Roštiljijada ("barbecue week"), an annual grilled-meat festival held in Leskovac *(see p30)*, is a mecca for carnivores that lasts for five days and attracts over 700,000 visitors.

Ćevapčići are finger-sized pieces of rolled minced beef served with flatbread, onions and sour cream or sauces.

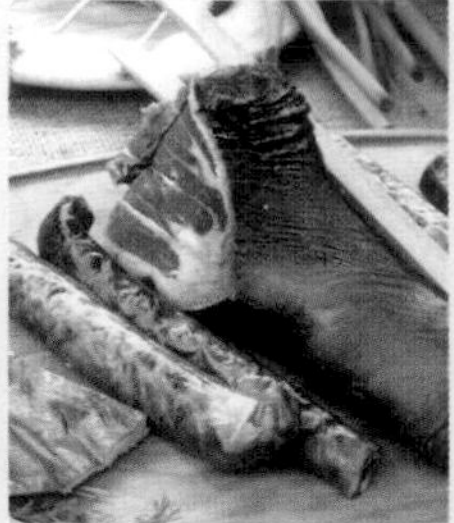

Kobasice, spiced pork or beef sausages, come in a variety of shapes and sizes, including straight, U-shaped and thick.

Selection of wines and rakias (fruit brandies) from the Negotin region

Central Serbia

Famed for its prolific orchards, central Serbia has an abundance of plums that are used primarily for *šljivovica* (plum brandy) and also for *pekmez od šljiva* (plum jam) and *knedle sa šljivama* (potato dumplings encasing a whole plum).

Cabbage is another staple eaten in many forms – *kiseli kupus* (pickled) and *salata od svežeg kupusa* (raw salad) – but the best known use for it is in *svadbarski kupus* ("wedding cabbage"), a spicy dish of pork or mutton and cabbage slow-cooked for hours in traditional Serbian ceramic pots.

Šljivovica, a potent plum brandy

Eastern Serbia

Riblja čorba (fish soup) has been on the menu for millennia along the Danube. Traditionally cooked outdoors in a cauldron, it is made from the heads of carp, catfish, pike or perch and is spiced generously with hot paprika; some say it tastes best when made with river water.

Many of the best wines of Serbia are produced in the countryside around Negotin where the riverside vineyards benefit from sunlight reflecting off the water. Popular local varieties include Smederevka, Prokupac and Začinak.

Western Serbia

The salty clotted cream known as *kajmak* is made throughout Serbia, but the mountainous region of Zlatibor is thought to produce the country's best. Consumed both as a snack and an ingredient, one of its most sought-after guises is *lepinja sa kajmakom*, a baked bread bun stuffed with *kajmak* and fried egg.

Among the region's popular Turkish-influenced dishes are *ćevapčići*, mildly spiced fingers of grilled meat served with raw onions, and a circular meat pastry called *mantije*. The city of Novi Pazar is known for its veal *ćevapčići*, produced with high-quality meat from cattle grazed in the verdant Pešter highlands west of town. The area is also noted for Sjenica *sudžuk*, a cold smoked and dried beef sausage.

Kajmak from Western Serbia, a salty clotted cream eaten as a snack

Ražnjići, Serbia's version of a kebab, is grilled pork or veal on a skewer. The name is derived from *ražnjevi* or "skewers".

Pljeskavice is a flat, round meat patty made with a mixture of ground meats – typically veal, beef, pork or lamb.

WHAT TO DRINK

Šljivovica, Serbia's national drink, is a plum brandy typically served as an apéritif.

Rakia is a strong fruit brandy that is commonly produced from plums *(šljivovica)*, apricots *(kajsija)* or grapes *(lozova)*.

Wines from Vršać, Negotin and Sremski Karlovci are renowned for their quality.

Šumadijski čaj is a popular winter drink consisting of rakia boiled with sugar.

Coffee in Serbia is traditionally brewed Turkish-style in a pot and served with a lump of *ratluk* or *lokum* (Turkish Delight).

Beers, including a pale lager, are locally produced and widely available in Serbia, although not well known outside the country.

Jogurt is a watery, sour yogurt drink that is often served with *burek* and grilled meat.

Limunada made with freshly squeezed lemon juice and sugar is a refreshing drink in summer.

Where to Eat and Drink

Belgrade

Black Turtle Pub RSD
Serbian **City Map** B2
Kosančićev venac 30, Stari grad
Tel *(011) 3286591*
Characterful pub on a historic old town street with river views. It offers a good choice of Serbian staples, including goulash, bean soup and fried chicken coated in sesame seeds, all served up with mugs of beer from the Black Turtle brewery.

Boutique RSD
Italian **City Map** C2
Trg republike 3/VI and Knez Mihailova 52a, Stari grad
Tel *(011) 2621373*
This reliable modern café offers shaded outdoor seating at two central locations, including one below the Boutique Rooms *(see p126)*. Good for snacks and more substantial pasta and meat dishes.

Kuhinja RSD
Serbian/Italian
Vojvode Stepe 93, Voždovac
Tel *(011) 2469492*
Great Serbian restaurant with an extensive menu that includes over 25 salads and every conceivable grilled meat option as well as a full pizza menu and various pasta options. Friendly service and cozy interior.

O.U.R. Bar RSD
Serbian **City Map** E4
Beogradska 71, Vračar
Tel *(011) 3238846*
Busy bar with wooden furniture and walls covered with images of Yugolsav films. It attracts a lively crowd and hosts regular music and DJ nights. Serves good steak and chips and Serbian grilled meat dishes until past midnight. Gets very crowded and smoky, especially at weekends.

Dijagonala 2.0 RSD RSD
International/Serbian **City Map** D5
Skerlićeva 6, Vračar
Tel *(011) 2449099*
Set in an old villa once owned by Serbian sculptor Đoka Jovanović across the road from the National Library, near the Temple of St Sava, this buzzing restaurant attracts a young crowd and is one of the places to be seen in Belgrade. It has a good choice of Serbian and international cuisine.

Diwali RSD RSD
Indian
Ljubićka 1b, Šumice
Tel *(011) 3446235* **Closed** *Mon*
Formerly known as Maharaja, Diwali is one of Belgrade's only Indian restaurants. On the menu are plenty of vegetarian options along with tandoori, rice and curry dishes – beware that some are very hot. Best reached by taxi from the city centre.

DK Choice

Dva jelena RSD RSD
Serbian **City Map** D2
Skadarska 32, Skadarlija
Tel *(011) 7234885*
A legendary establishment on Skadarska, the Two Stags has been serving hearty Serbian fare since the 19th century. Popular with both locals and tourists, it is one of the city's best places to enjoy Serbia's traditional grilled meat dishes while being serenaded by Roma musicians.

Kafana Question Mark RSD RSD
Serbian **City Map** B2
Kralja Petra 6, Stari grad
Tel *(011) 2635421*
Belgrade's oldest *kafana* or traditional tavern, this historic establishment is most famous for its unique name. In 1892 its owner wished to call it "By the Cathedral Church" but the church authorities objected. The owner hung a "?" sign above the door in protest and it soon became the official name. It is a great place to enjoy local dishes and soak up the atmosphere *(see p47)*.

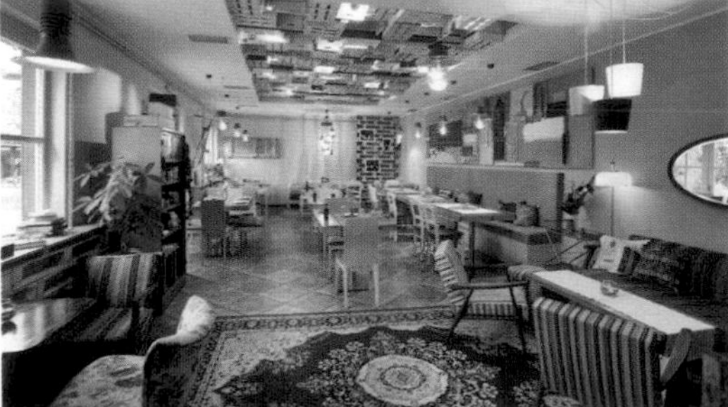
The cheerful, eclectic interior decor of the Greek restaurant Mezestoran Dvorište

Price Guide
Prices are based on an evening meal for one person, including service tax but no alcohol.

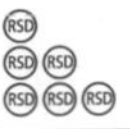

RSD	under 1,800 dinars
RSD RSD	1,800 to 3,000 dinars
RSD RSD RSD	over 3,000 dinars

Manufaktura RSD RSD
Serbian/Balkan **City Map** B2
Kralja Petra 13–15, Stari grad
Tel *(011) 2180044*
Popular place just off the main drag with a capacious interior that artfully combines vaguely industrial features with rustic shelving. Serves a good selection of Serbian and Balkan dishes and lists the origins of ingredients. Service is occasionally lethargic.

Mezestoran Dvorište RSD RSD
Greek **City Map** E3
Svetogorska 46, Stari grad
Tel *(011) 3246515*
Well-established Greek restaurant with bright interior decor, quirky design features and a delightful secluded garden. The choice of flawlessly prepared dishes includes stuffed aubergine, mussels in various sauces, fried courgettes and plenty of salads.

Milošev Konak RSD RSD
Serbian
Topčiderska 1, Topčider
Tel *(011) 2663146*
Traditional Serbian restaurant located within the old stables of the Mansion of Prince Miloš (Konak kneza Miloša) in Topčider Park *(see p59)*. Its excellent dishes include spit-roasted pork and lamb, tripe soup and goulash. There's also pleasant outdoor seating with views of the park.

Radost Fina Kuhinjica RSD RSD
Vegan/Vegetarian **City Map** B2
Pariska 3, Stari grad
Tel *(0) 616044445* **Closed** *Mon*
Wonderful vegan and vegetarian restaurant set in a tastefully converted old apartment with raw, vegetarian, vegan and gluten-free dishes. The portions can be small and service slow, but the food is superb. Try the vegan burger and the raw mint cake.

Šaran RSD RSD
Fish/Serbian
Kej oslobođenja 53, Zemun
Tel *(011) 2618235*
One of several riverside city restaurants, Šaran is known for its fresh fish dishes and seafood. The smoked carp is sublime, as is the fish soup. The live band provides a perfect accompaniment to the food and the fine river views.

Smokvica RSD RSD
International **City Map** C1
Kralja Petra 73, Stari grad
Tel *(0) 694464056*
Charming place with a lovely walled garden and an eclectic menu with falafel, ravioli, samosa and beefsteak. The home-made lemonade is perfect on a hot day.

Tchaikovsky (Čajkovski) RSD RSD
Serbian **City Map** C3
Terazije 20, Terazije
Tel *(011) 3642069*
Expect impeccable service and faultless Serbian cuisine when dining in the remarkable Art Nouveau interior of Hotel Moskva *(see p126)*. The portions are generous and the desserts fantastic.

Voulez-Vous RSD RSD
International
Đorđa Vajferta 52, Vračar
Tel *(011) 2440777*
Hugely popular eatery that is highly ranked on review sites for its high-quality food and service and appealing ambience. The desserts are phenomenally good and the Serbian, Italian and international mains are all excellent.

Selection of colourful rakias (fruit brandies) available at Belgrade's Ambar restaurant

Ambar RSD RSD RSD
International **City Map** B2
Karađorđeva 2–4, Beton Hala
Tel *(011) 3286637*
Located on the riverfront within the cutting-edge Beton Hala complex of designer restaurants, Ambar serves international and Serbian cuisine and is famous for its selection of over 50 different rakias (fruit brandies).

Casa Nova RSD RSD RSD
French/Italian **City Map** D2
Gospodar-Jovanova 42a, Stari grad
Tel *(011) 3036868*
Well regarded for its exceptional service and cuisine, Casa Nova occupies an elegant mansion in the atmospheric Upper Dorćol quarter. Among its specialities is the Sicilian Wheel, a chicken or beef steak served atop a tortilla and doused in sauce.

Comunale RSD RSD RSD
Italian **City Map** B2
Karađorđeva 2–4, Beton Hala
Tel *(011) 3037337*
Another stunning Beton Hala eatery, with a wood and steel interior. Based on the concept of communal dining, the restaurant seats its guests around several large banquet-style tables. High-quality pizzas and grilled meat are on the menu.

Ebisu RSD RSD RSD
Japanese **City Map** C2
Studentski trg 9, Stari grad
Tel *(011) 3333575* **Closed** *Mon*
Refined Japanese restaurant on the roof of the exclusive Square Nine Hotel *(see p127)*. Serves sublime desserts and sushi that is good though not world class. The terrace has great city views.

Gnezdo Organic 
International **City Map** B2
Male stepenice 1a, Stari grad
Tel *(0) 607407408* **Closed** *Mon*
Hard to find but worth the effort for its wholesome, healthy food. One of the city's best organic restaurants, Gnezdo has meat dishes plus vegan, gluten free and vegetarian options. Try the tofu kebabs, steak with grilled polenta and chocolate truffles. Book in advance.

Kalemegdanska terasa RSD RSD RSD
Serbian **City Map** B1
Mali Kalemegdan bb, Stari grad
Tel *(011) 3283011*
Classically styled restaurant within Kalemegdan Fortress with pretty views of the Danube from its secluded terrace. Serves high-quality Serbian cuisine alongside a few international dishes.

Pire RSD RSD
International **City Map** C2
Cara Lazara 11, Stari grad
Tel *(011) 2634994*
The owner, Serbian couturier Dragana Ognjenović, designed this small, white, stylish place herself. The focus is on slow food, and locally sourced ingredients are used for its daily menu of tempting dishes.

Salon 5 RSD RSD RSD
International/Italian
Avijatičarski trg 5, 1st floor, Zemun
Tel *(011) 2614893*
With a well-deserved reputation as one of the best places to eat in Belgrade, Salon 5 occupies a sophisticated space within a historic Zemun apartment building. On offer is exquisitely presented food from a tiny menu as well as a list of superb wines.

Toro RSD RSD RSD
Latin American **City Map** B2
Karađorđeva 2–4, Beton Hala
Tel *(011) 3034342*
Amongst the restaurants run by the award-winning Mexican chef Richard Sandoval, Toro is part of Belgrade's buzzing Beton Hala riverside development. It serves fantastic Central and South American small plates and wines, as well as a variety of cocktails, in effortlessly sleek surroundings.

Central Serbia

ARANĐELOVAC: Aleksandar RSD
Serbian **Road Map** C3
Knjaza Miloša 173
Tel *(034) 725617*
Traditional Serbian food a short walk from Aranđelovac's huge Bukovička Park. Decorated with antique-style furniture in classical 19th-century fashion, this appealing restaurant has plenty of charm. Its garden, shaded by trees, is an added bonus.

ARANĐELOVAC: Stari Park RSD
Serbian **Road Map** C3
Kralja Petra 59/1
Tel *(034) 724440* **Closed** *Mon*
Set in a great location opposite the large Bukovička Park in an elegant building that is very popular for wedding banquets. There are mostly Serbian staples on the menu along with some reasonable pasta choices.

ARANĐELOVAC: Tarpoš RSD RSD
Serbian **Road Map** C3
Vrbica Winery, Vrbica bb
Tel (034) 725805
This splendid restaurant is set on a hill within the Vrbica Winery, 5 km (3 miles) northeast of Aranđelovac. Dining here provides a great opportunity to learn more about local wines and enjoy wonderful views from the restaurant's covered terrace, which is surrounded by vineyards. The wine list includes the winery's own Riesling, Sauvignon Blanc, Chardonnay, Cabernet Sauvignon and Merlot.

KRAGUJEVAC: Beerhouse Allectus (RSD)
International **Road Map** C4
Daničićeva 21
Tel *(034) 501228*
Characterful pub with battered antique oddments on its bare brick walls. Narrow choice of beers but good food menu with pasta, pizza, goulash, vegetable kebabs and grilled salmon.

KRAGUJEVAC: Kafana Jugoslavja (RSD)
Serbian **Road Map** C4
Daničićeva 52
Tel *(0) 66365200*
Entertaining Communist-themed pub decorated with Tito-related memorabilia. Simple Serbian fare served in generous portions. Gets very busy on weekend evenings when there's usually live music.

KRAGUJEVAC: Peron (RSD)
International **Road Map** C4
Kralja Petra I bb
Tel *(0) 646774311*
One of the coolest spots in town occupies a tastefully converted third-class railway carriage with wooden benches and vintage suitcases. Sweet and savoury pancakes dominate the menu. Also popular for evening beers.

KRAGUJEVAC: Vodenica (RSD)
Serbian **Road Map** C4
Starine Novaka 56
Tel *(034) 313104*
Buzzing *etno* ("national") restaurant with a cavernous interior that resembles a giant hay barn. Great atmosphere and an enjoyable range of imaginatively presented Serbian dishes.

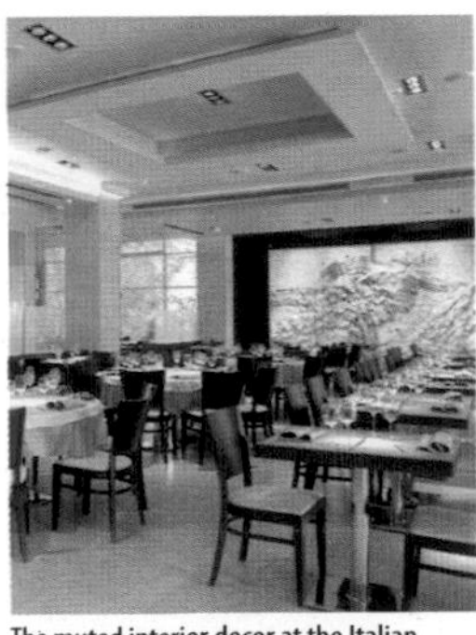

The muted interior decor at the Italian restaurant Zelengora in Kragujevac

KRAGUJEVAC: Zelengora (RSD)(RSD)
Italian/Serbian **Road Map** C4
Branka Radičevića 22
Tel *(034) 336254*
Sleek restaurant with a calm ambience within the hotel of the same name. Fine choice of pizza and pasta dishes and a selection of Serbian options too. There are over 60 local and international wines to choose from.

DK Choice

KRAGUJEVAC: Panorama (RSD)(RSD)(RSD)
International **Road Map** C4
Kralja Petra I 21
Tel *(034) 335533*
Very smart place with sweeping city views from its position atop Hotel Kragujevac *(see p127)*. Generous portions of immaculately presented dishes such as pork tenderloin in prune sauce, plus a marvellous wine list with many international options and local rakias. Flawless service. Well worth the higher price.

KRUŠEVAC: Laterna (RSD)(RSD)
Serbian **Road Map** C4
Dragomira Gajića 86
Tel *(037) 3538107*
Exceptionally well-presented Serbian food in a skillfully run restaurant with polite, attentive staff. The shabby-chic interior is a novel alternative to the more common *etno*-style traditional eateries. Highly recommended.

KRUŠEVAC: Olive Tree (RSD)(RSD)
International **Road Map** C4
Čolak Antina 3
Tel *(037) 3502008*
With its refreshing choice of Mediterranean, Lebanese, Chinese and Mexican dishes, the Olive Tree offers a welcome break from Serbia's typically meat-heavy cuisine. Delicious cakes as well as a good selection of local wines are available.

SMEDEREVO: Restaurant Grand (RSD)
Serbian **Road Map** C3
Trg republike
Tel *(026) 672703*
Lovely location just off the town's main square with shaded outdoor seating, classy interior and very good service. The menu features meaty Serbian staples such as *pljeskavica* but also has some vegetarian options and, occasionally, Danube trout.

SMEDEREVO: Talismano (RSD)
International **Road Map** C3
Knez Mihajlova 40
Tel *(026) 648400*
Good centrally located place with a modern interior, serving both Serbian specialities and a choice of international meat dishes, including pork fillet and Argentinian steak.

TOPOLA: Vožd (RSD)
Serbian **Road Map** C3
Jovana Skerlića 1/a
Tel *(034) 811365*
With its pleasant garden seating and smart interior, Vožd is a good year-round option. It's a great spot to try some hearty Serbian dishes and sample fine wines from respected local wineries.

TOPOLA: Knežev Han (RSD)(RSD)
Serbian **Road Map** C3
Karađorđeva 4
Tel *(034) 812111*
Set opposite the Royal Park, Knežev Han has a stylish interior, shaded outdoor seating and a good view of the Karađorđev House Museum *(see p75)*. The menu has grilled and smoked pork ribs, local cheese and wines from five regional vineyards.

Western Serbia

DRVENGRAD: Lotika (RSD)
Serbian **Road Map** B4
Mokra Gora
Tel *(031) 800686*
Huge choice of traditional meals in a cozy wooden building in the same complex as Hotel Mećavnik *(see p127)*. All the grilled meat favourites, *punjene paprike* (stuffed peppers) and *prebranac* (baked beans) are on the menu. Phlegmatic service may be due to the high turnover of diners.

KRALJEVO: Panorama (RSD)(RSD)
International **Road Map** C4
Trg srpskih ratnika 1
Tel *(036) 322366*
Smart modern place at the top of the Turist hotel *(see p127)* with a large terrace and fabulous views. Good choice of pizzas including a Nutella dessert one. Trout fillet with almonds and turkey with curry sauce are also on the menu.

MAGLIČ: Jerinin Grad (RSD)
Serbian **Road Map** C4
Maglič 46
Tel *(036) 5826009*
Simple roadside restaurant set below Maglič Fortress that does a great *šopska* salad and excellent fish soup alongside the standard choice of grilled meat.

NOVI PAZAR: Med Caffe (RSD)
International **Road Map** C5
28. novembra
Tel *(0) 659027902*
Popular retro-themed place on a busy pedestrianized street. Offers sandwiches, salad, omelette, pizza, pasta, chicken and fish dishes at very reasonable prices.

Key to Price Guide *see page 134*

NOVI PAZAR: Ras (RSD)
Serbian **Road Map** C5
Turističko naselje "Ras" Pazarište bb
Tel *(020) 361578*
Lovely spot outside Novi Pazar beneath the ancient hilltop fortress of Stari Ras on the road to Sopoćani Monastery. Ras serves well-presented Serbian food in a traditional interior; there are pretty gardens outside.

OVČAR-KABLAR GORGE: Kablar (RSD)
International **Road Map** C4
Ovčar Banja, Čačak
Tel *(032) 5596102, 5596106*
Wellness Centar Kablar's pleasant restaurant serves a broad choice of pasta, pizza, salads, beef dishes and pancakes as well as *žito sa šlagom*, a wheat paste mixed with nuts, cinnamon and nutmeg traditionally eaten by families celebrating their *slava* (saint day).

DK Choice

PRIJEPOLJE: Kanjon (RSD)
Serbian **Road Map** B4
Prijepolje
Tel *(033) 671767*
A charming restaurant about a kilometre (half a mile) beyond Mileševa Monastery, Kanjon has its own trout farm and a pretty garden as well as an outdoor play area and a small zoo with goats, rabbits and ducks to keep children entertained. It is a great spot to try fresh trout, a wide range of local dishes, delicious home-made bread and Serbian wine. The restaurant can be reached by taxi from Prijepolje or the monastery.

SIROGOJNO: Krčma (RSD)
Serbian **Road Map** B4
Old Village (Staro selo)
Tel *(031) 3802291*
Part of the open-air museum village, which also has cabins for guests *(see p127)*, this characterful tavern has a tremendous menu of traditional Serbian food that includes moussaka made with nettles, *heljda* (buckwheat) pie and homemade rakia as well as a tempting choice of pastries.

UŽICE: Aleksandar (RSD)
Serbian **Road Map** B4
Kralja Petra I 16a
Tel *(031) 518110*
Featuring classical styling with a traditional touch, Aleksandar is considered one of Užice's better restaurants. It serves a broad range of Serbian food in small or regular portions. The staff provide excellent service.

UŽICE: Moja reka (RSD)
Serbian **Road Map** B4
1300 Kaplara 24a
Tel *(031) 555075*
This highly rated eatery offers generous portions of Serbian staples as well as risotto, pizza and various other international dishes. It is set in a great location overlooking the river and offers splendid value for money.

UŽICE: Riblji restoran Pećina (RSD)
Serbian **Road Map** B4
Selo Potpeće, Sevojno
Tel *(031) 546737*
Marvellous fish restaurant in picturesque mountainous surroundings just outside Užice. An on-site trout farm provides fresh fish and there is plenty of grilled meat too. The flavoured home-made rakias are among the best in the region.

VALJEVO: Paviljon (RSD)
Serbian **Road Map** B3
Markova Stolica, Poparski put bb
Tel *(014) 3520216*
Housed within a large old house on the hillside above Valjevo, Paviljon has wonderful views from its shaded outdoor terrace. The Serbian menu includes an outstanding fish soup and all the usual grilled meat options.

VALJEVO: Intermeco (RSD)(RSD)
International **Road Map** B3
Birčaninova 36
Tel *(014) 230461*
Elegant and secluded spot with comfortable, shaded outdoor seating overlooking the river from the northern side of town. International menu with plenty of chicken options, good grilled trout and some imaginative salads. Wines from Serbia and Macedonia. Superb service.

ZLATIBOR: Miris dunja (RSD)
Serbian **Road Map** B4
Rujno 140
Tel *(031) 841529*
Delightful bucolic restaurant with wood panelling, sheepskin rugs and rustic ornamentation. Typical Serbian food dominates the menu, with an emphasis on grilled meat options.

ZLATIBOR: Grand (RSD)(RSD)
International **Road Map** B4
Tržni centar bb
Tel *(031) 848123*
Enormously popular central restaurant spread over two floors with an Irish pub and nightclub attached. Serves a good standard of Serbian and European cuisine, but can get uncomfortably smoky inside when crowded.

Home-made liqueur from Krušedol, flavoured with herbs, berries and fruits

Northern Serbia

FRUŠKA GORA: Krušedolka (RSD)
Serbian **Road Map** B2
Dragoljuba Jankovića 3, Krušedol
Tel *(0) 652060390*
Convenient location next to Krušedol Monastery with outdoor seating overlooking the monastery complex. Tasty local dishes include goulash, grilled trout and various chicken choices at very reasonable prices.

FRUŠKA GORA: Lisine (RSD)
Serbian **Road Map** B2
Strmosten bb, Vrdnik
Tel *(0) 631189063*
Idyllic rustic restaurant built over a stream in picturesque countryside on the outskirts of Vrdnik; the small waterfall in the garden is an additional attraction. Its popularity with tour groups means service can be slow, but it is enjoyable nonetheless.

FRUŠKA GORA: Lugarnica (RSD)
Serbian **Road Map** B2
Iriški venac bb, Fruška Gora
Tel *(022) 463125*
Situated around 10 km (6 miles) north of Novo Hopovo monastery, Lugarnica restaurant is a simple place ensconced within a glade of pine and fir trees. Wild boar, local mushrooms and fresh fish are on the menu and accommodation is also available.

KOVAČICA: Jarmočisko Vojvodina Pub (RSD)
Serbian **Road Map** C2
Ive Andrića 90
Tel *(0) 643512296*
This lively rock bar features a characterful bare-brick interior and plenty of music memorabilia scattered about. The basic menu covers most Serbian grilled meat dishes along with goulash and some delicious thick soups.

For more information on types of restaurants *see pages 130–31*

NOVI SAD: Café Veliki RSD RSD
Serbian **Road Map** B2
Nikole Pašića 24
Tel *(021) 553420*
This is an unpretentious place in the Hotel Veliki *(see p128)* with a distinctive interior of stripped brick walls and the original 19th-century brick floor. It offers a great choice of typical Vojvodina cuisine such as goulash and Banac meat balls. Desserts include plum dumplings and a remarkable four-layered pie.

NOVI SAD: Osam tamburaša RSD RSD
Serbian **Road Map** B2
Petrovaradinska tvrđava
Tel *(021) 421144*
Wonderful location near Hotel Leopold I *(see p128)* within Petrovaradin and an atmospheric interior with a vaulted ceiling and classic furniture. The terrace outside has sublime views over the Danube and Novi Sad. Good standards of food, but the service is not always up to scratch.

DK Choice

NOVI SAD: Project 72 RSD RSD RSD
International **Road Map** B2
Kosovska 15a
Tel *(021) 6572720*
This highly rated restaurant is renowned not only for its cuisine but also for its astonishingly good service. Staff greet all guests personally and introduce them to a menu designed to encourage sharing. Tapas-sized portions of veal cheeks, foie gras, octopus, scallops, venison kebabs and wild boar can be ordered as tasters. Main dishes include veal or pork fillet and a choice of salmon, tuna or sea bass fillet; 70 per cent of the accompanying vegetables are organically produced. Project 72's prices – higher than the norm – are well worth it.

Project 72's raspberry *milfei* (millefeuille) with mascarpone, honey and hazelnuts

PALIĆ: Mala gostiona RSD
Serbian **Road Map** B1
Park Heroja 15
Tel *(024) 753477*
Part of the historic Park Hotel *(see p128)*, Mala gostiona has Serbian and Hungarian cuisine with good fish options – the trout in white wine sauce is outstanding. There is shaded outdoor seating and distant views of the lake.

SREMSKA MITROVICA: Sojenica RSD
Serbian **Road Map** B2
Ribarska obala
Tel *(022) 618631*
Traditional-style restaurant built on stilts beside the river, locally renowned for its spicy *pljeskavica* and home-made wine. It has a cozy interior with open fires in winter and a terrace with great views in summer.

SREMSKI KARLOVCI: Bermet RSD RSD
Serbian **Road Map** B2
Trg Branka Radičevića 5
Tel *(021) 884544*
Central spot on the main square with a stylish modern interior and shaded outdoor seating decked out with flowers. Well-presented local cuisine. Great selection of regional wines.

SUBOTICA: Boss RSD RSD
International **Road Map** B1
Matije Korvina 7–8
Tel *(0) 656551111*
A smart yet casual affair that attracts a fashionable crowd. The broad menu has a choice of Chinese dishes, pizzas and European standards such as beef steak, but no traditional Serbian dishes. Polite, efficient service.

SUBOTICA: Stara Pizzeria RSD RSD
Italian **Road Map** B1
Matije Korvina 5
Tel *(024) 551835*
Located directly opposite the Boss restaurant, Stara Pizzeria has equally high standards but a rather more bohemian style. Its menu has a range of fabulous pizzas, some Mexican options and an exquisitely presented selection of desserts.

VRŠAC: Etno kuća Dinar RSD
Serbian **Road Map** C2
Dimitrija Tucovića 82
Tel *(013) 830024*
This fantastic *etno* restaurant is spread across several floors and features a big garden decked out with an engaging array of antique rural paraphernalia. It offers diners a superb choice of local cuisine and wines.

Eastern Serbia

GOLUBAC: Boga RSD
Serbian/Fish **Road Map** D3
Gorana Tošića Mačka
Tel *(012) 678066*
Simple restaurant with neat interior and a garden with river views. Wonderful home-cooked Serbian food and fresh fish prepared by the owners.

GOLUBAC: Zlatna ribica RSD
Serbian/Fish **Road Map** D3
Cara Dušana 28
Tel *(0) 691056407*
Smart place with shaded terrace overlooking the Danube. It offers a fine choice of Serbian dishes and delicious baked or grilled catfish, carp, perch and trout straight out of the river.

KLADOVO: Natura RSD
Serbian **Road Map** E3
Dunavska bb
Tel *(019) 807600*
A lovely family-run restaurant set in a meadow beside the Danube River. Expect a friendly welcome from the owners alongside some great fish soup and many other delightful Serbian dishes.

KLADOVO: Imperator RSD RSD
International **Road Map** E3
Dunavski kej 1
Tel *(019) 810810*
Pleasant riverside restaurant at the Aquastar Danube *(see p129)* with impeccable service. House specials include grilled Danube catfish and the legendary Đerdap roll: pork fillet stuffed with cheese and rolled in prosciutto.

KNJAŽEVAC: Kod Saše RSD
Serbian **Road Map** D4
Knjaža Miloša 131a
Tel *(019) 732446*
This is a tiny traditional *etno* restaurant with a few rural knick-knacks on the walls. It serves hearty local fare, which includes such dishes as tripe soup and calf's head in sauce.

NEGOTIN: Pizzeria Castello RSD
Italian **Road Map** E3
Trg Đorđa Stanojevića 46
Tel *(019) 541126*
Modern restaurant with a decent range of pizzas, salads and stylishly presented desserts.

RAM: Kod tvrđave RSD RSD
Serbian **Road Map** C3
Kneza Lazara 1
Tel *(012) 672152*
Set in a splendid spot facing the river below Ram Fortress. Serves speciality Danube fish dishes

with carp, catfish and trout and an outstanding fish soup. Diners can watch fishermen at work from the terrace.

DK Choice

SOKOBANJA: Stara vodenica (RSD)
Serbian **Road Map** D4
14. avgusta
Tel *(0) 638036104*
Set in an enchanting location in wooded gardens just outside Sokobanja, the Old Mill serves great Serbian dishes accompanied by home-baked bread. Children can amuse themselves in the play area and visit farm animals in a small petting zoo.

SOKOBANJA: Vidikovac (RSD)
Serbian **Road Map** D4
Dragoljuba Jovanovića 5
Tel *(018) 830866*
Situated on the hillside above Sokobanja with sweeping views of the area, this simple traditional restaurant serves excellent local cuisine including the famed *lepinja sa kajmakom* – a baked bread bun filled with egg, clotted cream and butter that is also known as a calorie bomb.

ZAJEČAR: Dva brata (RSD)
Serbian **Road Map** D4
Karađorđev venac 6
Tel *(019) 424443*
An unpretentious place, Zaječar's Two Brothers features a bright interior festooned with pretty flowers. Friendly staff are on hand to make recommendations and explain the origins of local dishes.

ZAJEČAR: Rivendell (RSD)
International **Road Map** D4
Vojvode Mišića 10a
Tel *(0) 63403323*
This is a laid-back Irish pub with a shaded terrace and warm brick-lined interior. Although there's no Guinness, there is a selection of local beer, pizzas and plenty of grilled meat dishes.

Southern Serbia

NIŠ: Riblja konoba (RSD)
Fish/Serbian **Road Map** D4
Kralja Stefana Prv. 5
Tel *(018) 257728*
This is a wonderfully atmospheric fish restaurant decorated in traditional Serbian style. Grilled, baked and smoked local fish are on Riblja konoba's menu along with a wide selection of other typical Serbian dishes.

NIŠ: Biser (RSD)(RSD)
Serbian **Road Map** D4
Koste Stamenkovića 1
Tel *(018) 248205*
Packed with locals, this highly regarded traditional Serbian restaurant has characterful decor, reasonable prices and fabulous cuisine. A great place to sample *roštilj* (grilled meat).

NIŠ: Elit (RSD)(RSD)
International **Road Map** D4
Prijezdina 5A
Tel *(018) 514514*
Elegant restaurant where crystal chandeliers, subdued lighting and impeccable waiting staff create an ambience of exclusivity. On offer is Chinese, Serbian and Italian cuisine prepared to a consistently high standard.

Pleasure, a popular restaurant and cocktail bar located in central Niš

NIŠ: Pleasure (RSD)(RSD)
International/
Serbian **Road Map** D4
Kopitareva 7
Tel *(018) 517551*
Hugely popular central restaurant with a reputation for fine cocktails that attracts a stylish crowd. Imaginative international dishes are served in large portions, but expect slow service at peak times.

PIROT: Dukat (RSD)
Serbian **Road Map** F5
Vuka Pantelića 55
Tel *(0) 66310510*
Typical Serbian restaurant that is highly rated by locals. Red and white checked tablecloths, antique knick-knacks and rural styling create a cozy ambience. The menu covers the full range of Serbian grilled meat options and Roma bands occasionally turn up to serenade diners.

PIROT: Kafana Oaza (RSD)
Serbian **Road Map** E5
Manastir Poganovo
Tel *(0) 63485438*
Occupying a gorgeous spot opposite the isolated Poganovo Monastery, this simple eatery is a very popular dining spot, with pleasant outdoor seating beneath pine trees. The menu includes local trout and a choice of salads and grilled meat.

PIROT: Krčma Ladna voda (RSD)
Serbian **Road Map** E5
Nikole Pašića 40
Tel *(010) 323422*
This traditional restaurant set next to Pirot's Museum of Ponišavlje has won several awards for its grilled meat dishes. Make sure you try the *pohovan kačkavalj* – a slab of Pirot's famous cheese fried in breadcrumbs. Waiting staff clad in folk dress add character.

PROLOM BANJA: Božiji raj (RSD)
Serbian **Road Map** D5
Prolom Banja
Tel *(027) 88288*
This idyllically sited fish restaurant, whose name translates to "God's Paradise", has its own trout farm in Prolom Banja that supplies fresh fish for the delicious Serbian dishes that are served here. Young children are well catered for with a play area and small petting zoo with farm animals.

VRANJE: Gradska meana (RSD)
Serbian **Road Map** D6
Jovana Hadživasiljevića 33
Tel *(017) 7424066*
A charming restaurant with a lovely garden and remarkably good food, Gradska meana has a wide choice of salads made from fresh local ingredients, along with the usual range of Serbian grilled meat dishes.

VRANJE: Hobbit kuća vilenjaka (RSD)
Serbian **Road Map** D6
Partizanska
Tel *(0) 631244191*
This fun, hobbit-themed cellar restaurant features a log balcony and rickety wooden fences. It serves great Serbian food, but be aware that it can get uncomfortably smoky when busy.

VRANJE: Stari bunar (RSD)
Serbian **Road Map** D6
Save Kovačevića 21
Tel *(0) 644468123*
The Old Well restaurant serves up a mind-boggling choice of traditional Serbian food in classy surroundings. Among the dishes on the menu is the legendary *Karađorđeva šnicla*, a large sausage-like dish of rolled pork steak stuffed with *kajmak* – rich, salty clotted cream, a Serbian speciality – then covered with breadcrumbs and fried.

For more information on types of restaurants *see pages 130–31*

SHOPPING IN SERBIA

Town and city centres across the country are as important for socializing as they are for shopping. Locals promenade, meet friends and shop throughout the day and gather in central cafés to smoke, drink coffee and chat, which goes some way to explaining why the influx of suburban shopping malls and online shops hasn't affected their popularity and vitality. New supermarkets are opening up all over the country, but Serbians still prefer to buy their fruit and vegetables from local farms, so traditional covered produce markets are as busy as ever. Most souvenirs and crafts available in the country tend to be regional variations on a theme, such as folk costumes, embroidery and ceramics, but some, such as Subotica's straw pictures, are unique to a town or region and difficult to find elsewhere.

Opening Hours

Shops in towns and cities open from around 9am to 7–8pm Monday to Saturday and are closed on Sundays and public holidays. Supermarkets and grocery stores are usually open by 7am and close at 10pm; they also open on Sundays any time between 7am and 3pm. Shopping malls in large cities are open daily from 10am to 10pm. Stores in smaller towns often close at around 5pm, earlier on Saturdays; they don't open at all on Sundays. Markets open by around 6am and close in the early afternoon.

Payment Methods

Cash is the most common form of payment, although credit and debit cards are becoming increasingly popular and are now accepted in large hotels, restaurants, shops and petrol stations. While haggling is not customary in shops, it is not unusual to see locals bargaining with traders at outdoor markets using the phrase *"može jeftinije?"* ("can that be cheaper?").

Markets

Every town has an outdoor market or *pijaca* where seasonal fruit, vegetables, herbs, meat and dairy products and even live chickens are sold by local farmers who take great pride in the quality of their produce. Belgrade's largest market is **Kalenićeva pijaca**, a five-minute walk east of the Temple of St Sava. It sells fresh produce as well as a quirky assortment of bric-a-brac. Stalls selling antique jewellery and Communist-era medals and militaria set up in the evenings at the entrance to Kalemegdan Fortress from Knez Mihailova street.

Fruit, vegetables and other fresh produce at an open-air market, Belgrade

Crafts and Souvenirs

Belgrade has a number of good souvenir shops stocked with popular items such as fridge magnets, snow globes, dolls in folk costumes, *kilims* (rugs), embroidery, *šajkača* (traditional men's hats), *opanci* (traditional shoes with the toe curled back), musical instruments and decorative ceramic pots and plates. For quirky retro Socialist souvenirs pop into the gift shop at Belgrade's **Museum of Yugoslav History** *(see p58)*, and for knick-knacks inspired by and themed around the city, stop by the café, bookstore and souvenir shop, **Belgrade Window**.

The capital was known for its perfume industry in the 1950s, but today there is only one tiny shop left that mixes its own fragrances. **Parfimerija Sava** is unmissable, not just for its wonderful handmade perfumes but also its sense of history.

Look out for pictures made from straw in Subotica, colourful woollen socks in Knjaževac and thick woollen jumpers and shawls at Sirogojno; traditional ceramicware and embroidered tablecloths can be found in most of the country's tourist

A range of brightly coloured ceramicware for sale at a craft stall

Mannequins in the glittering shop window of an upmarket clothing store in Central Belgrade

spots. Monasteries usually have small shops selling icons and religious texts and a few, such as **Ljubostinja** *(see p69)* and **Studenica** *(see p81)*, even bottle their own rakia (fruit brandy) and wine. Online stores such as **Mala srpska prodavnica** sell a broad range of Serbian souvenirs that can be shipped directly to your home address.

Designer Goods

International designer brands can be found in shopping malls and boutiques in Serbia's main cities, but for those keen on jewellery and clothing by local designers the best place is the **Belgrade Design District**, Čumićevo sokače, where over 30 fashion designers and jewellers have shops under one roof.

Books

Bookshops in larger towns and cities usually have a good choice of glossy books in various languages about Serbia's monasteries, historic sights and natural beauty. They also stock guidebooks to towns, regions and individual sights as well as road maps, hiking maps and town plans.

Food

Serbia offers an enormous array of delicacies that make excellent presents. Made using roasted peppers, aubergines and garlic, delicious *ajvar* can be eaten as a side dish or a sandwich spread and is available at supermarkets throughout Serbia. Cheese from Pirot is said to be the country's best, as is smoked meat from Užice, Zlatibor and Srem; both can be bought all over Serbia. The popular *ratluk* or *lokum* (Turkish Delight) is sold loose or in gift boxes at sweet shops such as **Ratluk Bosiljčić**, while presentation boxes of rich, sweet baklava are available at specialist Turkish confectioners, including **Sultans of Istanbul**.

Wine, Rakia and Šljivovica

Visiting wineries in the major wine-producing regions is the most enjoyable way to sample and buy quality local wines and spirits, but these can also be found in several Belgrade wine shops – **Vinoteka Beograd** and **Vinoteka Royal** both have excellent selections. Among the oldest and best-known wines in the country are Tamjanika, a Muscat, and Prokupac, a red or rosé; both have been produced in Serbia since medieval times. Bottles of the pear brandy *viljamovka*, with a whole pear inside, and rakia, a strong fruit brandy most commonly made from plums, apricots or grapes, make great gifts and souvenirs *(see pp132–3)*.

Viljamovka, a brandy made from pears

DIRECTORY

Markets

Kalenićeva pijaca, Belgrade
City Map F5. Njegoševa.

Crafts and Souvenirs

Belgrade Window, Belgrade
City Map C2. Cultural Centre of Belgrade, Knez Mihailova 6
W kcb.org.rs

Mala srpska prodavnica
W malasrpskaprodavnica.com

Parfimerija Sava, Belgrade
City Map C1. Kralja Petra 75.
Tel (011) 2632869.

Designer Goods

Belgrade Design District, Belgrade
City Map C/D2. Čumićeva 2, lok. 16B. **W belgradedesigndistrict.blogspot.co.uk**

Food

Ratluk Bosiljčić, Belgrade
City Map C3. Gavrila Principa 14.
W ratluk-bosiljcic.co.rs

Sultans of Istanbul, Belgrade
City Map E4. Bulevar kralja Aleksandra 114.
W sultansofistanbul.rs

Wine, Rakia and Šljivovica

Vinoteka Beograd, Belgrade
Bulevar oslobođenja 117.
W vinotekabeograd.com

Vinoteka Royal, Belgrade
City Map B2. Karađorđeva 3.
Tel (011) 3033024.

ENTERTAINMENT IN SERBIA

As the unrivalled cultural capital of Serbia, Belgrade hosts an eclectic choice of events throughout the year at venues that range from tiny jazz bars and boats with pounding sound systems to grand concert halls and a 25,000 capacity stadium. It is usually the first port of call for visiting international artists and performers, although Novi Sad has a smaller but equally intense cultural scene that culminates each year with the massive EXIT Music Festival and Niš has the renowned Nišville International Jazz Festival.

Classical Music

Most classical music concerts in Belgrade are held at **Kolarac Hall** (Kolarčeva zadužbina) or at the **Belgrade Philharmonic Orchestra** (Beogradska filharmonija). Both these venues are famed for their fine acoustics and have hosted some of the world's top artists. Some smaller classical concerts are performed in **Guarnerius Hall** (Centar lepih umetnosti Guarnerius). The only other Serbian city with its own philharmonic orchestra is Niš; its **Symphony Orchestra** (Niški simfonijski orkestar) hosts regular concerts. Novi Sad's main venue for classical music, opera and theatre is the **Cultural Centre** (Kulturni centar).

Brightly coloured marionettes used in children's puppet theatre performances, Belgrade

Opera, Ballet, Folklore and Theatre

With no opera house, operatic productions in Belgrade take place at the **National Theatre** (Narodno pozorište) and at the **Madlenianum Theatre** (Teatar Madlenianum) in Zemun, which also host musicals, ballet and folklore shows. Belgrade's theatrical productions are more often than not in Serbian, although foreign-language performances are staged occasionally.

Children's Theatre

Several Belgrade theatres cater to children – the oldest is the **Boško Buha Theatre** (Pozorište Boško Buha) with its two stages, one for shows for adults, the other for children. The **Pinokio Puppet Theatre** (Pozorište lutaka Pinokio) stages shows based on fairy tales and myths. The **Snail Theatre** (Pozorište Puž) is dedicated to children's shows of modernized fairy tales, and the **Little Duško Radović Theatre** (Malo pozorište Duško Radović) puts on productions that engage children via social and multicultural themes.

Performance of Tchaikovsky's popular ballet *Swan Lake* at the National Theatre in Belgrade

Nightclubs

Belgrade is now well known throughout the Balkans for its high-energy nightlife. Clubs open, close and change names so frequently that it is hard to keep pace with the scene. The situation is further complicated by the annual shift of clubs from the city centre to boats moored along the river that become nightclubs *(splavovi)* during the summer. Most nightclubs are located in the Old Town and the riverside Savamala area, which has gradually developed from an industrial wasteland into the city's hippest district. The most popular stretch of riverside clubs is to the left of Old Sava Bridge (Tramvajski most) where the boats with the loudest dance music are moored.

For a full list of city nightclubs visit the **Beograd Noću** website, and check **Gdeizaci.com** for up-to-date listings of events throughout the capital.

Members of a band playing jazz on clarinet and saxophones

Rock and Jazz

Rock and pop music concerts in Belgrade are usually staged at **Dom Omladine**, the **Sava Centar** and, for the largest events, the **Belgrade Arena**. The city's best jazz clubs are **Ptica**, **Muha** and, during the summer, the outdoor **Bašta** club.

Cinema

Multiplex cinemas in shopping malls have now superceded independent cinemas in most Serbian towns and cities. Two of the capital's biggest multiplexes are the **Cineplexx Ušće Shopping Centre** and the **Cineplexx Delta City** in New Belgrade across the Danube River from the Old Town. Novi Sad has the **Arena Cineplex**, while the main multiplex in Niš is the **Vilin Grad Cinema**.

Animations for children are usually dubbed, but all other films are generally shown in their original language with Serbian subtitles.

Ticket Sales

Tickets for all events can be bought directly from the venue's own box office or online at the **Eventim** website, which handles sales for major theatre and concert performances.

DIRECTORY

Classical Music

Belgrade Philharmonic Orchestra
City Map C2.
Studentski trg 11, Belgrade.
Tel (011) 3282977.
W bgf.rs

Cultural Centre
Road Map B2.
Katolička porta 5, Novi Sad.
Tel (021) 528972.
W kcns.org.rs

Guarnerius Hall
City Map D2. Džordža Vašingtona 12, Belgrade.
Tel (011) 3345237.
W guarnerius.rs

Kolarac Hall
City Map C2.
Kolarčeva zadužbina, Studentski trg 5, Belgrade.
Tel (011) 635073.
W kolarac.rs

Symphony Orchestra
Road Map D4. Generala Milojka Lešjanina 16, Niš.
Tel (018) 246620.
W simfonijski.com

Opera, Ballet, Folklore and Theatre

Madlenianum Theatre
Glavna 32, Zemun, Belgrade.
Tel (011) 3162797.
W operatheatre madlenianum.com

National Theatre
City Map C2.
Francuska 3, Belgrade.
Tel (011) 2620946.
W narodnopozoriste.rs

Children's Theatre

Boško Buha Theatre
City Map C2.
Trg republike 3, Belgrade.
W buha.rs

Little Duško Radović Theatre
City Map E3.
Aberdareva 1, Belgrade.
W malopozoriste.co.rs

Pinokio Puppet Theatre
Goca Delčeva 1, Zemun, Belgrade. **W pinokio.rs**

Snail Theatre
City Map F5. Radoslava Grujića 21, Belgrade.
W pozoristepuz.com

Nightclubs

Beograd Noću
W beogradnocu.com

Gdeizaci.com
W gdeizaci.com

Rock and Jazz

Bašta
City Map B3.
Karađorđeva 43 (Male stepenice 1a), Belgrade.
W jazzbasta.com

Belgrade Arena
Bulevar Arsenija Čarnojevića 58, Belgrade.
W kombankarena.rs

Dom Omladine
City Map D2.
Makedonska 22/IV, Belgrade.
W domomladine.org

Muha
City Map B2.
Kralja Petra 18, Belgrade.
W muhabar.com

Ptica
City Map F3.
Dalmatinska 98, Belgrade.
W jazzclubptica.com

Sava Centar
Milentija Popovića 9, Belgrade
W savacentar.net

Cinema

Arena Cineplex
Road Map B2.
Bulevar Mihajla Pupina 3, Novi Sad.
W arenacineplex.com

Cineplexx Delta City
Jurija Gagarina 16, Belgrade. **W cineplexx.rs**

Cineplexx Ušće Shopping Centre
Bulevar Mihajla Pupina 4, Belgrade. **W cineplexx.rs**

Vilin Grad Cinema
Road Map D4.
Obrenovićeva 19, Niš. **W vilingrad.rs**

Ticket Sales

Eventim
W eventim.rs

SPORTS AND OUTDOOR ACTIVITIES

The largely untamed wilderness of valleys, mountains, lakes and rivers in Serbia is ripe for active tourism, and there are a number of local operators that organize trips throughout the region. Several mountain resorts offer great downhill and cross-country skiing and snowboarding in winter; in summer the ski centres make excellent bases for hiking and biking. Riding is steadily gaining in popularity and off-roading is also catching on. Serbia's great rivers provide ample opportunities for rafting and kayaking – the Ibar has some exhilarating rapids while the Danube offers a more leisurely experience. Climbers can scale the country's spectacular cliffs, cavers can explore its labyrinthine karst caves, and canyoners can plunge into the freezing waters of mountain streams. With its varied habitats attracting native and migratory birds, Serbia offers rich rewards for bird-watchers. Nature lovers can simply enjoy the country's broad diversity of flora and fauna.

A solo hiker trekking across the beautiful landscape of the Stara planina Mountains

Hiking

With its abundance of hills and mountains crisscrossed with marked walking routes, there are countless opportunities for hiking in Serbia that are suitable for all levels. One of the most challenging routes popular with alpinists is the ascent of Midžor, Serbia's highest mountain at 2,169 m (7,116 ft). Local visitor information centres can usually provide detailed local maps, and the **Extreme Summit Team** and **Serbian Mountaineering Association** are both very useful sources of information about hiking trips of varying lengths.

Canyoning and Caving

Canyoning is relatively new to Serbia, but it hasn't taken long to catch on. The country has some ideal locations for it, of which Tara National Park is a favourite. **Wild Serbia** runs caving and canyoning trips with equipment and qualified guides, and **Extreme Canyoning** is also a good source of information.

Rock Climbing

Popular throughout Serbia, rock climbing takes place at many spectacular climbing sites, as well as several indoor and outdoor climbing walls. The **Climbing Tribe** group is an excellent resource for visiting climbers and also run climbing courses at various locations.

Paragliding

Paragliding is well established in Serbia, with most of the country's sites located in the south and west regions around Kopaonik, Zlatibor, Čačak and Raška. **Paragliding Serbia** and Wild Serbia are useful sources of information about paragliding experiences, courses and longer trips that take in several sites.

Biking

The country is ideal territory for mountain biking. Its well-marked hiking trails are suitable for biking but are not as well developed as those in countries where the sport is taken more seriously. Extreme Summit Team run exhilarating tours in the Zlatibor region and in the Stara planina Mountains where there is plenty of scope for fast down-hill action. Cyclists interested in a more straightforward road route should follow all or part of the Serbian section of Route 6 of the **EuroVelo** cycle network, which follows the Danube across the country *(see p163)*.

Paraglider preparing to take off from a verdant Serbian hillside

Winter Sports

Kopaonik is Serbia's premier ski resort, with 55 km (34 miles) of alpine runs, 12 km (7 miles) of cross-country runs and snow cover from November to May. The **Babin Zub Ski Resort** in the Stara planina Mountains is a smaller affair, with 13 km (8 miles) of runs. In the west, the **Tornik Ski Centre** at Zlatibor has 8 km (5 miles) of runs with plans to expand to 15 km (9 miles).

Rafting enthusiasts running exciting rapids on the Ibar River

Riding

Although riding is not hugely popular in Serbia, the country's mountainous terrain is ideal for it. **Equestrian Adventure Serbia** is an excellent source of information about riding tours in central Serbia; it also arranges stays in characterful rural houses.

Riding in the mountainous region of Zlatibor in Western Serbia

Kayaking and Rafting

Wild Serbia runs a variety of kayaking and rafting trips on several Serbian rivers. All levels of kayakers can run the Ibar River's Category III rapids close to Maglič Fortress or opt for a more sedate three-day rafting trip on the Danube from Novi Sad south to Belgrade.

Off-roading

Serbia has plenty of wild open spaces where roads are little more than rough tracks and mountain ranges can be traversed using rutted forestry routes, but rather than attempt these solo it is best to join an organized tour with your own or a borrowed vehicle. **Serbian Outdoor** is a good source of information. Quad bikes and buggies are available to rent in Zlatibor for off-road fun.

Bird-watching

Serbia's position on a migratory crossroads and its broad diversity of natural habitats mean that despite being landlocked and relatively small, it is an ornithologist's paradise. It is home to 140 bird species that are of conservation concern on the IUCN Red List and five globally endangered species. **Birdwatch Serbia** runs year-round trips of varying lengths.

Rural Tourism

Visitors interested in country life and the outdoors can spend time at a farmstead or village that has been unchanged for generations, where it is possible to learn traditional skills or relax and try home-made wine and *šljivovica* and hearty food. Stays can be booked online or at local tourist offices *(see p125)*.

DIRECTORY

Hiking

Extreme Summit Team
W extremesummitteam.com

Serbian Mountaineering Association
W pss.rs

Canyoning and Caving

Extreme Canyoning
City Map E2. Venizelosova 21, Belgrade. **W extremecanyoning.com**

Wild Serbia
W wildserbia.com

Rock Climbing

Climbing Tribe
Braće Jerković 120, Belgrade.
Tel (0) 637442115, (0) 63267738, (0) 638230488, (011) 3961681.
W serbianclimbing.com/en

Paragliding

Paragliding Serbia
W paraglidingserbia.com

Biking

EuroVelo
W eurovelo.com

Winter Sports

Babin Zub Ski Resort
Road Map E4. Ski resort: 50 km (31 miles) N of Pirot; company office: Milutina Milankovića 9, New Belgrade.
Tel (011) 2223986.
W skijalistasrbije.rs

Kopaonik Ski Centre
Road Map C5. 275 km (171 miles) S of Belgrade.
W skijalistasrbije.rs

Tornik Ski Centre
Road Map B4. 200 km (125 miles) SW of Belgrade.
Tel (031) 3150004.
W skijalistasrbije.rs

Riding

Equestrian Adventure Serbia
Road Map C4. Kamenica, Bare. **W equestrianadventure-serbia.org**

Off-roading

Serbian Outdoor
W 4x4.serbianoutdoor.com

Bird-watching

Birdwatch Serbia
Road Map B2. Magelan Corp., Pasiceva 7, Novi Sad. **Tel** (021) 4724088.
W birdwatchserbia.rs

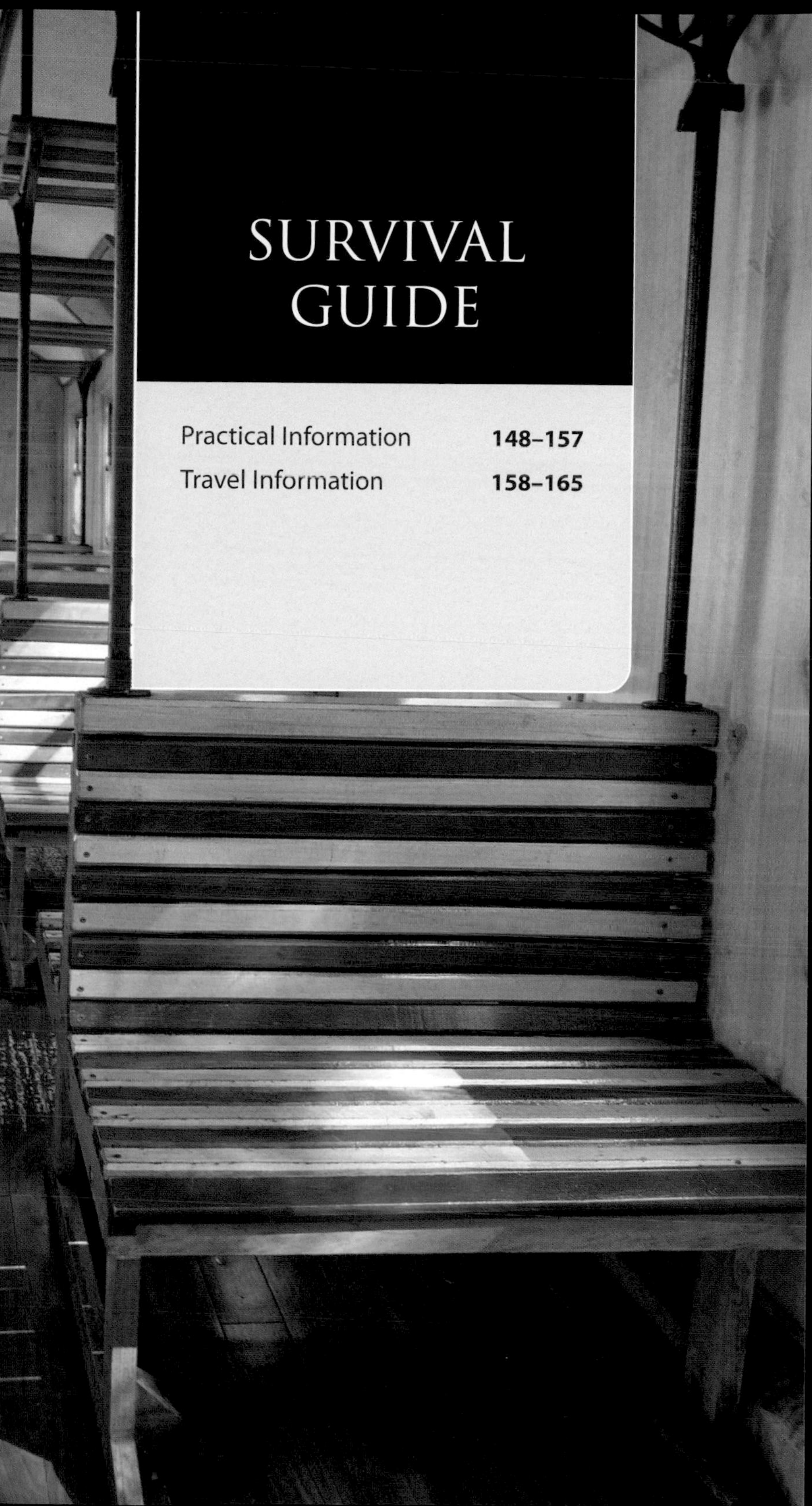
SURVIVAL GUIDE
Practical Information 148–157
Travel Information 158–165

PRACTICAL INFORMATION

Serbians are keen to dispel any negativity associated with memories of the Yugoslav Wars in the 1990s, and as a result foreign visitors are always made to feel welcome, with locals often going out of their way to be helpful despite the language barrier. Thanks to its relaxed visa regime, comprehensive network of well-run visitor information centres and the increasingly high standards of its hotels and restaurants, Serbia has developed rapidly into a hugely attractive tourist destination, where the country's burgeoning number of visitors can expect to enjoy a stress-free travel experience.

Passports and Visas

Citizens of the EU, Switzerland, the US, Canada, Australia and New Zealand can visit Serbia as tourists for up to 90 days without a visa as long as their passport is valid for the duration of their stay. Visa-free entry is also allowed for holders of other passports who have a valid visa for the US, any Schengen state, the UK or any other EU member state, as well as for those who have a US Green Card or a residence permit for an EU or Schengen country. For longer stays, a visa must be obtained in advance from the Serbian embassy. All other visitors should check if they need a visa on the website of Serbia's **Ministry of Foreign Affairs** or at the closest Serbian embassy. Most countries have consular representation in Belgrade, including **Canada**, the **US**, the **UK** and **Australia**. The **New Zealand** embassy in Rome is accredited to Serbia.

Entry and Exit

When entering Serbia all visitors must ensure that they get an entry stamp in their passports as failure to do so will cause problems upon departure. The country does not currently recognize its border crossings with Kosovo, so any visitors who try to enter Serbia via Kosovo will be denied entry as they will not have an official Serbian border passport stamp. This also means that all those who exit via Kosovo will not receive a Serbian exit stamp and will therefore run the risk of technically overstaying their visa, which will negatively affect future visits to the country.

Registration

All foreign visitors to Serbia are required to register with the local police within 24 hours of their arrival. Hotels, B&Bs and other categorized accommodation will automatically register their guests at check in. At check out guests will receive a document confirming their registration, which should be retained for border inspections when leaving the country.

Travel Safety Advice

Visitors can get up-to-date travel safety information from the **US Department of State**, the **Australian Department of Foreign Affairs and Trade** and the **UK Foreign and Commonwealth Office**.

Customs Information

Visitors can bring up to €10,000 of foreign currency, one litre of wine, 750 ml (25 oz) of strong alcohol and 200 cigarettes into Serbia without declaration; anything more must be declared upon entry. Visitors travelling with pets are expected to have a valid veterinary certificate translated into Serbian.

Take care when purchasing anything in Serbia that may be deemed to have archaeological, historic or ethnographic value. All such items will require an export license from the government. Make sure that the vendor is able to arrange this before you pay for it.

When to Go

Best visited between late spring and early autumn, Serbia has a typical southeast European climate with summers that are rarely too hot, although August in Belgrade can be stifling. The winters are cold and wet and best avoided unless you're an adventure sports enthusiast on a skiing or snowboarding holiday.

Kopaonik ski resort with winter sports enthusiasts skiing down a gentle slope

What to Take

Pack light for a summer trip to Serbia as it is likely to be consistently hot with the occasional torrential downpour. Take warm clothes and a raincoat for the cooler and wetter spring and autumn months, and full winter gear for December and January when the temperature dips well below zero. While almost everything you will need can be bought in Serbia, plug adaptors for electrical devices that don't have an EU two-pin plug are hard to find, so be sure to bring your own. If you're planning to stay longer than a few days consider bringing a spare mobile phone to carry a Serbian pay-as-you-go SIM card that can be utilised for both cheap local calls and Internet data.

◀ One of the heritage carriages of Western Serbia's Šargan Eight railway

Responsible Travel

With five national parks, 325 natural monuments, 102 areas with varying degrees of environmental protection and several more likely to receive protected status in the near future, Serbia has made great progress towards preserving its natural heritage.

Organic food production is being actively encouraged and a lot of the fresh vegetables and fruit on sale at local markets are produced without chemicals.

Travellers can also support local communities by opting for smallholdings and ecotourism farms over chain hotels. This will let you stay with local families, experience traditional lifestyles, enjoy local food and observe rural customs and farming techniques. For details contact the local visitor information centre and visit the website of **Seoski turizam Srbije** *(see p125)*.

Visitor Information

Serbia has an excellent network of visitor information centres across the country run by the National Tourism Organisation of Serbia (NTOS). The centres are manned by knowledgeable local staff who speak several languages and can help visitors with maps, local advice, hotels, day trips, guides and more. The information centres in **Belgrade**, **Niš**, **Novi Sad** and **Subotica** are located in the heart of each city. Opening hours for each vary so it is best to check in advance on the **NTOS** website, which has details of all the centres across the country and is itself also an excellent source of information.

Visiting Places of Worship

While Serbia's churches and mosques are open to the public, all visitors are expected to be respectful of local customs. This means hats off, no shorts or miniskirts and sometimes no bare arms in churches. Some of the country's more popular churches offer black sarong-like garments to underdressed visitors, but most do not. When visiting mosques, guests must take off their shoes and women should cover their heads. Visits should be avoided during prayers. Ask permission before taking any photographs.

Ravanica Monastery, one of Serbia's most popular places of worship

Admission Fees

Although they vary from place to place, admission fees at most local sights and museums tend to be around 250 dinars (€2) or less. Popular attractions, such as Belgrade's Nikola Tesla Museum, generally charge higher fees (around 500 dinars/€4 or more).

Opening Hours

Supermarkets and groceries are open by 7am and close at 10pm Monday to Saturday; on Sundays they shut around 3pm. Malls in towns and cities are usually open from 10am to 10pm daily *(see p140)*. Banks are open from 9am to 5pm on weekdays, and from 9am to 1pm on Saturdays *(see p154)*. Post offices are usually open from 8am to 7pm on weekdays and 8am to 2pm on Saturdays *(see p156)*. Not all museums keep the same hours, but they are normally open from 10am to 5pm on weekdays and closed on Mondays.

Sign showing opening times at Belgrade's Palace of Princess Ljubica

DIRECTORY

Passports and Visas

Embassy of Australia, Belgrade
Vladimira Popovića 38–40, New Belgrade. **Tel** (011) 3303400.
W serbia.embassy.gov.au

Embassy of Canada, Belgrade
City Map C5. Kneza Miloša 75. **Tel** (011) 3063000. **W canada.rs**

Embassy of New Zealand, Rome, Italy
Via Clitunno 44. **W nzembassy.com/italy**

Embassy of the United Kingdom, Belgrade
City Map C4. Resavska 46. **Tel** (011) 3060900.
W ukinserbia.fco.gov.uk

Embassy of the United States, Belgrade
Bulevar kneza Aleksandra Karađorđevića 92.
Tel (011) 7064000.
W belgrade.usembassy.gov

Ministry of Foreign Affairs
W mfa.gov.rs

Travel Safety Advice

Australian Department of Foreign Affairs and Trade
W dfat.gov.au/smartraveller.gov.au

UK Foreign and Commonwealth Office
W www.gov.uk/foreign-travel-advice

US Department of State
W travel.state.gov

Visitor Information

Belgrade
City Map C2. Knez Mihailova 5. **Tel** (011) 2635622. **W tob.rs**

Niš
Road Map D4. Vožda Karađorđa 7. **Tel** (018) 521321, 524877.
W visitnis.com

Novi Sad
Road Map B2. Trg slobode 3/3. **Tel** (021) 421811, 421812, 6617343. **W novisad.travel**

NTOS
W serbia.travel

Subotica
Road Map B1. Trg slobode 1. **Tel** (024) 670350, 753111.
W visitsubotica.rs

Female Travellers

The majority of Serbian men are extremely respectful towards women. There are no particular dangers here for women travelling alone, but sexual harassment is a possibility so the usual safety precautions should be observed: travel during the day whenever possible and don't walk in poorly lit streets or parks at night; stay in control by not drinking to excess in social situations and refuse drinks from strangers; avoid overcrowded public transport and use only recommended taxi services (if in doubt ask staff in a restaurant or hotel to book a taxi for you).

Travelling with Children

Serbs love children and the country has an abundance of parks and playgrounds, so travelling with a young family should be relatively trouble-free. Restaurants can usually provide high chairs and hotels can arrange for cots and extra beds in rooms, but they should be booked in advance. Be prepared for few public toilets other than those in shopping malls to be equipped with nappy changing facilities. Supermarkets have a good range of baby food and disposable nappies and there are well-stocked pharmacies in towns and cities. Bear in mind that if only one parent is accompanying their children into the country, they will need to produce at the border a translated letter of permission to travel from the absent parent.

Belgrade's trolleybus no. 22 with automated wheelchair ramps for disabled travellers

Disabled Travellers

Despite the efforts of several non-governmental organizations, local attitudes towards disabled people are a long way behind those in western Europe. Disabled Serbians tend to be cared for in residential homes and institutions, with little effort to integrate them into the mainstream. This is reflected in the woeful state of facilities around the country – pavements in most cities are uneven, nonexistent or used as parking spaces; public toilets are inaccessible, as are most cafés and restaurants; and only the most expensive hotels can offer anything better than a ground-floor room.

That said, getting to Serbia via the fully accessible facilities at Belgrade's Nikola Tesla Airport is a straightforward process for wheelchair users. Some of the capital's pedestrian crossings have been fitted with sloped kerbs, its large shopping malls are equipped with facilities for disabled customers and a number of attactions have been fitted with disabled access ramps. Belgrade's trolleybus no. 22 and trams no. 7, 12 and 13 have automated wheelchair access ramps with space for one wheelchair on board. The drivers on these lines are trained to help wheelchair users access the vehicle. For more information about people living with disabilities in Serbia visit the website of the **Centre for Independent Living of PWDs** (persons with disabilities).

Gay and Lesbian Travellers

Threats from homophobic groups in Serbia have led to the cancellation of several Gay Pride marches; the marches in 2014 and 2015 were only possible with the protection of hundreds of riot police supported by tanks and helicopters. Many Serbians consider homosexuality to be an aberration – a view supported by the church – and there have been numerous cases of openly gay men being attacked in the streets. To avoid the risk of such dangers, same-sex couples are strongly advised to abstain from public displays of affection. Serbia's LGBT community keeps a low profile with a scene that remains deeply underground, but plenty of information for gay travellers is available online at **Belgrade Gay Guide**, **Gay Serbia Guide** and **Gaymost**.

Children enjoying themselves at a fountain in Knez Mihailova, Belgrade

Visitor photographing the magnificent meanders of the Uvac River *(meandri Uvca)* in Western Serbia

Language

Serbian is a phonetic language that is easy to pronounce once you've mastered the handful of accented letters in its Latin alphabet or have familiarized yourself with its more challenging Cyrillic alphabet. Although signs often appear in both their Cyrillic and Latin forms, it is a good idea to tackle the Cyrillic alphabet before you arrive to be on the safe side. Learning a few Serbian words or phrases will certainly be worth the effort as Serbs will be appreciative of your attempts to speak their language. While many people in the towns and cities speak at least some English, this will not necessarily be the case further afield so a good phrasebook will be handy. Many restaurants are able to provide foreign guests with an *engleski jelovnik* (English menu) when asked.

Smoking

In Serbia smoking is something of a national pastime. It is estimated that every third adult is a smoker. Smoking in enclosed public areas was banned in 2010, but restaurants, bars and cafés are exempt from this rule and are therefore inevitably frequented by heavy smokers. Things may be about to change as EU pressure mounts for a full smoking ban in the hospitality sector, but few Serbs are likely to view this as beneficial.

Photography

There are no restrictions on taking photographs in Serbia, but it is a good idea to ask permission before taking close-up shots of strangers in order to avoid causing offence. When in a place of worship, be respectful and considerate while using a camera. Ensure you do not take pictures of military, police or border installations, personnel or vehicles anywhere in the country as this could create problems with the authorities.

Public Toilets

Serbia's larger towns and cities usually have public toilet facilities. These tend to be looked after by attendants who keep them clean and charge users a small fee. It is worth noting that women's toilets often have nothing more than the letter "Ž" or "Ж" (in Serbian *žena/жена* means "woman") on the door to differentiate them from the men's, which have the letter "M" (*muški* means "men"). If there are no public toilets in sight, just ask to use the facilities in any nearby café, restaurant or hotel.

Time

Serbia is one hour ahead of GMT in London, six hours ahead of New York and nine hours ahead of Los Angeles, 10 hours behind Sydney and 12 hours behind Auckland.

Electricity

Serbia uses standard European plugs with two round pins and a voltage and frequency of 220V/50Hz. UK, EU, Australian, and most Asian and African visitors will be able to use their own electrical appliances as their home countries' voltage is also 220V–240V, but they may need plug adaptors. Visitors from North America will need both adaptors and voltage converters.

Standard European plug with two round pins used across Serbia

DIRECTORY

Disabled Travellers

Centre for Independent Living of PWDs
W cilsrbija.org

Gay and Lesbian Travellers

Belgrade Gay Guide
W belgrade-gay.com

Gaymost
W gaymost.info

Gay Serbia Guide
W gej.rs

Personal Security and Health

As safe to visit as any other European country, Serbia actually has fewer tourist-related dangers than many of the more popular destinations on the continent. Despite fairly high unemployment, towns and cities throughout the country have a thriving outdoor café culture that keeps them buzzing until late into the night and engenders a safe and welcoming atmosphere. Health risks are low and a thriving private healthcare sector provides a high standard of treatment to compensate for the ailing state-run system.

One of the main buildings of Belgrade's University Hospital Centre

Emergency Services

Belgrade is patrolled by police on foot, in cars, on motorcycles and occasionally on horseback. Most other cities also have regular foot and car patrols, giving visitors a good sense of security. Serbian police officers are generally approachable and will usually speak a little English. In an emergency dial the **all-Europe emergency number** or the individual **fire**, **police** or **ambulance** numbers.

Tourists shopping for produce at a crowded street market in Serbia

Personal Security

Despite Serbia being safe to visit, the usual common-sense precautions should be taken. Watch out for pickpockets in crowded areas, especially at markets, railway stations, airports and on public transport. Hide bags or high-value items in the boot of the car when parked; luxury vehicles should be left only in guarded car parks to prevent them being targeted by thieves. It is always best to travel with others in a group if you are planning to visit remote areas. Avoid poorly lit areas at night, only use recommended taxis, never change money with strangers who approach you on the street and stay in control by not drinking to excess.

Political protests take place from time to time in Belgrade and other large cities. Most are peaceful, but have the potential for violence when extremist groups are involved and are therefore best avoided. The **UK Foreign and Commonwealth Office**, the **US Department of State** and the **Australian Department of Foreign Affairs and Trade** *(see p149)* have the most up-to-date security advice.

Medical Treatment

Britain and a number of other EU countries have reciprocal healthcare agreements with Serbia that allow their citizens to receive free treatment for genuine emergencies. All non-emergency medical treatment must be paid for, so it is wise to have a comprehensive travel health insurance policy in place before you travel. It should cover theft, lost luggage, and costs run up by cancellations and delays, plus the potentially high price of emergency medical evacuation. State hospitals tend to be ill maintained due to chronic underfunding, so private clinics are often preferable. The **Belgrade Emergency Clinical Centre** and **University Children's Hospital** are not far from the main railway station, and just east of them is a **24-Hour Dental Service**. Outside the capital, **Kragujevac Clinical Centre**, **Niš Clinical Centre** and **Novi Sad Clinical Centre of Vojvodina** are reliable hospitals.

Pharmacies

Well-stocked pharmacies or *apoteke* can be found in all large towns and cities. Some medications may be hard to find, so those with specific requirements or prescriptions should bring sufficient supplies for the duration of their trip. Your hotel will know the location of the nearest 24-hour pharmacy. Near the National Assembly and the

Serbian ambulance, easily recognized by the red stripes and blue logo

Farmland and animals in the rural parts of Zlatibor, Western Serbia

Old Palace is the 24-hour **Apoteka Prvi maj**, and about 700 m (765 yd) south of it, near the central railway station, is the 24-hour **Apoteka Sveti Sava**.

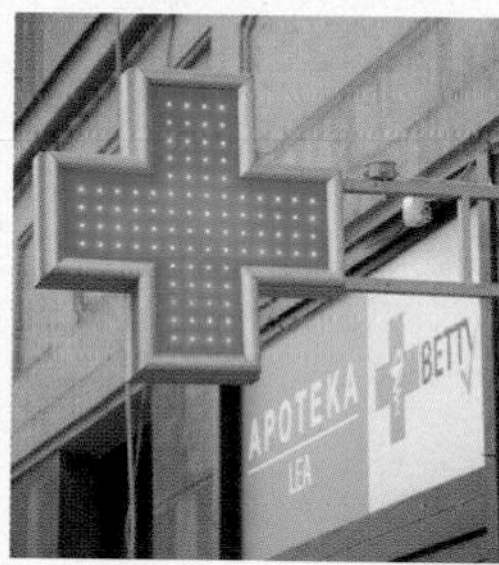

Green and white sign with a green cross advertising an *apoteka* or pharmacy

General Precautions

Tap water in Serbia is generally safe to drink although there have been occasional issues with drinking water quality, so it is best to stick to bottled water. Visit your doctor or travel clinic at least four weeks before your departure to discuss your vaccinations. You will need to be inoculated against tetanus and hepatitis A and should consider having a rabies vaccination as Serbia is classed as a high-risk rabies country. If you plan to visit rural areas, the Ticovac vaccine for tick-borne encephalitis might also be necessary. Apart from this, the worst health danger you are probably likely to come across is excessive passive smoking in public spaces. The latest information regarding health issues can be found online at **Travel Health Pro**.

Animals and Insects

By far the worst pests in Serbia are mosquitoes, especially near lakes and rivers. Insect repellents are available locally. Try to pick the one with the highest DEET content. Beware of street dogs – they are mostly harmless but can become aggressive in groups. Serbia has a high risk of rabies and the disease can be transmitted through the saliva of an infected animal so it is unwise to stroke or feed stray dogs. If you do get bitten, seek medical assistance without any delay. In rural areas there is a danger of tick-borne encephalitis, spread by tick bites. Simple precautions that can be taken against ticks include wearing a hat and long trousers tucked into socks, applying insect repellent and having a Ticovac vaccination before travelling. Hikers should watch out for the venomous long-nosed adder.

Unexploded Mines

In the mountainous areas to the north and east of Kosovo there is a danger of mines and other unexploded munitions from the 1999 conflict in Kosovo and Serbia. Be extremely careful in these areas and do not stray from marked paths and roads. Local tourist organizations will be able to provide you with up-to-date information.

Narcotics

Drug possession of any amount is strictly illegal and punishable by a lengthy prison sentence.

DIRECTORY

Emergency Services

All-Europe Emergency Number
Tel 112.

Ambulance
Tel 194.

Fire
Tel 193.

Police
Tel 192.

Medical Treatment

24-Hour Dental Service, Vračar, Belgrade
City Map E5.
Kneginje Zorke 15, Belgrade.
Tel (011) 3402522.

Belgrade Emergency Clinical Centre
City Map D5.
Pasterova 2, Belgrade.
Tel (011) 3618444.
W kcs.ac.rs

Kragujevac Clinical Centre
Road Map C4. Zmaj Jovina 30, Kragujevac. **Tel** (034) 505050.
W kc-kg.rs

Niš Clinical Centre
Road Map D4. Bulevar Dr Zorana Đinđića 48, Niš. **Tel** (018) 506906.
W kcnis.rs

Novi Sad Clinical Centre of Vojvodina
Road Map B2. Hajduk Veljkova 1, Novi Sad. **Tel** (021) 4843484.
W kcv.rs

University Children's Hospital, Belgrade
City Map D5.
Tiršova 10, Belgrade.
Tel (011) 3616061.
W tirsova.rs/eng

Pharmacies

Apoteka Prvi maj, Belgrade
City Map D3.
Kralja Milana 9, Belgrade.
Tel (011) 3240533.

Apoteka Sveti Sava, Belgrade
City Map C4.
Nemanjina 2, Belgrade.
Tel (011) 2643170.

General Precautions

Travel Health Pro
W travelhealthpro.org.uk

Banking and Currency

Serbs have a strong emotional attachment to their currency, the dinar, as its use dates back to the early 13th century. However, a number of leading economists advocate adopting the euro as the solution to many of Serbia's economic problems, despite the price hikes that will inevitably accompany such a move. Whatever happens, visitors will find that this rapidly modernizing country is increasingly user friendly. ATMs are common, both debit and credit cards are widely accepted and money transfers can be made in minutes.

A 24-hour ATM (cash machine) that can be used to withdraw dinars

Serbian Dinar

The Serbian dinar is a stable currency that replaced the old Yugoslav dinar in 2003 and is officially listed on exchanges as RSD. Foreigners can legally import or export a maximum of 120,000 dinars, the equivalent of around 1,000 euros, but in practice it is unlikely you would ever want to as dinars are hard to exchange outside Serbia. The high exchange rate of the dinar to the euro, pound sterling and US dollar means that most transactions are made with notes rather than coins, so be ready for a pocket or purse full of unfamiliar paper money. It is, thankfully, nowhere near as bad as the hyperinflationary period of 1993 when things got so out of hand that a 500 billion dinar banknote was printed.

Banks

Banks usually work from 9am to 5pm on weekdays (some until 7pm); some are also open from 9am to 1pm on Saturdays. With travellers' cheques now on the verge of obsolescence and the proliferation of bureaux de change throughout Serbia, there is little need to visit a bank other than to use its ATM. **Komercijalna Bank**, **Raiffeisen Bank** and **UniCredit Bank** are well-known, reliable names.

Changing Money

Serbia is awash with bureaux de change, instantly recognizable by their LED displays of currency exchange rates and *menjačnica* signs. Pick one that prominently displays a zero commission sign. Most are open from 8am to between 7 and 9pm during the week and from 9am to between 3 and 5pm on Saturdays. Some are open on Sundays from 9am until around 1pm. Euros usually get the best rates. Banks and post offices will change money at similar rates, but generally take longer to do so. The **Panter** bureau de change is not far from the Nikola Tesla Museum and **VIP** is near Republic Square.

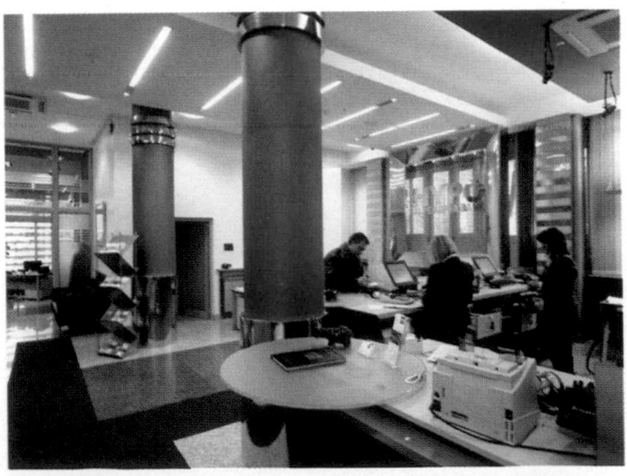
A branch of the Hypo Alpe-Adria-Bank, one of several commercial banks in Serbia

ATMs

Cash machines or ATMs can be found throughout the country and generally accept Maestro, Cirrus, Mastercard and Visa debit and credit cards. Your bank will levy a handling fee for each transaction. Avoid using credit cards to withdraw cash as the fees and interest will be very high. Opt for ATMs attached to banks rather than shops or petrol stations as it will be easier to retrieve your card in the event of it being swallowed.

DIRECTORY

Banks

Komercijalna Bank, Belgrade
City Map C2. Kralja Petra 19.
Tel (011) 3308033, 3308036.
W **kombank.com**

Raiffeisen Bank, Belgrade
City Map C2. Đure Jakšića 8.
Tel (011) 3202100.
W **raiffeisenbank.rs**

UniCredit Bank, Belgrade
City Map B2. Rajićeva 27-29.
Tel (011) 3777888.
W **unicreditbank.rs**

Changing Money

Panter, Belgrade
City Map E4.
Bulevar kralja Aleksandra 122.
Tel (011) 2459977.
W **menjacnica-panter.co.rs**

VIP, Belgrade
City Map D2. Makedonska 24.
Tel (0) 63273603.
W **vipsistem.rs**

Money Transfers

Western Union
Call centre. **Tel** (011) 3334999.
W **transfernovca.rs**

Money Transfers

To receive a foreign money transfer in a Serbian bank you will need to open a Serbian bank account. The funds will take from two to seven days to arrive and fees will be applied at both ends. **Western Union** is a more convenient option. Only the sender incurs a fee and the transfer takes just a few minutes. Funds can be collected in dinars from post offices or in euros from Raiffeisen Bank, UniCredit Bank and Komercijalna Bank.

Credit and Debit Cards

Visa and Mastercard credit and debit cards are widely accepted in hotels, petrol stations and larger shops and restaurants. Your bank will charge handling fees for each transaction; check the cost before you travel. Small towns in remote areas of the country are less likely to be able to accept cards, so it is essential to carry a cash reserve. Notify your bank of your travel plans before departure to prevent them from blocking your card when you try to use it abroad.

Banknotes

Serbian dinar banknotes come in nine denominations. The yellow 10 dinar note is the smallest, followed by the green 20 dinar note, violet 50 dinar note, blue 100 dinar note showing Nikola Tesla, amber 200 dinar note, green-yellow 500 dinar note, red 1,000 dinar note, grey 2,000 dinar note and purple 5,000 dinar note.

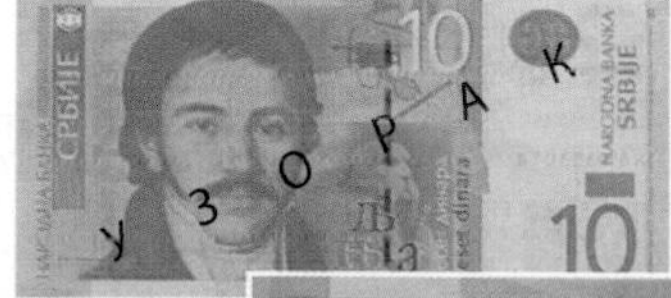

10 dinars

20 dinars

50 dinars

100 dinars

200 dinars

500 dinars

1,000 dinars

Coins

Serbian dinar coins currently come in denominations of 1, 2, 5, 10 and 20 dinars. For 10 and 20 dinars, coins and banknotes are both commonly used.

2,000 dinars

5 dinars

2 dinars

1 dinar

5,000 dinars

Communications and Media

Serbia's numerous online English-language media services allow travellers to get up to speed with the latest in Serbian current affairs and culture before even setting foot in the country. Three mobile phone networks provide country-wide coverage and high-speed Wi-Fi and mobile Internet is widely available, so visitors can expect to be well connected unless they venture into remote mountainous regions. Post offices are open late and can be used for international phone calls, changing money and receiving Western Union transfers as well as sending postcards and packages.

Postal Services

Regional post offices work from 8am to 7pm during the week and from 8am to 2pm on Saturdays. Central post offices in larger towns and cities may have longer Saturday hours and be open on Sundays too; check before visiting. In Belgrade, the **Central Post Office** is located at Takovska 2; **Post Office 2** is also convenient for tourists.

Letters up to 20g cost 70 dinars to send within Europe; postcards cost 60 dinars. If sending a package, you'll need to leave it open for inspection and fill in a customs declaration form. Post to most European countries is sent by airmail and takes 5 to 10 days to arrive. Major courier companies such as **DHL**, **FedEx**, **UPS** and **TNT** have offices in Belgrade.

A red 19th-century Serbian postbox still in active use in Belgrade

Mobile Phones

To use your mobile phone in Serbia you need to make sure it is a dual- or tri-band device and enabled for roaming. As Serbia is not in the EU, it falls into the most expensive "rest of the world" price band for nearly all European mobile operators. You'll be charged a substantial amount to make and to receive calls and text messages, so it is a good idea to purchase a Serbian pay-as-you-go SIM card upon arrival. Apart from being handy for domestic calls and to pay for parking by text message, a local SIM card will have cheap mobile Internet data that can be used for Skype, Viber, WhatsApp and other online calling platforms (VoIP calls). Serbia's three mobile phone operators, **Telenor**, **MTS** and **VIP**, have shops in most towns and sell SIM cards that can be topped up online or over the counter.

Telephone Calls

For local calls it is easiest to get a Halo phonecard *(Halo kartica)* for use in Serbia's orange public phone booths, unless you prefer to buy a local SIM card for use in your mobile phone instead. Street kiosks and post offices sell Halo phonecards at either 300 or 600 dinars, and it costs 8 dinars per minute for calls to mobiles within Serbia, 25 dinars per minute for calls to most European numbers and 45 dinars per minute for calls to the US, Canada and Australia. To use a public telephone, lift the handset, wait for the dialling tone, then insert the phonecard. Select the language by pressing the "i" button, then dial the number you wish to call. If you are not communicating through Skype or other internet phone platforms (VoIP), the cheapest way to make domestic and international calls is to use the telephone centres at local post offices, which generally stay open until 7pm in the evening. Visitors will be shown to phone booths to make the call, and payment will be taken after the call has ended.

Travellers can call from most hotels, but international calls are extremely expensive; local calls are a bit cheaper, but still quite costly. It is best to avoid using hotel phones if possible.

Standard modern orange public telephone booth found across the country

Internet

The Internet had a slow start in Serbia due to the all-inclusive sanctions imposed by the UN from 1992 to 1995. It came into its own in 1999 when NATO bombs wiped out the country's television and radio broadcasting infrastructure. Serbs relied on the Internet for information and to communicate with the outside world.

Since then a sophisticated cable broadband network has been installed which supplies high-speed Internet to much of the country. Internet cafés can still be found in Serbia, but many are used exclusively for gaming now that Wi-Fi is so widely available. Restaurants, cafés, bars, hotels and some parks and public areas now offer Wi-Fi, but most require a password that is only available to patrons. The remoter areas of the country are less likely to be well connected, so heavy

Modern Serbian café offering customers free Wi-Fi and Internet access

Internet users should consider buying a local SIM card with a large data allowance.

Television and Radio

The state television and radio broadcaster, RTS, is very popular, as are the privately owned television channels Pink and Prva. Famed for its role in organizing the anti-government demonstrations of the 1990s, **B92** is a popular independent television and radio outlet. Far less politically active today, it also has a English-language website with regularly updated news and entertainment information.

Newspapers and Magazines

Although it ceased to exist as a national news agency in 2015, **Tanjug** still publishes its stories online in English. The English-language *Belgrade Insight* is a free newspaper distributed to hotels, restaurants, bookshops and cafés. Published fortnightly, it carries in-depth business and political analysis along with entertainment listings and lifestyle and cultural features, and is a great way to familiarize yourself with current affairs across Serbia. *Cord* is a monthly English-language magazine that offers similar content. Both also have excellent websites that are regularly updated. Belgrade visitors will enjoy the beautifully designed *BelGuest* magazine, which offers both print and online versions. It is published quarterly, as are *Welcome to Belgrade*, available at National Tourism Organisation of Serbia centres, and *Belgrade In Your Pocket*. The latter series also has editions of other Serbian cities as well as a very good website. *Yellow Cab* is in Serbian, but has up-to-date Belgrade listings. Foreign magazines and newspapers are usually available in Serbia's high-end hotels.

Useful Dialling Information

- To call Serbia from abroad, dial the international access code of the country you are in (usually 00), then Serbia's country code 381, the city code, and finally the phone number.
- To make a domestic long-distance call in Serbia, dial 0 followed by the city code and phone number.
- Serbian city codes: Belgrade 11; Niš 18; Novi Sad, Sremski Karlovci 21; Despotovac 35; Novi Pazar 20; Kragujevac, Topola, Aranđelovac 34; Pirot 10; Kraljevo 36; Kruševac 37; Sremska Mitrovica 22; Užice 31; Kuršumlija 27; Smederevo 26; Subotica 24; Valjevo 14; Vranje 17; Vršac, Bela Crkva 13; Zaječar, Knjaževac, Negotin 19.
- Mobile phone numbers usually have 9 or 10 digits always starting with 06, while landline numbers have 6 to 8 digits and a 2- or 3-digit city code.
- To make an international call from Serbia, dial 00 (note that it is no longer 99), followed by the country code, city code, and phone number.
- Useful country codes: UK 44; USA and Canada 1; Australia 61; New Zealand 64.

DIRECTORY

Postal Services

Central Post Office, Belgrade
City Map D3. Takovska 2.
Tel (011) 3210068. **W posta.rs**

DHL, Belgrade
City Map D3. Takovska 6.
Tel (011) 3105500. **W dhl.rs**

FedEx, Belgrade
Flying Cargo Yugoslavia, Autoput 22. **Tel** (011) 3109400.
W fedex.com/rs

Post Office 2, Belgrade
City Map C4. Savska 2.
Tel (0) 700 100300. **W posta.rs**

TNT, Belgrade
City Map E2. Venizelosova 29.
Tel (011) 3332555. **W tnt.com**

UPS, Belgrade
Nikola Tesla Airport. **Tel** (011) 2286422. **W ups.com**

Mobile Phones

MTS, Belgrade
City Map D3. Takovska 2
Tel (0) 800 100100 (within Serbia).
W mts.rs

Telenor, Belgrade
City Map C2.
Knez Mihailova 24. **Tel** (0) 639000.
W telenor.rs

VIP, Belgrade
City Map C2.
Knez Mihailova 9. **Tel** (0) 601234 (only within Serbia).
W vipmobile.rs

Television and Radio

B92
W b92.net

Newspapers and Magazines

Belgrade Insight
W belgradeinsight.com

Belgrade In Your Pocket
W inyourpocket.com

BelGuest
W belguest.rs

Cord
W cordmagazine.com

Tanjug
W tanjug.rs

Yellow Cab
W yc.rs

TRAVEL INFORMATION

The easiest way to get to Serbia is to fly directly to the capital Belgrade. Air Serbia, the country's flag carrier, has regular direct and indirect flights from many European destinations as well as from parts of the Middle East, Asia and Australia. Several major European carriers, including Lufthansa, Alitalia, Swiss and Austrian Airlines, fly direct to Belgrade, which is also serviced by the budget airlines Wizzair, Eurowings and easyJet. Serbia's many land border crossings facilitate entry by car or bus from all directions, the most popular being the E70 motorway route from Croatia and the E75 from Hungary.

Arriving by Air

Visitors who fly into Serbia will usually arrive at Terminal 2 of Belgrade's **Nikola Tesla Airport**. **Air Serbia** has direct flights to and from most European capitals and serves destinations as far afield as Beijing and Sydney with indirect flights. It has recently started flights from New York to Belgrade, and American visitors can also fly in via European hubs such as London or Paris. With the exception of British Airways, almost all the major European airlines, including **Lufthansa**, **Alitalia**, **Swissair** and **Austrian Airlines**, offer direct flights to Belgrade.

Wizzair offers budget flights to Belgrade from London, Paris, Stockholm, Dortmund and other EU cities. **Eurowings** has cut-price flights to Belgrade from Stuttgart and **easyJet** flies to Belgrade from Geneva.

Located 18 km (11 miles) west of Belgrade, the modern Nikola Tesla Airport comes complete with restaurants, shops, bureaux de change, ATMs and free Wi-Fi (log on to the UniFi network using the password "unifi"). The airport also has a **Visitor Information Centre** that is open every day until 9.30pm.

Cars on a Serbian motorway, with the buildings of Belgrade in the distance

Getting from the Airport to the City

For taxis into Belgrade and beyond, head to the taxi information desk in the baggage reclaim area where prepaid vouchers can be purchased for your journey. Taxis to the centre of Belgrade cost between 1,400 and 1,800 dinars for up to four passengers with luggage.

Minibuses to Trg Slavija in the centre leave every 30 minutes from outside the airport, stopping at several points; tickets from the driver cost 300 dinars. The cheapest option is local bus no. 72, leaving every 40 minutes from outside the terminal to Zeleni venac in the city centre. Tickets from the driver cost 150 dinars. A large number of car rental agencies, including **Avis**, **Hertz**, **Europcar** and **Budget**, have their offices in the arrivals area of Terminal 2 at the airport.

Arriving by Boat

River cruisers arriving in the capital dock at the passenger terminal on the Sava below Kalemegdan *(see pp52–3)*. Services include a visitor information centre, restaurants, gift shops, ATMs and bureaux de change. Most cruise passengers join guided sightseeing tours, but it is also possible to visit the city by foot or taxi from here.

Cruisers docked at the marinas on the river below Belgrade's imposing Kalemegdan Fortress

Sailors arriving in their own vessel must register their boat and crew at the port authority inside the passenger terminal. They are then free to sail and dock in Serbian waters. **Nautec**, **Nautilus** and **Vidra** Marinas in Belgrade can carry out repairs and have all the usual facilities, including security cameras and guards, fuel, water, electricity, maintenance, cleaning and Wi-Fi. For more information, see **The Danube** website run by the Danube Competence Centre.

Long-distance buses at the Belgrade Central Bus Station or Autobuska stanica (BAS)

Arriving by Car

To drive in Serbia, visitors need an international driving permit, car ownership documents and valid car insurance. If the vehicle is registered and insured in the EU, additional insurance will not be required. If not, you will need to buy a short-term insurance policy at the border for around €80. Most roads are free to use, but motorways have toll fees that can be paid in euros, dinars or by credit or debit card. Note that foreign-registered cars are charged higher fees *(see p164)*.

Arriving by Bus

International buses arrive at **Belgrade Central Bus Station**, located next to the central railway station in a part of the city known as Savski venac. From here you can either walk for about 15 minutes or take tram no. 2 to Kalemegdan and the Old Town. Serbia's Eurolines partner **Lasta** has an office in the bus station where you can book international bus tickets. There are direct bus routes from and to much of Europe, but long journey times (from London to Belgrade via Frankfurt takes 38 hours) mean that flying is a better option.

Arriving by Train

International trains arrive at **Belgrade Central Railway Station** in Savski venac. The **Visitor Information Centre** in the station is open from Monday to Saturday from 7am to 1.30pm. For train times visit the **Serbian Railways** website.

DIRECTORY

Arriving by Air

Air Serbia
City Map D3. Bul. kralja Aleksandra 17, Belgrade.
Tel (011) 3112123.
W airserbia.com

Alitalia
Call centre only. **Tel** (011) 3245000. **W alitalia.com**

Austrian Airlines
Call centre only.
Tel (011) 3248077.
W austrian.com

easyJet
Call centre only.
Tel (011) 2094863.
W easyjet.com

Eurowings
Call centre only.
Tel (011) 2094863.
W eurowings.com

Lufthansa
City Map C3.
Terazije 3/VII, Belgrade.
Tel (011) 3034389.
W lufthansa.com

Nikola Tesla Airport
Belgrade. **Tel** (011) 2094000. **W beg.aero**

Swissair
Call centre only. **Tel** (011) 3030140. **W swiss.com**

Visitor Information Centre
Nikola Tesla Airport.
Tel (011) 2097828.

Wizzair
Call centre only.
Tel (0) 900 232321 (within Serbia). **W wizzair.com**

Getting from the Airport to the City

Avis
Belgrade Airport. **Tel** (011) 2097062. **W avis.rs**

Budget
Belgrade Airport. **Tel** (011) 2286361. **W budget.rs**

Europcar
Belgrade Airport. **Tel** (011) 228640. **W europcar.rs**

Hertz
Belgrade Airport.
Tel (011) 2286017.
W hertz.rs

Arriving by Boat

Nautec Marina
Danube River,
Kej oslobođenja 3a,
Zemun, Belgrade.
Tel (011) 3077792.
W nautec.co.rs

Nautilus Marina
Danube River,
Višnjička 115a,
Ada Huja, Belgrade.
Tel (0) 669251630.
W nautilusmarina.rs

The Danube
W dunav-info.org

Vidra Marina
Sava River, Omladinskih brigada bb, Blok 70a, New Belgrade.
Tel (0) 656811022.
W marinavidra.com

Arriving by Bus

Belgrade Central Bus Station
City Map B3.
Železnička 4. **Tel** (011) 2636299. **W bas.rs**

Lasta, Belgrade
City Map B3.
Železnička 2. **Tel** (011) 3348555, 3402300.
W lasta.rs

Arriving by Train

Belgrade Central Railway Station
City Map C3.
Glavna železnička stanica.
Tel (011) 3602899.
W serbianrailways.com

Serbian Railways
W serbianrailways.com

Visitor Information Centre
City Map C3. Belgrade Central Railway Station.
Tel (011) 3612732.

Getting Around Belgrade

There is little need for public transport in Belgrade's Old Town as it is compact enough to cover on foot, but sights that lie further afield are best reached with some form of transport. Buses, trams and trolleybuses are the cheapest and most characterful option – friendly locals will often go out of their way to help you find the right bus and the availability of smartphone travel apps such as BeoGSP reduces the risk of becoming lost. Taxis are the best choice for quick, stress-free trips through the city, while for those with some time on their hands a cycle tour is a wonderful way to experience Belgrade.

Cyclist riding along a street on the east bank of the Sava River in Belgrade

Buses

Belgrade has an extensive bus network operated by **Lasta** in the suburbs and **GSP Beograd** in town. Services run from 4am to midnight every day, while limited night bus services from Republic Square (Trg republike) continue until around 3am. Single tickets can be bought from the driver for 150 dinars, but it is cheaper to opt for a paper **BusPlus** travelcard sold for 40 dinars at news kiosks throughout the city. These can be charged with up to 500 dinars credit and are valid for three months. A trip lasting up to 90 minutes with an unlimited number of rides costs 89 dinars. Those planning on staying longer can buy a BusPlus plastic travelcard for 250 dinars, which has no limit to the number of times it can be charged and is valid for three years. Tickets for night buses are 150 dinars for Zone 1; these can only be purchased from the bus driver.

Travelcards must be swiped across a card reader upon entering a bus. It is also possible to use a plastic BusPlus card with adequate credit to pay for a group travelling together by selecting "group ticket" on the card reader and keying in the number of travellers.

Useful bus routes from the central Studentski trg include no. 31 to St Sava and no. 41 to the House of Flowers. Bus no. 83 from Belgrade's Central Bus Station travels to Zemun and no. 72 goes to the airport from Zeleni venac. Smartphone users can download the PlanPlus or BeoGSP apps to find the fastest way around the city using only public transport.

Belgrade's BusPlus plastic travelcard

Minibuses

Belgrade has nine public and several private minibus lines. Express minibuses are air-conditioned and more comfortable and have fewer stops than regular buses. Most stops do not show the route and travellers must wait for the minibus to arrive to discover the route. They run until midnight from Monday to Saturday and tickets from the driver cost 150 dinars for trips within the city centre. Visitors are likely to make most use of the A1 line, which runs between Nikola Tesla Airport and Trg Slavija every 30 minutes; tickets cost 300 dinars from the driver *(see p158)*.

Trams and Trolleybuses

Trams were first introduced to Belgrade in the late 19th century. Today there are 11 tram lines that run until midnight every day. They use the same ticket pricing system as the city buses. The most useful trams for visitors are nos. 2, 11 and 13, which connect the Old Town with the central bus and railway stations. Tram no. 2 is famous for its sightseeing circular route, known as *krug dvojke*, which

Belgrade tram no. 2, well known for its circular route passing many key sights

Red trolleybuses powered by electricity running on fixed routes along Belgrade streets

passes through much of the Old Town and central Belgrade. The seven trolleybus lines are powered by overhead electric cables and run along fixed routes like ordinary buses. Ticket prices are the same as for buses. Trams and trolleybuses are both operated by GSP Beograd.

Easily recognizable blue oval roof plate of an officially registered Belgrade taxi

Taxis

If you follow a few simple rules to avoid being ripped off, taxis can be an efficient and relatively inexpensive way to get around Belgrade – short city journeys are likely to cost between 300 and 500 dinars. Make sure you use only officially registered taxis, recognizable by the blue oval registration plate that is mounted on the roof. These taxis are all metered and charge a standard rate. Always ensure that the meter is running and never agree to a fixed price offered in advance by the driver. To reduce the risk of being cheated, avoid taxis waiting outside the bus and railway stations; instead flag down a taxi in a nearby street or ask the railway station visitor information centre to order one for you.

Use the taxi booking service *(see p158)* from the international airport to the centre when you arrive and ask your hotel receptionist to book you a taxi to the airport upon departure. **Pink**, **Lux**, **Beotaxi** and **Beogradski** are reliable taxi companies.

Cycling

Cycling is not recommended in the Old Town as the streets are narrow and often jammed with cars that pay scant attention to cyclists. New Belgrade, with its broad streets, is more appealing, but the city's three purpose-built cycle routes are by far the safest, most attractive options.

One route follows the east bank of the Sava River from Dorćol to Ada Ciganlija where it joins a second route that loops around the island's lake. The third route starts from Hotel Jugoslavija on the west bank of the Danube River and runs south past the confluence of the Sava and the Danube towards Blok 45, a residential district on the Sava. Cycle maps are available from visitor information centres and bikes can be hired at Ada Ciganlija, Dorćol and Hotel Jugoslavija.

iBikeBelgrade run various scheduled daily tours of the city with English-speaking guides. They also offer private group and individual cycling tours.

Group of visitors on an iBikeBelgrade cycling tour of the city

DIRECTORY

Buses

BusPlus
Tel (011) 7155155.

GSP Beograd, Belgrade
City Map D1. Kneginje Ljubice 29. **Tel** (011) 3664000. **W gsp.rs**

Lasta, Belgrade
City Map B3. Železnička 2.
Tel (011) 3348555, 3402300.
W lasta.rs

Taxis

Beogradski Taxi, Belgrade
Tel (011) 2099920.
W beogradski-taxi.com

Beotaxi, Belgrade
Tel (011) 2415555.
W radiobeotaxi.co.rs

Lux Taxi, Belgrade
Tel (011) 3033123. **W luxtaxi.rs**

Pink Taxi, Belgrade
Tel (011) 19803. **W pinktaxi.info**

Cycling

iBikeBelgrade, Belgrade
City Map B3. Braće Krsmanović 5.
Tel (0) 669008386.
W ibikebelgrade.com

Getting Around Serbia

Travelling by long-distance bus is the most popular form of public transport in Serbia and, short of hiring a rental car, this is the best way to reach the remotest sights in the country. Train journeys are a fair bit cheaper and certainly more scenic, but the lack of comfort and sluggishness of the trains often detract from the overall experience. However you decide to make your way across the country, there are several Serbian websites with excellent public transport journey planners that make life a lot easier for independent travellers.

Modern building housing the Belgrade Autobuska stanica (BAS) central bus station

Travelling by Bus

Belgrade Central Bus Station has regular services to several Serbian towns and cities from where local buses serve smaller destinations and fast intercity buses connect regional centres. Tickets should be bought in advance from booths within the bus station. The price usually includes a seat reservation. You will be given either a turnstile token *(žeton)* or a platform ticket *(peronska karta)* that will allow access to your departure platform. If you are in a hurry and want to jump on a bus that is about to leave, it is possible to buy a *peronska karta* and purchase a ticket directly from the driver. Any luggage stowed under the bus will incur a small charge in exchange for a ticket from the driver or conductor.

While some of the larger bus companies in Serbia, such as **Lasta**, have invested in modern air-conditioned coaches for their intercity and international services, regional buses in the country's rural areas are most likely to be less comfortable older models that can become stiflingly hot in summer. Seat reservations are honoured, but buses often get overcrowded on popular routes because drivers frequently stop to pick up standing passengers along the way. Smoking is forbidden on public transport, but don't be surprised if the driver has a cigarette with his window open. The rest of the smokers on board have to wait for the five- or 10-minute cigarette and toilet breaks that punctuate most longer journeys.

Bus Stations

Most bus stations across the country offer passengers either covered or indoor waiting areas, which generally have cafés or snack kiosks and toilets, as well as left luggage facilities.

Travelling by Train

Decades of underinvestment in Serbia's passenger rail infrastructure mean that breakdowns and delays are common and carriages on domestic routes are often old, uncomfortable and overcrowded. That said, trains are the cheapest way to travel around Serbia if you're not in a hurry, and the scenery can be spectacular, especially on the mountainous Belgrade to Bar (Montenegro) line. International routes have much more

Train travelling along the Šargan Eight narrow-gauge line from Mokra Gora station, Western Serbia

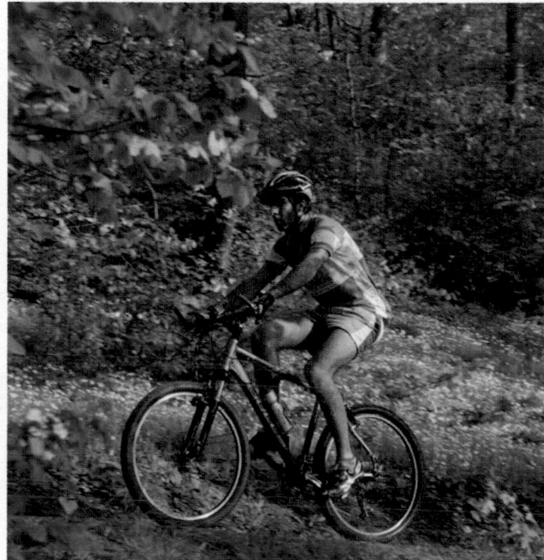

Cyclist tackling a hilly patch on the Serbian section of EuroVelo Route 6

DIRECTORY

Travelling by Bus

Lasta, Belgrade
City Map B3. Železnička 2.
Tel (011) 3348555, 3402300.
W lasta.rs

Planning your Journey

Belgrade Central Bus Station
W bas.rs

Niš Bus Station
W nis-ekspres.rs

Polazak
W polazak.com

Serbian Railways
W serbianrailways.com

Cycling

EuroVelo
W eurovelo.com

comfortable trains with sleeper compartments for longer journeys. Ensure you book sleeper tickets well in advance during summer. Domestic and international trains rarely have buffet cars so stock up on food and drinks before departure.

Planning your Journey

The timetable on the website of the **Belgrade Central Bus Station** is a great resource for planning bus journeys from Belgrade, as is the website of the **Niš Bus Station**. The **Serbian Railways** website also lists train schedules. The **Polazak** website has gone a step further by successfully integrating Serbian bus and train schedules to offer a choice of travel options. It also has a customer review tab that gives travellers an idea of what standards to expect from the various transport providers. Local visitor information centres can be relied upon for travel information. Determined visitors can have a go at deciphering the Cyrillic timetables posted in bus and train stations, but be aware that they are not always kept up to date. Departures are listed as *polasci*, arrivals are *dolasci*.

Cycling

If congested cities and busy main roads are avoided, cycling in Serbia can be delightful. Its country lanes see very little traffic and the short distances between villages mean you are never too far from civilization. In remote rural areas, however, you will have to wild camp or rely upon local hospitality as hotels and guest houses will be thin on the ground. Many cyclists follow the Serbian section of Route 6 of the **EuroVelo** cycle network. This begins at the Bački Breg border crossing with Hungary and follows the Danube for 736 km (457 miles) past Novi Sad, Belgrade and Negotin before finally entering Bulgaria at Bregovo.

Hitchhiking

Hitchhikers are a common sight in Serbia, especially in summer. Hitching from motorway toll gates is a popular strategy but try not to be dropped off at motorway junctions as they are often far from the cities they service. Approaching drivers at petrol stations is a good idea as they are more likely to offer a lift if they have had a chance to talk to you. It is illegal to hitchhike on motorways, but it is acceptable to hitch from slip roads if you choose a safe spot. It is difficult and dangerous to hitchhike at night as street lighting is often poor or nonexistent and drivers are unlikely to pick up hitchhikers after dark. Women should avoid hitchhiking alone.

Backpacker waiting by the roadside to hitch a ride in Serbia

Travelling by Road

In terms of independence and convenience, you will see far more of Serbia by car than by any other method of touring. Car hire is easy to arrange or you can bring your own vehicle. Motorways link Subotica in the north to Novi Sad, Belgrade, Niš and the Macedonian border, and Belgrade to the Croatian border; the rest of the country is covered by A and B roads and the occasional gravel track. Rural lanes are often littered with potholes and blocked by tractors and other slow-moving agricultural vehicles, so cautious driving is essential. Satellite navigation can be a great help, but keep a traditional paper road map within reach for when the system is unable to distinguish between a B road and a rutted forestry track.

Serbian vehicle with a car hire firm's contact details prominently displayed

Car Rental

All the major car hire firms, including **Hertz**, **Budget** and **Avis**, have offices in Belgrade and in large towns and cities across Serbia. Their vehicles range from budget hatchbacks to minibuses and luxury saloons and can be booked online through either the company website or intermediary price comparison sites. Satellite navigation systems, booster seats, and baby car seats should be ordered at the time of booking as demand is high in summer and availability may be limited.

All visitors intending to drive in Serbia will need a valid EU or international driving permit and must pay a substantial deposit upon collecting the car. If a credit card is used the deposit amount will be blocked for the rental period; if a debit card is used the deposit will be withdrawn and then refunded once the vehicle has been returned. Inspect the car for any signs of damage before signing for it and insist that even the smallest scratches are marked on the rental document to avoid being charged for them upon your return. Keep the vehicle registration documents with you at all times and do not leave them in the car. In the event of an accident make sure that the police issue you with a European accident claim form for the hire company or your car insurer.

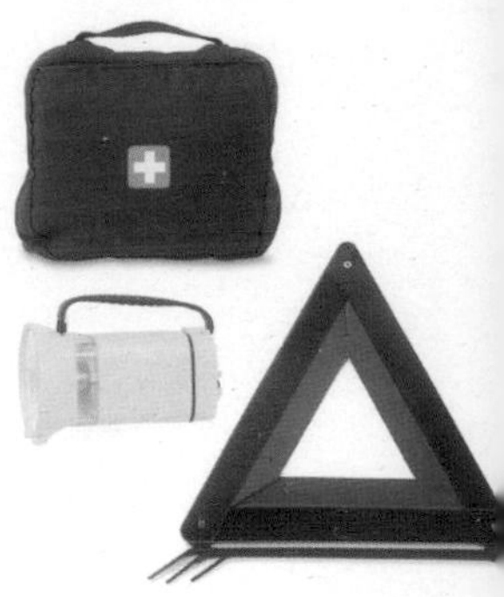

A reflective triangle, first-aid kit and torch, required by law in vehicles in Serbia

Bringing your own Car

As with rental cars, drivers who bring their own vehicles must carry their passport, valid EU or international driving permit, car ownership documents and valid car insurance. If your vehicle is registered and insured in the EU, additional insurance will not be required; if it is not, you will need to buy a short-term insurance policy at the border for around €80 *(see p159)*. All vehicles are required to carry a reflective jacket (in the passenger compartment), first-aid kit, warning triangle, spare bulb set, spare tyre and a tow rope at least 3 m (10 ft) long. From 1 November to 1 April winter tyres are mandatory and snow chains must be carried at all times.

Fuel

Petrol stations with cafés, shops, and toilets are located along motorways and on the outskirts of towns and cities. A growing number of petrol stations have

Large petrol station along a Serbian motorway, with fuel prices displayed clearly and a small shop for essentials

Serbian motorway displaying large, clear signage indicating motorway numbers, destinations, road rules and speed limits

LPG *(autogas)* and unleaded petrol and diesel is sold everywhere. Most large petrol stations accept card payments.

Emergencies

If you are involved in a road accident ask a local to call the **Traffic Police** or dial the **all-Europe emergency number** to request police and medical assistance if necessary. Hire car breakdowns should be dealt with by the rental company; if your own vehicle has problems contact **AMSS**, Serbia's roadside assistance association.

Rules of the Road

At unmarked crossings give way to vehicles coming on the right. Your car's side lights or dipped headlights must be used during the day and the use of seatbelts is compulsory. Using a mobile phone while driving is forbidden. If drivers are flashed by vehicles travelling in the opposite direction it means that there is either a police speed trap or a hazard on the road ahead.

The speed limit is 120 kmph (75 mph) on motorways, 100 kmph (62 mph) on main roads and 50 kmph (31 mph) in built up areas. The traffic police will not hesitate to issue on-the-spot fines to any driver caught speeding. The permissible blood alcohol content for drivers is like most European countries at 0.03 per cent – be aware that this is the equivalent of just one glass of wine or one glass of beer. For motorcyclists and novice drivers this limit is 0 per cent. Children under the age of 12 and those travellers who are visibly under the influence of alcohol are not allowed to sit in the front. On motorcycles, helmets are compulsory for all drivers and their pillion passengers.

Car Repair Garages

Auto servisi or car repair garages are easy to find in Serbia and can handle basic repairs such as punctures and flat batteries. Few of the smaller places will have the computer technology required to deal with newer vehicle models so it is always advisable to visit the main dealer for more complex issues.

Vehicle parked outside a Serbian mechanic's shop at an *auto servis*

Getting Around

Motorways and main roads are well marked with signposts, but minor roads in rural areas often have none, so a good satellite navigation system or paper map is essential. If in doubt ask locals for directions. Most roads are free to use, but there are tolls on some motorways, including the A1/E75 from Subotica to Novi Sad, Belgrade and Niš, and from Niš to Leskovac. The toll can be paid in euros, dinars or by credit or debit card *(see p159)*. Note that foreign-registered cars are charged a different toll fee.

DIRECTORY

Car Rental

Avis, Belgrade
Pivljanina Baje 43/6, Dedinje.
Tel (011) 3676644. **W avis.rs**

Budget, Belgrade
Omladinskih brigada 90a, Zemun.
Tel (011) 3113050. **W budget.rs**

Hertz, Belgrade
City Map A3. Vladimira Popovića 6. **Tel** (011) 2028200. **W hertz.rs**

Emergencies

All-Europe Emergency Number
Tel 112.

AMSS
Tel (011) 1987.
W www.amss.org.rs

Traffic Police
Tel 192.

General Index

Page numbers in **bold** refer to main entries

A

Abstract Expressionism 25
Accommodation 124–9
  see also Hotels
Ada Bridge (Belgrade) 27
Ada Ciganlija (Belgrade) 12, 43, 44, **59**
Addresses, street names 27
Admission fees 149
Air travel 158, 159
Alcohol
  customs information 148
  driving regulations 165
Alexander II (Karađorđević), Crown Prince 59
Alexander I Karađorđević, King 35, 51, 59, 92
Alexander I Obrenović, King 54
Aleksić, Dragan 25
Alexander Nevsky, St 50–51
Ali Paša, Grand Vizier 52
Altun-alem Mosque (Novi Pazar) 23
Amidža's Mansion (Kragujevac) 74
Animals
  safety 153
  see also Wildlife
Antić, Ivan 27, 58
Apartment hotels 124
Aranđelovac 75
  hotels 127
  restaurants 135
Architecture 26–7
Armistice Day 31
Art 24–5
  see also Museums and galleries
Art Nouveau 27
  Subotica 27, 41, 89, 98
Arts and crafts see Crafts
ATMs 154
Automobile Museum (Belgrade) 12, **54**
Autumn in Serbia 30
Avramović, Dimitrije 48

B

Babin Zub Ski Resort 121
Bač 89, 90, **96**
Bačka Bishop's Palace (Novi Sad) 89, **92**
Bajrakli Mosque (Belgrade) 50
Balkan League 35
Balkan Wars 35
Ballet 142, 143
Banking 154–5
Banknotes 155
Baroque art 18, 25
Baumhorn, Lipot 93
Bela Crkva 99
  festivals 28
  hotels 128
Belgrade 10, **43–63**
  climate 29
  festivals 17, 28–31
  hotels 126–7
  Kalemegdan Fortress 52–3
  map, city 44–5
  map, street finder 60–63
  Old Town: Street-by-Street map 46–7
  restaurants 134–5
  street names 27
  travel 44, 160–61
  Two days in Belgrade 12
Belgrade, Siege of (1456) 34
Berlin, Congress of (1878) 34
Bicycles *see* Cycling
Birds 20–21, 145
Bireš, Mihal 98
Black Wave cinema 25
Boats 158–9
Book shops 141
Borač 74
Bosnia and Herzegovina 33, 36, 37
Bosnian War (1992–95) 37
Branković, Đurađ 65, 68, 99
Broz, Jovanka 58
Brutalism 27
Budget accommodation 125
Bugarski, Alexander 26
Bukovo Monastery 108
Bulgaria 35
Bureaux de change 154
Burek Days (Niš) 30, 132
Buses 159, 160, 161, 162, 163
Byzantine art and architecture 18, 24, 26, 54, 59, 68, 97, 113, 116, 120
Byzantine Empire 33, 34, 80, 96, 101, 120

C

Canyoning 144, 145
Caričin Grad 113, **120**
Carpathians 14, 15
Cars 164–5
  Automobile Museum (Belgrade) 12, **54**
  driving to Serbia 159, 164
  emergencies 165
  fuel 164–5
  rental 164, 165
  repairs 165
  rules of the road 165
  see also Tours
Castles *see* Fortresses
Cathedrals and churches 22–3, 149
  Cathedral Church of St Michael (Belgrade) 43, 46, **48**
  Cathedral of St George (Novi Sad) 89, **92**
  Cathedral of St Nicholas (Sremski Karlovci) 91, 96
  Cathedral of St Nicholas (Vršac) 89, 99
  Cathedral of the Holy Trinity (Niš) 117
  Chapel of St Petka (Belgrade) 53
  Church of St Alexander Nevsky (Belgrade) 50–51
  Church of St Mark (Belgrade) 54
  Church of St Nicholas (Belgrade) 58
  Church of the Holy Trinity (Sremski Karlovci) 91, 96
  Church of the Name of Mary (Novi Sad) 89
  Church of the Virgin Mary (Studenica Monastery) 26
  Holy Trinity Church (Kraljevo) 81
  Holy Trinity Cathedral (Vranje) 121
  Karađorđe Mausoleum Church of St George (Topola) 11, 65, 66, 75
  Lazarica Church (Kruševac) 65, 69
  Old Church (Negotin) 108
  St George's Church (Petrovaradin) 94
  St Nicholas Church (Novi Sad) 92–3
  St Petka's Church (Vranje) 121
  St Sava's Church (Belgrade) 8–9
  Sts Peter and Paul (Novi Pazar) 23, 24, 82
  Temple of St Sava (Belgrade) 23, **55**
  see also Monasteries
Caves 144, 145
  Ceremošnja 108
Caves (cont.)
  Rajkova 104, 108
  Ravništarka 108
  Resavska 13, **68**
  Risovača (Aranđelovac) 75
  Stopića 86
Central Serbia 65–75
  the Flavours of Serbia 133
  hotels 127
  Manasija Monastery 70–71
  map 66–7
  restaurants 135–6
  travel 66
Ceremošnja Cave 108
Četniks 36
Chalupova, Zuzana 16, 17
Charles I, King of Hungary 96
Charles VI, Emperor 52
Children 150
  in hotels 124
  in restaurants 130
  theatre 142, 143
Christmas 18, 31
Churches *see* Cathedrals and churches
Cinema *see* Film
City Hall (Subotica) 27, 98
City Museums
  City Museum (Knjaževac) 109
  City Museum (Petrovaradin Fortress, Novi Sad) 95
  City Museum (Sremski Karlovci) 96
  City Museum (Subotica) 98
  City Museum (Vršac) 99
  Pasha's Residence (Vranje) 121
  see also Museums and galleries
Climate 29, 148
Clothes
  in churches and mosques 149
  what to take 148
Coins 155
Communications 156–7
Communist Party 18–19, 36
Constantine the Great, Emperor 32, 113, 116, 117
Constantine the Philosopher 70
Constantinople School, icons 22
Constructivism 25
Contemporary art 25
Crafts shops 140–41
Credit cards 155
  in restaurants 131
  in shops 140
Crime 152
Crna Reka Monastery 23, 79, **83**
Croatia 36, 37
Croatian Peasant Party 35
Ćuprija
  hotels 127
Currency 154–5
  see also Credit cards; Debit cards
Customs information 148
Cycling 144, 161, 163
  Belgrade 44, 59, 160, 161
  Danube Cycling Route 104
  EuroVelo 144, 145, 163
  Kraljevo 81
  Novi Sad 93
  Palić 98
  Sokobanja 109
  Tara National Park 87
  Tour de Serbie 28

D

Dance 142, 143
  festivals 28, 30

Danilo II, Archbishop 81
Danube River 10, 14, 15, 33, 43, 65, 89, 90, 93, 94, 95, 102, 145, 159
  Along the Danube 104–5
  cycling 104, 161
  festivals 28
  Iron Gates 21, 100, 101, 103, 105 106–7
Debit cards 155
December Group 25
Deliblato Sands 21
Dental care 153
Đerdap Dam 104, 105
Desmaisons, Emile 34
Devil's Town 11, 13, 41, 113, **120**
Dialling codes 157
Diana Roman Fort 101, 105
Dinaric Alps 14, 20
Đinđić, Zoran 19
Đipša (Divša) Monastery 97
Disabled travellers 150, 151
  hotels 124
Doctors 152
Dogs, rabies 153
Đoković, Novak 19
Donji Milanovac
  hotels 128
Draga, Queen 54
Drinks *see* Food and drink
Drugs, illegal 153
Drunken Boat (Šumanović) 25
Drvengrad 77, 79, 84–5, 87
  festivals 31
  hotels 127
  restaurants 136
Dunavska (Novi Sad) 92

E

Eastern Orthodox Church 23
Eastern Serbia 101–12
  Along the Danube 104–5
  Felix Romuliana (Gamzigrad) 110–11
  the Flavours of Serbia 133
  hotels 128–9
  map 102–3
  restaurants 138–9
  travel 102
Economy 19
Electricity 151
Embassies 149
Embassy of France (Belgrade) 46
Emergencies 152, 153, 165
Entertainment 142–3
  children's theatre 142, 143
  cinema 143
  classical music 142, 143
  nightclubs 143
  opera, ballet, folklore and theatre 142, 143
  rock and jazz 143
  tickets 143
Ethnic groups 18
  Bosniaks 18, 37, 82
  Bunjevci 18, 23, 98
  Croats 18, 23, 33, 35, 37, 52, 58, 98
  Germans 23, 89, 99
  Hungarians 18, 23, 27, 89, 98, 104, 132
  Romanians 18, 23, 36, 51, 98, 121
  Slovaks 16, 17, 18, 23, 89, 98
  Ukrainians 23
Ethnographic Museum (Belgrade) 12, **48**
European Union (EU) 19, 37
Events 28–31
EXIT Music Festival (Novi Sad) 29, **95**
Expert, Roger-Henri 46

F

Faculty of Fine Arts (Belgrade) 47
Felix Romuliana (Gamzigrad) 41, 101, 108, **110–11**
Festivals 17, 28–31
Film 143
  Black Wave cinema 25
  festivals 29, 30, 31
Food and drink
  festivals 29, 30
  the Flavours of Serbia 132–3
  shops 141
  see also Restaurants; Wine
Fortresses
  Golubac Fortress 101, 103, 104, 106–7
  Kalemegdan Fortress (Belgrade) 12, 40, 43, **52–3**
  Maglič Fortress 79, **81**
  Mileševac Fortress 83
  Momčilov Grad (Pirot) 115, 120–21
  Niš Fortress 13, 26, 113, 114, **116**
  Petrovaradin Fortress 89, **94–5**
  Ram Fortress 101, 104
  Smederevo Fortress 12–13, 34, 65, 67
  Sokograd Fortress 102
  Vršac 99
Franz Ferdinand, Archduke 35
Freedom Square (Novi Sad) 93
Fresco Gallery (Belgrade) 49
Fruška Gora 19, 89
  hotels 128
  monasteries 13, 89, 90, 97
  restaurants 137
  wineries 13
Fruška Gora National Park 97

G

Gabrjelčič, Peter 27
Galerius, Emperor 41, 96, 101, 108, 110–11
Galleries see Museums and galleries
Gallery of Naïve Art (Kovačica) 98
Gallery of the Natural History Museum (Belgrade) 52, 53
Gay and lesbian travellers 150
Golubac Fortress 101, 103, 104, 106–7
  restaurants 138
Government 19
Great Migrations 18, 25, 83
Great Morava River 15, 41, 65, 66, 67
Grgeteg Monastery 13, 97
Guča Trumpet Festival 17, 29

H

Habsburg dynasty 18, 89, 94, 96
Hajduk Veljko Museum (Negotin) 108
Health 152–3
Heritage Museum (Knjaževac) 109
Hiking 144, 145
History 33–7
Hitchhiking 163
Hitler, Adolf 36
Holidays, public 31
Holy Mother of God (fresco) 22
Holy Trinity Church (Kraljevo) 81
Holy Trinity Cathedral (Vranje) 121
Horses
  festivals 30
  riding 145
Hospitals 152, 153
Hotels 124–9
  apartment hotels 124
Hotels (cont.)
  Belgrade 126–7
  boutique hotels 125
  budget accommodation 125
  Central Serbia 127
  children in 124
  disabled travellers 124
  Eastern Serbia 128–9
  facilities 124
  family-friendly hotels 124
  how to book 124
  Northern Serbia 128
  Southern Serbia 129
  spa hotels 124
  Western Serbia 127–8
House of Flowers (Belgrade) 12, **58**
Huršid Paša 117

I

Imperial Palace (Sremska Mitrovica) 96
Insect bites 153
International Monetary Fund 19
Internet 156–7
Iron Gates 21, 100, 101, 103, 105
Isa-beg Hammam (Novi Pazar) 82
Islam 23, 34, 77
  see also Mosques

J

Jakab, Dezső 98
  City Hall (Subotica) 27
Jakšić, Đura 25
Jazak Monastery 97
Jazz 143
  festivals 28, 29, 30
Jews 23
  Jewish Historical Museum (Belgrade) 50
  see also Synagogues
Jonaš, Martin 98
Joseph II, Emperor 58
Jovanović, Pavle "Paja"
  Migration of the Serbs 25, 92
Justinian, Emperor 96, 105, 113, 120

K

Kafana Question Mark (Belgrade) 47
Kalemegdan Fortress (Belgrade) 12, 40, 43, **52–3**
Kalenić Monastery 64, 65, 66, 69
Karađorđe (Đorđe Petrović) 11, 34, 35, 65, **75**, 95
Karađorđe House Museum (Topola) 75
Karađorđe Mausoleum Church of St George (Topola) 11, 65, 66, 75
Karađorđe Monument (Belgrade) 35
Karađorđević dynasty *see* Alexander I Karađorđević; Alexander II (Karađorđević); Karađorđe; Peter I (Karađorđević); Peter II Karađorđević
Karadžić, Radovan 19
Karadzić, Vuk 48, 174
Karas River 21
Katherine, Crown Princess 59
Kayaking 145
King Alexander Boulevard (Belgrade) 54
King Peter's House (Topola) 75
Kingdom of Serbs, Croats and Slovenes 35, 58
Kladovo
  hotels 129
  restaurants 138
Knez Mihailova (Belgrade) 47

Knjaževac 109
festivals 29
hotels 129
restaurants 138
Komor, Marcell 27, 98
Kopaonik 20, 77, 78, **82**
Kosaničićev venac (Belgrade) 46
Kosovo 14, 15, 19, 33, 35, 36, 37
border crossings 148
Kosovo, Battle of (1389) 34, 65, 69
Kovačica 17, **98**
hotels 128
restaurants 137
Kračun, Teodor 25, 96, 97
Kragujevac 13, 65, **74**
climate 29
festivals 28
hotels 127
restaurants 136
Krajina Museum (Negotin) 108
Kralja Petra (Belgrade) 46
Kralja Petra School (Belgrade) 47
Kraljevo 13, 77, **80–81**
festivals 29, 30
hotels 127
restaurants 136
Krstić, Branko 54
Krstić, Đorđe 25
Krstić, Petar 54
Krušedol Monastery 13, 25, 97, 137
Kruševac 13, 65, **69**
festivals 30
hotels 127
restaurants 136
Kučevo 108
Kuršumlija 113, **120**
Kurtović, Ivo 55
Kusturica, Emir 31, 87

L

Lakes 20
Ada Ciganlija 59
Bela Crkva 99
Ludaš 20, 90
Međuvršje 80
Palić 20, 29, 90, 98, 128, 138
Spajići 2–3, 4
Šumaričko 74
Zaovine 4, 5
Lamartine, Alphonse de 117
Landscape 17, 20–21
Lazar, Prince 34, 48, 65, 69, 97
Lazarević, Stefan 52, 65, 69, 70, 71
Lazarica Church (Kruševac) 65, 69
Leopold I, Emperor 52
Lepenski Vir 33, 101, 105
Leskovac
hotels 129
Leskovac Grill Festival (Roštiljijada) 30, 132
Ljubica, Princess 43, 49
Ljubostinja Monastery 11, 13, 65, 66, 69, 141
Ludaš *see* Lakes
Lukovska Banja 113, 120
hotels 129

M

Macedonia 35, 37
Magazines 157
Maglič Fortress 79, **81**
restaurants 136
Manasija Monastery 5, 11, 13, 41, 65, 67, **70–71**
Mansion of Prince Miloš (Belgrade) 59, 134
Maps
Along the Danube 104–5
Maps (cont.)
Belgrade 43, 44–5
Belgrade Old Town Street-by-Street 46–7
Belgrade street finder 60–63
Central Serbia 65, 66–7
climate 29
Discovering Serbia 10–11
Eastern Serbia 101, 102–3
Europe 14
Fruška Gora monastery tour 97
Niš 117
Northern Serbia 89, 90–91
Novi Sad 93
Serbia 14–15
Serbia Area by Area Front endpaper
Serbia at a Glance 40–41
Serbia road map Back endpaper
Southern Serbia 113, 114–15
Western Serbia 77, 78–9
Maritsa, Battle of (1371) 34
Markelj, Viktor 27
Markets 140, 141
Martin Jonaš Memorial House (Kovačica) 98
Media 156–7
Mediana (Niš) 116, **117**
Medical treatment 152, 153
Medieval art 24
Medieval church architecture 26
Međuvršje *see* Lakes
Mehmed II, Sultan 34, 68
Mesolithic 33, 101
Meštrović, Ivan
Monument of Gratitude to France 53
The Victor (Pobednik) 52
Migration of the Serbs (Jovanović) 25
Mihailo Obrenović, Prince 48, 49, 50, 51, 75
Mihailović, Draža 36
Milan I (Obrenović), King 81
Milan Obrenović, Prince 54
Mileševa Monastery 32, 33, 76, 77, 78, **83**, 99, 127, 137
Mileševac Fortress 83
Miletić, Svetozar 93
Milica, Princess 69
Military Museum (Belgrade) 52
Millennium Tower (Belgrade) 58
Miloš Obrenović, Prince 34, 35, 43, 48
Aranđelovac 75
Cathedral Church of St Michael (Belgrade) 46, 48
Kragujevac 65, 74
Kraljevo 81
Old Town (Belgrade) 46
Palace of Princess Ljubica (Belgrade) 46, 47, 49
Prince Miloš Street (Belgrade) 54–5
Sokobanja 109
Topčider Park (Belgrade) 59
Milošević, Slobodan 19
Kosovo 37
protests against 51, 95
Yugoslav Wars 37
Milovanović, Milan 25
Mines, unexploded 153
Minibuses 160
Miroslav's Gospel 22
Mitrović, Mihajlo 27
Mladić, Ratko 19
Mobile phones 156, 157
Modern architecture 27
Modern Art Gallery (Subotica) 98
Modernist art 25
Mokra Gora 19, 87, 162
hotels 127
restaurants 136
Mokranjac, Stevan 108
Mokranjac House Museum (Negotin) 108
Molnàr, Geörgy 26
Momčilov Grad (Pirot) 115, 120–21
Monasteries 23, 24
Bukovo 108
Crna Reka 23, 79, **83**
Đipša (Divša) 97
Fruška Gora monasteries 13, 89, 90, **97**
Grgeteg 13, 97
Jazak 97
Kalenić 64, 65, 66, 69
Krušedol 13, 25, 97, 137
Ljubostinja 11, 13, 65, 66, 69, 141
Manasija 5, 11, 13, 41, 65, 67, **70–71**
Mileševa 32, 33, 76, 77, 78, **83**, 99, 127, 137
Novo Hopovo 97
Ovčar-Kablar Gorge 80
Poganovo 4, 112, 113, 115, 121, 139
Pustinja 78, 80
Rakovac 97
Ravanica 18, 22, 26, 48, 65, 67, **69**, 149
Sopoćani 24, 40, 49, 77, 79, **83**
Staro Hopovo 33, 97
Studenica 22, 24, 26, 40, 49, 77, 79, **81**, 127, 141
Vrdnik 13, 97
Žiča 5, 13, 24, 77, 79, 81
Money 154–5
Montenegro 33, 37
Monuments
Karađorđe Monument (Belgrade) 35
Monument of Gratitude to France (Belgrade) 53
Monument to the Kosovo Heroes (Kruševac) 69
Monument to the Liberators of Niš (Niš) 114, 116
October 21st memorial monuments (Kragujevac) 74
Stefan Lazarević Monument (Belgrade) 52, 53
Morava School 26, 50, 51, 65, 69, 70, 97
Mosques 26, 34, 43, 77, 78, 149
Altun-alem Mosque (Novi Pazar) 23, 82
Bajrakli Mosque (Belgrade) 26, 45, **50**
Bali-beg Mosque (Niš) 26, 116, 117
Motorways 165
Mountains 20
Babin Zub 115, 121, 145
Bukulja, Mount 75
Carpathian Mountains 14, 15, 33, 40, 99, 105, 109
Dinaric Alps 14, 20, 40, 48, 78
Fruška Gora 13, 89, 97
Gledić Mountains 15, 66
Gobelja 79, 82
Kopaonik Mountains 20, 77, 79, **82**, 122–3, 144, 145, 148
Kotlenik Mountains 66
Kučaj Mountains 15, 66, 67
Midžor 115, 121, 144
Ovčar-Kablar Gorge 19, **80**
Ozren 103, 109
Pančićev vrh 15, 66, 79, 82
Radan, Mount 41, **120**
Rhodope Mountains 14, 15
Rtanj 15, 103, 109
Stara planina Mountains 14, 15, 20, 115, 118-19, 120, **121**, 144, 145
Suva planina Mountains 20, 115
Tara Mountains 2–3, 5, 77, 78, 87, 144
Tornik 14, 78, **86**,145
Zlatibor Mountains 78, **86**, 144, 145

Murad I, Sultan 34
Museum of Contemporary Art (Belgrade) 24, 43, **58**
Museum of Ponišavlje (Pirot) 121
Museum of the Serbian Orthodox Church (Belgrade) 46, 48
Museum of Srem (Sremska Mitrovica) 96
Museum of Vojvodina (Novi Sad) 92
Museum of Yugoslav History (Belgrade) 12, 58
Museums and galleries
- admission fees 149
- Amidža's Mansion (Kragujevac) 74
- Automobile Museum (Belgrade) 12, **54**
- City Museum (Knjaževac) 109
- City Museum (Petrovaradin Fortress, Novi Sad) 95
- City Museum (Sremski Karlovci) 96
- City Museum (Subotica) 98
- City Museum (Vršac) 99
- Drvengrad 87
- Ethnographic Museum (Belgrade) 12, **48**
- Fresco Gallery (Belgrade) 49
- Gallery of Naïve Art (Kovačica) 98
- Gallery of the Natural History Museum (Belgrade) 52, 53
- Hajduk Veljko Museum (Negotin) 108
- Heritage Museum (Knjaževac) 109
- House of Flowers (Belgrade) 12, **58**
- Jewish Historical Museum (Belgrade) 50
- Karađorđe House Museum (Topola) 75
- Krajina Museum (Negotin) 108
- Lepenski Vir 33, 104, 105
- Mansion of Prince Miloš (Belgrade) 59
- Martin Jonaš Memorial House (Kovačica) 98
- Mediana (Niš) 117
- Military Museum (Belgrade) 52
- Millennium Tower (Belgrade) 58
- Modern Art Gallery (Subotica) 98
- Mokranjac House Museum (Negotin) 108
- Museum of Contemporary Art (Belgrade) 24, 43, **58**
- Museum of Ponišavlje (Pirot) 121
- Museum of the Serbian Orthodox Church (Belgrade) 46, 48
- Museum of Srem (Sremska Mitrovica) 96
- Museum of Vojvodina (Novi Sad) 92
- Museum of Yugoslav History (Belgrade) 12, 58
- Muselim's Residence (Valjevo) 80
- National Museum (Aranđelovac) 75
- National Museum (Belgrade) 12, 43, **51**
- National Museum (Kragujevac) 74
- National Museum (Kraljevo) 81
- National Museum (Kruševac) 69
- National Museum (Niš) 116
- National Museum (Užice) 87
- National Museum (Valjevo) 80
- National Museum (Zaječar) 108, 110
- Natural History Museum (Belgrade) 52, 53
- Nikola Tesla Museum (Belgrade) 12, 43, **55**
- October 21st Memorial Museum (Kragujevac) 74
- Old Museum (Belgrade) 58
- opening hours 149

Museums (cont.)
- Pasha's Residence (Vranje) 121
- Pharmacy on the Steps (Vršac) 99
- Prijepolje Museum 83
- Ras Museum (Novi Pazar) 82
- Red Cross Camp Museum (Niš) 116
- Sirogojno 77, **86**
- Small Art Gallery (Kragujevac) 74
- Smederevo Museum (Smederevo) 68
- Zastava Industrial Museum (Kragujevac) 74

Music
- classical music 142, 143
- festivals 17, 28–9, 30, 31, 95
- rock and jazz 143

Muslims *see* Islam; Mosques
Muselim's Residence (Valjevo) 80

N

Načić, Jelisaveta 47
Narcotics 153
National Library of Serbia (Belgrade) 55
National Museums
- National Museum (Aranđelovac) 75
- National Museum (Belgrade) 12, 43, **51**
- National Museum (Kragujevac) 74
- National Museum (Kraljevo) 81
- National Museum (Kruševac) 69
- National Museum (Niš) 116
- National Museum (Užice) 87
- National Museum (Valjevo) 80
- National Museum (Zaječar) 108, 110
- *also see* Museums and galleries

National parks, nature parks and special nature reserves
- Deliblato Sands 21
- Fruška Gora National Park 97
- Kopaonik Mountains 77
- Stara planina Nature Park 113, 115, 121
- Tara National Park 77, **87**
- Zasavica Special Nature Reserve 17

National Theatre (Belgrade) 26, 51
NATO 18, 19, 37, 55, 92
Natural History Museum (Belgrade) 52, 53
Nature parks *see* National parks, nature parks and special nature reserves
Nazis 36, 81, 87
- Jewish Historical Museum (Belgrade) 50
- King Alexander Boulevard (Belgrade) 54
- Kragujevac 13, 74
- Kralja Petra (Belgrade) 27
- Kraljevo 81
- National Library of Serbia (Belgrade) 55
- Novi Sad 93
- Red Cross Camp Museum (Niš) 13, 116
- Užice 87
- World War II 36

Negotin 19, 101, 103, **108**
- festivals 30
- hotels 129
- restaurants 138
- wineries 108

Nemanjić dynasty 22, 33
Nenadović, Jakov 80
Nenadović Tower (Valjevo) 80
Neo-Renaissance architecture 26
Newspapers 157
Nightclubs 143
Nikola Tesla Museum (Belgrade) 12, 43, **55**
Nikolić, Vladimir 26
Niš 11, 13, 113, **116–17**
- climate 29
- festivals 17, 29, 30
- hotels 129
- restaurants 139

Niš Fortress 13, 26, 114, **116**
Nišville International Jazz Festival (Niš) 29, 142
Northern Serbia 89–99
- the Flavours of Serbia 132
- Fruška Gora monastery tour 97
- hotels 128
- map 90–91
- Novi Sad 92–3
- Petrovaradin Fortress 94–5
- restaurants 137–8
- travel 91

Novi Pazar 23, 77, **82**
- festivals 29
- hotels 127
- restaurants 136–7

Novi Sad 10, 12, 13, 89, **92–3**
- climate 29
- festivals 17, 28, 29, 30
- hotels 128
- map 93
- restaurants 138

Novo Hopovo Monastery 97

O

Obradović, Dositej 48
Obrenović dynasty 34, 54, 81
- *see also* Mihailo Obrenović; Miloš Obrenović

Obrenovićeva (Niš) 116
October 21st Memorial Museum (Kragujevac) 74
Off-roading 145
Old Museum (Belgrade) 58
Old Town (Belgrade) 12
- Street-by-Street map 46–7

Opening hours 149
- banks 154
- restaurants 130
- shops 140, 149

Opera 142, 143
Orfelin, Jakov 96, 97
Orthodox Church see Serbian Orthodox Church
Ottoman Empire 18, 26, 34–5, 65, 70, 77, 83, 94, 96, 101, 104, 113, 116, 120
- *see also* Islam

Outdoor Activities 19, 144–5
Ovčar-Kablar Gorge 19, **80**
- hotels 127
- restaurants 137

P

Palaces
- Bačka Bishop's Palace (Novi Sad) 89, **92**
- Palace of the Bishop of Banat (Vršac) 99
- Palace of Princess Ljubica (Belgrade) 12, 46, **49**
- Patriarch's Palace (Sremski Karlovci) 96
- Royal Palaces (Belgrade) 12, 56–7, **59**

Palić 98
- hotels 128
- lake *see* Lakes
- restaurants 138

Pančevo
- festivals 28

Pannonian
- basin 21
- sea 89

Paragliding 144, 145

Parks and gardens
Topčider Park (Belgrade) 59
see also National parks, nature parks and special nature reserves
Pasha's Residence (Vranje) 121
Passports 148, 149
Patriarch's Palace (Sremski Karlovci) 96
Paul, Prince Regent 36, 59
Personal security 152–3
Peter I (Karađorđević), King 27, 75
Peter II Karađorđević, King 36
Peter of Koriša, St 83
Petka, St 53
Petković, Bratislav 54
Petrol 164–5
Petrovaradin Fortress 11, 89, **94–5**
Petrović, Dimitrije 48
Petrović, Đorđe see Karađorđe
Petrović, Nadežda 25
Pharmacies 152–3
Pharmacy on the Steps (Vršac) 99
Photography 151
Pieta (Vozarević) 25
Pirot 120–21
festivals 29
hotels 129
restaurants 139
Planetarium
Belgrade 52
Play of the Black Horses (Rosandić) 44
Pobednik (Meštrović) 52
Poganovo Monastery 4, 112, 113, 115, 121, 139
Police 148, 152, 165
Popović, Svetozar and Vidosava 109
Post-war art 25
Postal services 156, 157
Požarevac
festivals 30
Prijepolje 83
hotels 127
restaurants 137
Prijepolje Museum 83
Prince Miloš Street (Belgrade) 54–5
Princip, Gavrilo 35
Prolom Banja 11, 13, 113, 120
hotels 129
restaurants 139
Public holidays 31
Public toilets 151
Pustinja Monastery 78, 80

R

Rabies 153
Radan, Mount 41
Radio 157
Rafting 145
Raichle Mansion (Subotica) 88, 98
Railways see Trains
Rainfall 29
Rajkova Cave 104, 108
Rakia (fruit brandy) 141
Rákóczi 96
Rakovac Monastery 97
Ram Fortress 101, 104
restaurants 138–9
Ras Museum (Novi Pazar) 82
Raška School 18, 26, 77, 81, 120
Raspopović, Ivanka 27, 58
Ravanica Monastery 18, 22, 26, 48, 65, 67, **69**, 149
Ravništarka Cave 108
Realism 25
Red Cross Camp Museum (Niš) 116
Registration, with police 148
Religion 18
Islam 23, 34, 77
Serbian Orthodox Church 18, 22–3
Religion (cont.)
see also Cathedrals and churches; Monasteries; Mosques; Synagogues
Renting cars 164, 165
Republic Square (Belgrade) 51
Republika Srpska 37
Resavska Cave 13, **68**
Responsible travel 149
Restaurants 130–39
Belgrade 134–5
bills and tipping 131
Central Serbia 135–6
children in 130
Eastern Serbia 138–9
the Flavours of Serbia 132–3
menus 130
Northern Serbia 137–8
opening hours 130
reservations 130
smoking in 131
Southern Serbia 139
vegetarians and vegans 131
Western Serbia 136–7
see also Food and drink
Rhodope Mountains 14, 15
Riding 145
Risovača Cave (Aranđelovac) 75
Rivers 21, 133, 143
beaches 40, 43, 59
Beli Timok 41, 102
confluence of Danube and Sava 12, 14, 43, 52, 58, 161
Crna Reka 83
Crni Timok 103
Danube 10, 14, 15, 21, 33, 43, 65, 89, 90, 93, 94, 100, 101, 102, 103,**104–5**, 106–7, 145, 159, 161
Drina 15, 40, 78
festivals 28, 29
Great Morava 15, 41, 65, 66, 67
Ibar 15, 29, 40, 77, 78, 79, 81, 144, 145
Karas 21
kayaking and rafting 77, 81, 83, 145
Kolubara 79, 80
Lim 77, 78, 83
Moravica 103, 109
Nišava 41, 113, 115, 116
Raška 82, 83
Resava 67, 70
Sava 14, 15, 31, 38–9, 40, 43, 44, 46, 59, 79, 89, 90, 158, 161
South Morava 15, 41, 66, 113, 114, 121
Studenica 81
Svrljiški Timok 109
Tamis 15, 21, 91
Timok 15, 103
Tisa 15, 40, 89, 91
travel 158–9, 161
Uvac 15, 40, 78, 151
West Morava 15, 19, 40, 66, 67, 79, 80
Rock climbing 144, 145
Rock music 143
Roksandić, Simeon
Struggle 52
Roman Catholic Church 18, 23
Roman Empire 33, 54, 68, 82, 89, 92, 114, 120
Along the Danube 104–5
Caričin Grad 120
Diana Roman Fort 101, 103, 105
Felix Romuliana (Gamzigrad) 101, 108, **110–11**
Mediana (Niš) 113, 116, **117**
Sirmium 89, 96
Viminacium 13, 101, 102, 104
Romania 35
Rosandić, Toma
Play of the Black Horses 44
Royal Palaces (Belgrade) 12, 56–7, **59**
Rudno
hotels 127
Rural tourism 125, 145

S

Safety 148, 149, 152–3
St George's Church (Petrovaradin) 94
St John the Baptist 24
St Nicholas 22
St Nicholas Church (Novi Sad) 92–3
St Petka's Church (Vranje) 121
St Sava's Church (Belgrade) 8–9
St Sava's Day 31
St Trifun 18
Saints 22
Sts Peter and Paul Church (Novi Pazar) 23, 24, 82
Sarajevo, Siege of (1992–96) 37
Šargan Eight 77, **87**
Sarrabezolles, Carlo 46
Sava, St 18, 22, 33
Mileševa Monastery 83
relics 99
St Sava's Day 31
Temple of St Sava (Belgrade) 55
Sava River 14, 15, 31, 38–9, 40, 43, 44, 46, 59, 79, 89, 90, 158, 161
Serbian Orthodox Church 18, 22–3
festivals 28, 31
history 33
Serbian Uprisings (1804, 1815) 34, 35, 55, 59, 65, 74, 75, 80, 81, 108, 117
Serbo-Byzantine architecture 26
Shopping 140–41
Sinan Paša 55, 99
Sinđelić, Stevan 117
Sirmium 89, 96
Sirogojno 77, **86**
festivals 29
hotels 127
restaurants 137
Skardalija (Belgrade) 10, 12, **51**
Skiing 145
Babin Zub Ski Resort 121
Kopaonik 82
Tornik Ski Centre 86
Skull Tower (Niš) 11, **117**
Slava 18, 22, 132, 137
Šljivovica (plum brandy) 17, 141
Slovenia 37
Small Art Gallery (Kragujevac) 74
Smederevo 12, 65, **68**
festivals 30
hotels 127
restaurants 136
Smederevo Fortress 11, 12–13, 34, 65, 67
Smederevo Museum (Smederevo) 68
Smoking 151
in restaurants 131
Social Realism 18–19, 25, 27
Sokobanja 18, 101, **109**
hotels 129
restaurants 139
Sokograd Fortress 102
Sopoćani Monastery 24, 40, 49, 77, 79, **83**
Sokol, Jan 98
Southern Serbia 113–21
the Flavours of Serbia 132
hotels 129
map 114–15
Niš 116–17
restaurants 139
travel 114
Souvenir shops 140–41
Spajići *see* Lakes

Spas 19, 124
 Aranđelovac 75
 Lukovska Banja 113
 Prolom Banja 113
 Sokobanja 101, **109**
Special nature reserves *see* National parks, nature parks and special nature reserves
Sports *see* Outdoor Activities
Spring in Serbia 28
Sremska Mitrovica 89, **96**
 festivals 29
 hotels 128
 restaurants 138
 wineries 96
Sremski Karlovci 91, **96**
 festivals 30
 hotels 128
 restaurants 138
 wineries 96
Stalin, Joseph 18–19, 25, 36
Stanojević, Aca 109
Stara planina Mountains 14, 15, 20, 113, 115, 118–19, **121**
Staro Hopovo Monastery 33, 97
Statehood Day 31
Stefan II, King 33, 77
Stefan Dušan the Mighty, Emperor 33, 34, 54
Stefan Milutin, King 108
Stefan Nemanja, Grand Prince 33, 77, 81, 82, 120
Stefan Uroš I, King 77, 83
Stefan Vladislav, King 77, 83
Stojanović, Marko 47
Stopića Cave 86
The Strand (Novi Sad) 93
Street names 27
Struggle (Roksandić) 52
Studenica Monastery 22, 24, 26, 40, 49, 77, 79, **81**, 127, 141
 hotels 127
Subotica 17, 41, 89, **98**
 festivals 28, 29
 hotels 128
 restaurants 138
Šumadija 65
Šumanović, Sava 25
 Drunken Boat 25
Šumaričko *see* Lakes
Summer in Serbia 28–9
Sunshine 29
Suprematism 25
Surrealism 25
Synagogues
 Belgrade 62
 Novi Sad 93
 Subotica 90, 98

T

Tablet of Trajan 104, 105
Tara Mountains 77
Tara National Park 87
Taxis 158, 159, 161
Telephones 156, 157
Television 157
Temperatures 29
Temple of St Sava (Belgrade) 23, **55**
Tenecki, Stefan 25
Teodor of Vršac, St 99
Teodorovic, Arsa 25
Tesla, Nikola
 Nikola Tesla Museum (Belgrade) 12, 43, **55**
Theatre 142, 143
 children's theatre 142, 143
 festivals 28, 30
 National Theatre (Belgrade) 26, 51
Theft 152
Time zones 151
Tipping, in restaurants 131
Tito 36
 break with Stalin 18–19, 25, 36
 death 36, 55
 House of Flowers (Belgrade) 58
 Petrovaradin Fortress 95
 Prince Miloš Street (Belgrade) 55
 Royal Palaces (Belgrade) 59
 statue of 36
 tomb 58
 Užice 87
 World War II 36
Toilets, public 151
Topčider Park (Belgrade) 59
Topola 11, 13, **75**
 hotels 127
 restaurants 136
Tornik Ski Centre 77, 86
Tours
 Along the Danube 104–5
 Fruška Gora monastery tour 97
Trains 159, 162–3
 Šargan Eight 77, **87**
Trajan, Emperor 104, 105
Trams
 in Belgrade 160–61
Travel 158–65
 air 158, 159
 Belgrade 44, 160–61
 boats 158–9
 buses 159, 162, 163
 cars 159, 164–5
 Central Serbia 66
 cycling 161
 Eastern Serbia 102
 minibuses 160
 Northern Serbia 91
 Southern Serbia 114
 taxis 158, 159, 161
 trains 159, 162–3
 trams and trolleybuses 160–61
 Western Serbia 78
Trem 20
Trolleybuses
 in Belgrade 160–61
Tuđman, Franjo 37

U

UNESCO Intangible Cultural Heritage List 18
UNESCO World Heritage Sites
 Felix Romuliana (Gamzigrad) 41, 101, **110–11**
 Sopoćani Monastery 77, **83**
 Sts Peter and Paul Church (Novi Pazar) 82
 Studenica Monastery 40, 77, **81**
Unexploded mines 153
United Nations 37
Užice **87**
 festivals 29
 hotels 128
 restaurants 137

V

Vaccinations 153
Valjevo 77, **80**
 festivals 28, 30
 hotels 128
 restaurants 137
Vasa's Residence (Kraljevo) 81
Vauban, Sebastian 94
Vegan food 131
Vegetarian food 131
Veljko, Hajduk 108
The Viktor (Meštrović) 52
Viminacium 13, 101, 104
 hotels 129
Vinci
 hotels 129
Visas 148, 149
Visitor information 149
Vlachs 101, **109**
Vojvodina 17, 18, 25, 89
Vozarević, Lazar
 Pieta 25
Vranje 113, **121**
 hotels 129
 restaurants 139
Vrdnik Monastery 13, 97
Vršac 19, **99**
 festivals 29, 30
 hotels 128
 restaurants 138
 wineries 99

W

Walking 144, 145
Water, drinking 153
Weather 29, 148
West Morava River 19, 80
Western Serbia 77–87
 the Flavours of Serbia 133
 hotels 127–8
 map 78–9
 restaurants 136–7
 travel 78
Wheelchair access see Disabled travellers
White Angel on the Grave of Christ (fresco) 76, 83
Wildlife 20–21
 see also National parks, nature parks and special nature reserves
Wine 19, 133
 customs information 148
 driving regulations 165
 festivals 30
 shopping 141
 wineries of Fruška Gora 13
 wineries of Negotin 108
 wineries of Sremski Karlovci 96
 wineries of Vršac 99
Winter in Serbia 31
Winter sports 145
Women travellers 150
World Bank 37
World War I 35
World War II 23, 36, 50

Y

Yugo-Dada 25
Yugoslav Wars 37
Yugoslavia 35, 36–7

Z

Zadarska (Belgrade) 47
Zaječar 108
 festivals 29
 hotels 129
 restaurants 139
Zaovine *see* Lakes
Zasavica Special Nature Reserve 17
Zastava Industrial Museum (Kragujevac) 74
Zemun (Belgrade) 58
Žiča Monastery 5, 13, 24, 77, 79, 81
Žilnik, Želimir 25
Živković, Nikola 49
Zlatibor 86
 festivals 29
 hotels 128
 restaurants 137
Zuzoric, Cvijeta 52

Acknowledgments

Dorling Kindersley would like to thank the following people whose help and assistance contributed to the preparation of this book.

Author

Matt Willis is a seasoned travel guide author who wrote extensively about Serbia's neighbours – Bulgaria, Bosnia and Herzegovina, Montenegro and Romania for DK's Eyewitness Travel Guides – before finally tackling Serbia itself. Matt has also authored the DK Top 10 guides to Moscow and to Southwest Turkey, updated the Rough Guide to Bulgaria and the Rough Guide to Europe on a Budget, and spent months on the Trans-Siberian railway as part of his research for the DK Eyewitness Guide to Russia.

Fact Checker

National Tourism Organisation of Serbia (Zorica Jovanov, Smiljana Novičić, Ivan Vuković)

Proofreader

Debra Wolter

Indexer

Hilary Bird

Editorial Consultant

Scarlett O'Hara

Additional Picture Research

National Tourism Organisation of Serbia (Nataša Drulović, Marijana Markoska)

Picture Credits

a = above; b = below/bottom; c = centre; f = far; l = left; r = right; t = top

The publisher would like to thank the following individuals, organizations, companies and picture libraries for their kind permission to reproduce their photographs:

akg-images: 35tr; Erich Lessing 22cl.

Alamy Images: akg-images 36tl; Ancient Art and Architecture 22cla; Chronicle/Grenville Collins Postcard Collection 35cb; Peter Forsberg 37tr; Stuart Forster 36bc; ITAR-TASS Photo Agency 37cb; Falk Kienas 104bc; Shirlee Klasson 34br; Vova Pomortzeff 142b; Serbia Pictures/Adam Radosavljevic 23cr, 72-3, 124cra; Westend61 GmbH/Martin Moxter 51t; Wietse Michiels Travel Stock 142tr; World History Archive 36clb.

Ambar: 135clb.

Belgrade City Museum: Pavle Paja Jovanic "Migration of the Serbs" (1896) 25cra.

Avi Ben Simon: 31c, 132cr, 132c, 132fcra.

Dreamstime.com: Afroto 46tr; Akarelias 151cr; Andrej Antic 95cr; Vladimir Babic 12b; Banepetkovic 59tl; Sergiy Beketov 43b; Boggy 104c; Nadezhda Bolotina 41tl; Borisb17 46cb; Irina Brinza 132cb; Ioan Florin Cnejevici 5cr; Dedekk 20crb; Djama86 132crb; Dobok81 82tl; Draghicich 141cb; Electropower 42, 46cla; Elenathewise 66bl; Elena Elisseeva 158b; Geza Farkas 65b; Fotosergio 132clb; Gagyeos 52tr; Vladislav Gajic 84-5; Hakiagena 33br; Isselee 20cl, 97tr; Jevtic 21cl, 21cr; Khaleesii 70clb; Lunja87 53br; Maeklong 21br; Sasa Maricic 13l; Marinela84 13b; Pavle Marjanovic, 32, 41cra; Mikhail Markovskiy 88; Stanisa Martinovic 94tr; Masezdromaderi 94cla; Aleksandar Mijatovic 4tr, 35bl; Mikelane45 21tr; Miroslav110 97cl; Moonru 38-9; Guido Nardacci 20br; Natureimmortal 21crb; Nomadbeg 106-7; Ntcandrej 92br; Nyiragongo70 1; Alexander Podshivalov 20cr; Porojnicu 100; Rasica 31t; Polina Ryazantseva 130br; Saiko3p 52br; Sarah2 20bl; Selena 97crb; Valery Shanin 34crb; Andrey Shevchenko 117tl; Slasta20 97cra, 105t; Snowyns 89b, 93tl; Soloway 163br; Wang Song 143tc; Nikolai Sorokin 146-7; Darko Sreckovic 125br; Stanisa 95bl, 118-9; Stoyanh112; Tijanaa 44bl; Vigortakeda 34clb; Vladimirnenezic 10cla, 60b; Weblogiq 20clb; Yvdavyd 132cr; Zoransimin 10b, 90bl.

Dusan Maletic: maletic.org/Mihailo Maletic 22-3c.

Eco Hostel: Republik: 128tl.

EXIT Festival: EXIT Photo Team 95br.

FLPA: Imagebroker/Christain Hatter 21bl.

Gallery Babka, Kovačica: Zuzana Chalupova "Harvest" (1976) oil painting, 45cmx65cm 16.

Getty Images: De Agostini Picture Library 34tr; Greg Elms 161cl; John Freeman 47tr.

Hotel Moskva: 126br.

Kevin "Elvis" King: 47cb.

Mezestoran Dvorište: 134bl.

Museum of Contemporary Art, Belgrade: "Pietà" (1956) Lazar Vozarević, oil on canvas; 124 x 280, Inv. No. 8 25br.

National Tourism Organisation of Serbia: 50cr, 81tr; Dragan Bosnić 2-3, 4br, 5clb, 8-9, 11t, 16, 18bl, 18t, 19b, 20cra, 21cla, 22bl, 22bc, 22br, 23cl, 24tr, 24b, 25tl, 26tr, 26cla, 26cr, 26bl, 27t, 27bl, 28cra, 28br, 29c, 30b, 33cb, 33bl, 40bl, 40cl, 41br, 44c, 45bl, 46bl, 50tl, 53cr, 54tl, 54br, 56-7, 58tl, 59br, 64, 66cl, 67tr, 67br, 68tl, 68br, 69tl, 69br, 70cla, 71cra, 71crb, 71bl, 74cr, 74bl, 75tr, 75bl, 76, 77b, 78bl, 79br, 80t, 80crb, 81bl, 82br, 83tl, 83br, 86b, 87tl, 87c, 87br, 90tr, 91t, 91crb, 92tr, 92cl, 96tl, 97cb, 98tl, 98c, 99tl, 99b, 101b, 102bl, 103t, 103br, 104tr, 105crb, 105bl, 105cla, 108tl, 108br, 109tl, 109br, 113b, 115t, 115cr, 116tr, 116cr, 117cr, 120tl, 120br, 121tl, 121bc, 122-3, 125tl, 144br, 145tr,

145cl, 148cra, 149tc, 151t, 162br; Branko Jovanović 5t, 13t, 17b, 20cla, 21cra, 21clb, 23tr, 23br, 25cra, 25cl, 30tl, 41cr, 47br, 47cr, 48tr, 48bl, 49tr, 49b, 50br, 52ca, 53tl, 55br, 55cl, 58br, 70tr, 71tl, 79tr, 86tl, 94crb, 95tl, 102tr, 110tr, 110cla, 110br, 111tl, 111bl, 111cra, 130cla, 131tl, 131b, 132tr, 132cla, 132bc, 132br, 132r, 133tl, 133bl, 133clb, 133cr, 137tr, 140ca, 140br, 141t, 149bc, 150tr, 152tr, 152br, 152cl, 153tl, 153cl, 154tr, 154bl, 155 (all), 156bl, 156cr, 157tl, 158cra, 159tl, 160tr, 160c,160br, 161tl, 161br, 162tr, 163tl, 164cl, 164b, 165t, 165bc; Milan Kopčok 20tr; Milos Milenković 144cla, 150bl.

Nišville International Jazz Festival: 29tr.

Pleasure: 139c.

Project 72: 138bl.

Asif Quadri: 11cra, 92cr, 114bl, 114tr, 116cla, 133bc.

Square Nine: 127tl.

Vila Delux Negotin: 129clb.

Zelengora: 136bl.

Front Endpaper

Dreamstime.com: Leonid Andronov Lc; Mikhail Markovskiy Lt; Porojnicu Rc; Stoyanh Rb.
National Tourism Organisation of Serbia: Dragan Bosnic Lb, Rt.

Front Cover

Alamy Images: Shotshop GmbH main.
National Tourism Organisation of Serbia: Dragan Bosnić bl.

Phrase Book

Serbian is one of the only European languages with complete digraphia, using both Cyrillic and Latin scripts. The Serbian Cyrillic alphabet was standardized by Serbian philologist and linguist Vuk Karadžić (1787–1864) in 1814, who based it on phonemic principles. He also wrote the first Serbian dictionary. The Latin alphabet for Serbo-Croatian languages was devised by Croatian linguist Ljudevit Gaj (1809–72) in 1830. In this guide, all Serbian words and names of people, places and streets have been written using the Latin script. For some names, where a well-known English form exists, this has been used. In particular, names of Serbian rulers are given in their anglicized form – hence, Peter (not Petar), Paul (not Pavle) and Alexander (not Aleksandar).

Guidelines for Pronunciation

The Serbian alphabet has 30 letters, whose order varies in the Latin and Cyrillic scripts. The table below lists the alphabet in the Cyrillic order, with the uppercase and lowercase forms of each Cyrillic character and its Serbian Latin equivalent. The right-hand column of the table indicates how Cyrillic letters are pronounced by comparing them to sounds in English words. Exact transliterations are generally not possible as Serbian contains certain distinctions and sounds not found in English. On the following pages, the English word or phrase is given in the left-hand column, with the Serbian in the middle column. The right-hand column provides a literal system of pronunciation. Stress generally falls on the first syllable, but when words have a prefix, stress is on the middle syllable. The last syllable is never stressed. Because of the existence of genders in Serbian, in a few cases both the masculine and feminine forms of a phrase are given.

Cyrillic	Latin	English
А а	**A a**	*c**a**r*
Б б	**B b**	***b**oy*
В в	**V v**	***v**erb*
Г г	**G g**	***g**irl*
Д д	**D d**	***d**og*
Ђ ђ	**Đ đ**	***j**am*
Е е	**E e**	*l**e**t, **e**gg*
Ж ж	**Ž ž**	*plea**s**ure, vi**s**ion*
З з	**Z z**	***z**oo*
И и	**I i**	*fr**ee***
Ј ј	**J j**	***y**es*
К к	**K k**	***k**ing*
Л л	**L l**	***l**ike*
Љ љ	**Lj lj**	*mi**lli**on*
М м	**M m**	***m**an*
Н н	**N n**	***n**est*
Њ њ	**Nj nj**	*ca**ny**on*
О о	**O o**	*th**ough**t*
П п	**P p**	***p**ack*
Р р	**R r**	***r**at (rolling r)*
С с	**S s**	***s**and*
Т т	**T t**	***t**ime*
Ћ ћ	**Ć ć**	*fu**t**ure (tch)*
У у	**U u**	*b**oo**t*
Ф ф	**F f**	***f**ather*
Х х	**H h**	*lo**ch**, **h**at*
Ц ц	**C c**	*ca**ts***
Ч ч	**Č č**	***ch**urch*
Џ џ	**Dž dž**	***g**in*
Ш ш	**Š š**	***sh**eep*

In an Emergency

Help!	**Upomoć!**	*upomotch!*
Stop!	**Stanite!**	*staneete!*
Look out!	**Pazite!**	*pazeete!*
Thief!	**Lopov!**	*lopov!*
Call a doctor!	**Pozovite doktora!**	*pozoveete doktora!*
Call an ambulance!	**Pozovite hitnu pomoć!**	*pozoveete heetnoo pomotch!*
Call the police!	**Pozovite policiju!**	*pozoveete politseeyoo!*
Call the fire brigade!	**Pozovite vatrogasce!**	*pozoveete vatrogastse!*
There has been an accident!	**Dogodila se nesreća!**	*dogodila se nesretcha!*
Where is the nearest telephone?	**Gde je najbliži telefon?**	*gde ye naybleezhee telefon?*
Where is the nearest hospital?	**Gde je najbliža bolnica?**	*gde ye naybleezha bolneetsa?*

Communication Essentials

Yes	**Da**	*da*
No	**Ne**	*ne*
Please (offering)	**Izvolite**	*eezvoleete*
Please (asking)	**Molim**	*moleem*
Thank you	**Hvala**	*hvala*
No, thank you	**Ne, hvala**	*ne, hvala*
Excuse me, please	**Izvinite, molim Vas**	*eezveenite, moleem vas*
Hello	**Zdravo**	*zdravo*
Goodbye	**Doviđenja**	*doveedyenya*
Good morning	**Dobro jutro**	*dobro yootro*
Good afternoon	**Dobar dan**	*dobar dan*
Good evening	**Dobro veče**	*dobro veche*
Good night	**Laku noć**	*laku notch*
Here	**Ovde**	*ovde*
There	**Tamo**	*tamo*
Who?	**Ko?**	*ko?*
What?	**Šta?**	*shta?*
When?	**Kad?**	*kad?*
Where?	**Gde?**	*gde?*
Why?	**Zašto?**	*zashto?*
How?	**Kako?**	*kako?*

Useful Phrases

How are you?	**Kako ste?**	*kako ste?*
Very well, thank you	**Dobro, hvala**	*dobro, hvala*
Pleased to meet you	**Drago mi je da smo se upoznali**	*drago mee ye da smo se upoznalee*
See you soon	**Vidimo se uskoro**	*veedeemo se uskoro*
That's fine	**To je u redu**	*to ye u redoo*
Do you speak English?	**Govorite li engleski?**	*govoreete lee engleskee?*
I don't speak Serbian	**Ne govorim srpski**	*ne govoreem srpskee*
I don't understand	**Ne razumem**	*ne razoomem*
Could you speak slowly please?	**Možete li molim Vas govoriti sporije?**	*mozhete lee moleem vas govoreetee sporeeye?*
I'm sorry	**Žao mi je**	*zhao mee ye*
Can you help me?	**Možete li mi pomoći?**	*mozhete lee mee pomotchee?*
I have...	**Imam...**	*eemam...*
a pain	**bol**	*bol*
a stomach ache	**bolove u stomaku**	*bolove oo stomakoo*
a headache	**glavobolja**	*glavobolya*
a fever	**groznica**	*grozneetsa*
a cough	**kašalj**	*kashaly*
a cold	**prehladu**	*prehladoo*
diarrhoea	**proliv**	*proleev*
an allergy	**alergiju**	*alergeeyoo*

Useful Words

toilet	**toalet**	*toalet*
woman	**žena**	*zhena*
man	**čovek**	*chovek*
big	**veliki**	*veleekee*
small	**mali**	*malee*
hot	**vruć**	*vrootch*
cold	**hladan**	*hladan*
good	**dobar**	*dobar*
bad	**loš**	*losh*
open	**otvoreno**	*otvoreno*
closed	**zatvoreno**	*zatvoreno*
left	**levo**	*levo*
right	**desno**	*desno*
straight on	**pravo**	*pravo*
near	**blizu**	*bleezu*
far	**daleko**	*daleko*
up	**gore**	*gore*
down	**dole**	*dole*

early	**rano**	*rano*
late	**kasno**	*kasno*
entrance	**ulaz**	*ulaz*
exit	**izlaz**	*eezlaz*
vacant (unoccupied)	**slobodno**	*slobodno*
free (no charge)	**besplatno**	*besplatno*
danger	**opanost**	*opasnost*
prohibited	**zabranjen**	*zabranyen*
no entry	**zabranjen ulaz**	*zabranyen oolaz*
enough	**dovoljan**	*dovolyan*
well	**dobro**	*dobro*
ear	**uvo**	*oovo*
eye	**oko**	*oko*
head	**glava**	*glava*
stomach	**stomak**	*stomak*
heart	**srce**	*srtse*
teeth	**zubi**	*zoobee*
doctor	**doktor**	*doktor*
dentist	**zubar**	*zoobar*

Keeping in Touch

Can I call abroad from here?	**Mogu li telefonirati u inostranstvo odavde?**	*mogu lee telefoneeratee u inostranstvo odaavde?*
I'd like to make a reverse charge call	**Želim da obavim poziv o trošku onog koga pozivam**	*zheleem da obaveem pozeev o troshku onog koga pozeevam*
I'll call back later	**Uzvratiću poziv kasnije**	*uzvrateetchu pozeev kasneeye*
Can I leave a message?	**Mogu li ostaviti poruku?**	*mogu lee ostaveetee poruku?*
Hold on	**Sačekajte**	*sachekayte*
Could you speak up a little please?	**Možete li govoriti malo glasnije, molim Vas?**	*mozhete lee govoreetee malo glasneeye, moleem vas?*
local call	**lokalni poziv**	*lokalnee pozeev*
public phone box	**javni telefon**	*javnee telefon*
mobile phone	**mobilni telefon**	*mobeelnee telefon*
post office	**pošta**	*poshta*
letter, registered	**pismo, preporučeno**	*peesmo, preporoocheno*
courier	**kurir**	*kooreer*
address	**adresa**	*adresa*
street	**ulica**	*ooleetsa*
town	**varoš**	*varosh*
village	**selo**	*selo*
Internet café	**Internet café**	*internet kafe*
Wi-Fi	**Wi-Fi**	*veefee*
email	**email**	*email*

Shopping

How much does this cost?	**Koliko ovo košta?**	*koleeko ovo koshta?*
I would like...	**Želeo bih... (masc.)** **Želela bih... (fem.)**	*zheleo beeh...* *zhelela beeh...*
Do you have...?	**Imate li...?**	*eemate lee...?*
I'm just looking	**Samo gledam**	*samo gledam*
May I try this on?	**Mogu li bih probati?**	*mogoo lee bee probatee?*
Do you take credit cards?	**Primate li kreditne kartice?**	*preemate lee kredeetne karteetse?*
Do you take travellers' cheques?	**Primate li putničke čekove?**	*preemate lee putnichke chekove?*
What time do you open?	**Kada se otvara prodavnica?**	*kada se otvara prodavneetsa?*
What time do you close?	**Kada se zatvara prodavnica?**	*kada se zatvara prodavneetsa?*
This one	**Ovo**	*ovo*
That one	**Ono**	*ono*
expensive	**skupo**	*skoopo*
cheap	**jeftino**	*yefteeno*
size, clothes	**veličina, odeća**	*velicheena, odetcha*
size, shoes	**veličina, cipele**	*velicheena, tseepele*
red	**crveno**	*tsrveno*
blue	**plavo**	*plavo*
green	**zeleno**	*zeleno*
yellow	**žuto**	*zhuto*
white	**belo**	*belo*
black	**crno**	*tsrno*
brown	**braon**	*braon*

Types of Shop

antique	**antikvarnica**	*anteekvarneetsa*
bakery	**pekara**	*pekara*
bank	**banka**	*banka*
bar	**bar**	*bar*
bookshop	**knjižara**	*knyeezhara*
butcher	**mesara**	*mesara*
cake shop	**poslastičarnica**	*poslasteecharneetsa*
cheese shop	**prodavnica sireva**	*prodavneetsa seereva*
chemist (pharmacy)	**apoteka**	*apoteka*
dairy	**mlečni proizvodi**	*mlechnee proizvodee*
department store	**robna kuća**	*robna kutcha*
delicatessen	**delikatesna radnja**	*delikatessna radnya*
florist	**cvećara**	*tsvetchara*
fishmonger	**ribarnica**	*reebarneetsa*
gift shop	**suvenirnica**	*sooveneerneetsa*
greengrocer	**piljar**	*peelyar*
grocery	**bakalnica**	*bakalneetsa*
hairdresser	**frizer**	*freezer*
market	**pijaca**	*peeyatsa*
newsagent	**novinarnica**	*noveenarneetsa*
shoe shop	**prodavnica cipela**	*prodavneetsa tseepela*
shop	**prodavnica**	*prodavneetsa*
supermarket	**supermarket**	*supermarket*
tavern / inn	**kafana**	*kafana*
tobacconist	**prodavnica cigareta, kiosk**	*prodavneetsa tseegaretta, keeosk*
travel agent	**putnička agencija**	*putneechka agentseeya*

Sightseeing

art gallery	**umetnička galerija**	*umetneechka galereeya*
bus station	**autobuska stanica**	*autobuska staneetsa*
cathedral	**katedrala**	*katedrala*
church	**crkva**	*tsrkva*
garden	**bašta**	*bashta*
library	**biblioteka**	*beebleeoteka*
monastery	**manastir**	*manasteer*
museum	**muzej**	*moozey*
railway station	**železnička stanica**	*zhelezneechka staneetsa*
tourist information office	**turistički informativni centar**	*tooristeechkee informateevnee tsentar*
town hall	**gradska skupština**	*gradska skupshteena*
closed for a public holiday	**zatvoreno u dane državnih praznika**	*zatvoreno u dane drzhavneeh prazneeka*
Where is / are...?	**Gde je / su ...?**	*gde ye / su ...?*
How far is it to...?	**Koliko je daleko...?**	*koleeko ye daleko?*
Which way to...?	**Kojim putem do...?**	*koyeem pootem do...?*
I would like...	**Želeo bih... (masc.)** **Želela bih... (fem.)**	*zheleo beeh...* *zhelela beeh...*
one ticket	**jednu kartu**	*yednoo kartooo*
two tickets	**dve karte**	*dve karte*
a return ticket	**povratnu kartu**	*povratnoo kartoo*
a one-way ticket	**kartu u jednom pravcu**	*kartoo oo yednom pravtsoo*

Staying in a Hotel

Do you have a vacant room?	**Imate li slobodnu sobu?**	*eemate lee slobodnoo soboo?*
I have a reservation	**Imam rezervaciju**	*eemam rezervatseeyu*
room with a bath, shower	**soba sa kupatilom**	*soba sa koopateelom*
double room, with a double bed	**dvokrevetna soba, sa francuskim ležajem**	*dvokrevetna soba, sa frantsuskeem lezhayem*
twin room	**dvokrevetna soba**	*dvokrevetna soba*
single room	**jednokrevetna soba**	*yednokrevetna soba*
porter	**recepcioner**	*retseptseeoner*
key	**ključ**	*klyooch*
air conditioning	**klima uređaj**	*kleema oorejay*

Eating Out

Have you got a table?	**Imate li slobodan sto?**	*eemate lee slobodan sto?*
A table for... please?	**Sto za... molim Vas?**	*sto za... moleem vas?*
I want to reserve a table	**Želim da rezervišem sto**	*zheleem da rezerveeshem sto*
The bill please	**Molim Vas račun**	*moleem vas rachun*
I am a vegetarian	**Ja sam vegetarijanac (masc.)** **Ja sam vegetarijanka (fem.)**	*ya sam vegetereeyanats* *ya sam vegetereeyanka*
I don't eat meat	**Ne jedem meso**	*ne yedem meso*
Is it fasting food?	**Da li je posno?**	*da lee ye posno?*
wine bar	**vinski bar**	*veenskee bar*
café	**kafić**	*kafeetch*
wine list	**karta pića**	*karta peetcha*
menu	**jelovnik**	*yelovneek*
fixed-price menu	**jelovnik sa fiksnim cenama**	*yelovneek sa feexneem tsenama*

English menu	**engleski jelovnik**	*engleskee yelovneek*
cover charge	**platiti**	*plateetee*
tip	**napojnica**	*napoyneetsa*
waitress	**konobarica**	*konobareetsa*
waiter	**konobar**	*konobar*
bottle	**flaša**	*flasha*
glass	**čaša**	*chasha*
plate	**tanjir**	*tanyeer*
knife	**nož**	*nozh*
fork	**viljuška**	*veelyooshka*
spoon	**kašika**	*kasheeka*
cup	**šoljica**	*sholyeetsa*
breakfast	**doručak**	*doroochak*
lunch	**ručak**	*roochak*
dinner	**večera**	*vechera*
starter / first course	**predjelo**	*predyelo*
main course	**glavno jelo**	*glavno yelo*
side dish	**prilog**	*preelog*
dessert	**dezert / poslastice**	*dezert / poslasteeste*
dish of the day	**dnevni meni**	*dnevnee menee*
grilled meat dishes	**jela sa roštilja**	*yela sa roshtilya*
home-made	**domaće**	*domatche*
without cheese	**bez sira**	*bez seera*
rare	**slabo (pečen)**	*slabo (pechen)*
medium	**srednje (pečen)**	*srednye (pechen)*
well done	**jako (pečen)**	*yako (pechen)*
baked	**pečen**	*pechen*
boiled	**kuvan**	*koovan*
dry	**suv**	*soov*
grilled	**grilovano**	*greelovano*
poached	**poširan**	*posheeran*
roast	**pečenje**	*pechenye*

Menu Decoder

apple	**jabuka**	*yabooka*
aubergine	**plavi patlidžan**	*plavee patleezhan*
banana	**banana**	*banana*
beef	**junetina**	*yuneteena*
beer, draught	**pivo, točeno**	*peevo, tocheno*
brandy, apricot	**kajsija**	*kayseeya*
brandy, fruit	**rakija / rakia**	*rakeeya*
brandy, grape	**lozova**	*lozova*
brandy, pear	**viljamovka**	*veelyamovka*
brandy, plum	**šljivovica**	*shlyeevoveetsa*
bread	**hleb**	*hleb*
butter	**puter**	*pootter*
cabbage	**kupus**	*koopus*
cake	**kolač**	*kolach*
cheese	**sir**	*seer*
chicken	**piletina**	*peeleteena*
chips	**pomfri**	*pomfree*
chocolate	**čokolada**	*chokolada*
cocktail	**koktel**	*koktel*
coffee	**kafa**	*kafa*
cream, clotted	**kajmak**	*kaymak*
cucumber	**krastavac**	*krastavats*
duck	**pačetina**	*pacheteena*
egg	**jaje**	*yaye*
fish	**riba**	*reeba*
fruit (fresh)	**sveže voće**	*svezhe votche*
garlic	**beli luk**	*belee look*
ham	**šunka**	*shoonka*
ice	**led**	*led*
ice cream	**sladoled**	*sladoled*
lamb	**jagnjetina**	*yagnyeteena*
lemon	**limun**	*leemoon*
liver	**džigerica**	*dzeegereetsa*
lobster	**jastog**	*yastog*
meat	**meso**	*messo*
milk	**mleko**	*mleko*
mineral water	**mineralna voda**	*meeneralna voda*
mustard	**senf**	*senf*
oil	**ulje**	*ulye*
olives	**masline**	*masleene*
onion	**luk**	*look*
orange	**pomorandža**	*pomorandzha*
orange juice (fresh)	**sok od ceđene pomorandze**	*sok od tsedyene pomorandzhe*
lemon juice (fresh)	**limunada**	*leemoonada*
parsley	**peršun**	*pershoon*
pastry, filled	**burek**	*boorek*
pepper	**biber**	*beeber*
peppers	**paprika**	*papreeka*
pork	**svinjetina**	*sveenyeteena*
potato	**krompir**	*krompeer*
plum	**šljiva**	*shlyeeva*
prawns	**gambori**	*gamboree*
relish, of peppers and aubergines	**ajvar**	*ayvar*
rice	**pirinač**	*peereenach*
roll	**rolovan**	*rolovan*
salad	**salata**	*salata*
salt	**so**	*so*
sauce	**sos**	*sos*
sausage, fresh	**kobasica**	*kobaseetsa*
seafood	**morski plodovi**	*morskee plodovee*
shellfish	**ostriga**	*ostreega*
soup	**supa**	*soopa*
steak	**šnicla**	*shneetsla*
sugar	**šećer**	*shetcher*
tea	**čaj**	*chay*
toast	**tost**	*tost*
tomato	**paradajz**	*paradayz*
Turkish Delight	**ratluk / lokum**	*ratlook / lokoom*
vegetables	**povrće**	*povrtche*
vinegar	**sirće**	*seertche*
water	**voda**	*voda*
wine, red	**crno vino**	*tsrno veeno*
wine, white	**belo vino**	*belo veeno*

Numbers

0	**nula**	*noola*
1	**jedan**	*yedan*
2	**dva**	*dva*
3	**tri**	*tree*
4	**četiri**	*cheteeree*
5	**pet**	*pet*
6	**šest**	*shest*
7	**sedam**	*sedam*
8	**osam**	*osam*
9	**devet**	*devet*
10	**deset**	*deset*
11	**jedanaest**	*yedanaest*
12	**dvanaest**	*dvanaest*
13	**trinaest**	*treenaest*
14	**četrnaest**	*chetrnaest*
15	**petnaest**	*petnaest*
16	**šesnaest**	*shesnaest*
17	**sedamnaest**	*sedamnaest*
18	**osamnaest**	*osamnaest*
19	**devetnaest**	*devetnaest*
20	**dvadeset**	*dvadeset*
30	**tridest**	*treedeset*
40	**četrdeset**	*chetrdeset*
50	**pedeset**	*pedeset*
60	**šezdeset**	*shezdeset*
70	**sedamdeset**	*sedamdeset*
80	**osamdeset**	*osamdeset*
90	**devedeset**	*devedeset*
100	**sto**	*sto*
1,000	**hiljadu**	*heelyadoo*

Time, Days, Seasons and Weather

minute	**minut**	*meenoot*
half an hour	**pola sata**	*pola sata*
one hour	**sat**	*sat*
day	**dan**	*dan*
week	**nedelja**	*nedelya*
month	**mesec**	*mesets*
year	**godina**	*godeena*
morning	**jutro**	*yootro*
noon	**podne**	*podne*
afternoon	**popodne**	*popodne*
evening	**veče**	*veche*
night	**noć**	*notch*
yesterday	**juče**	*yooche*
today	**danas**	*danass*
tomorrow	**sutra**	*sootra*
now	**sada**	*sada*
What time is it?	**Koliko je sati?**	*koleeko ye satee?*
Monday	**ponedeljak**	*ponedelyak*
Tuesday	**utorak**	*utorak*
Wednesday	**sreda**	*sreda*
Thursday	**četvrtak**	*chetvrtak*
Friday	**petak**	*petak*
Saturday	**subota**	*soobota*
Sunday	**nedelja**	*nedelya*
season	**sezona**	*sezona*
spring	**proleće**	*proletche*
summer	**leto**	*leto*
autumn	**jesen**	*yesen*
winter	**zima**	*zeema*
weather	**vreme**	*vreme*
rain (it is raining)	**kiša (pada kiša)**	*keesha (pada keesha)*
wind	**vetar**	*vetar*
sunny	**sunčano**	*soonchano*
warm	**toplo**	*toplo*
cold	**hladno**	*hladno*

Road Map of Serbia

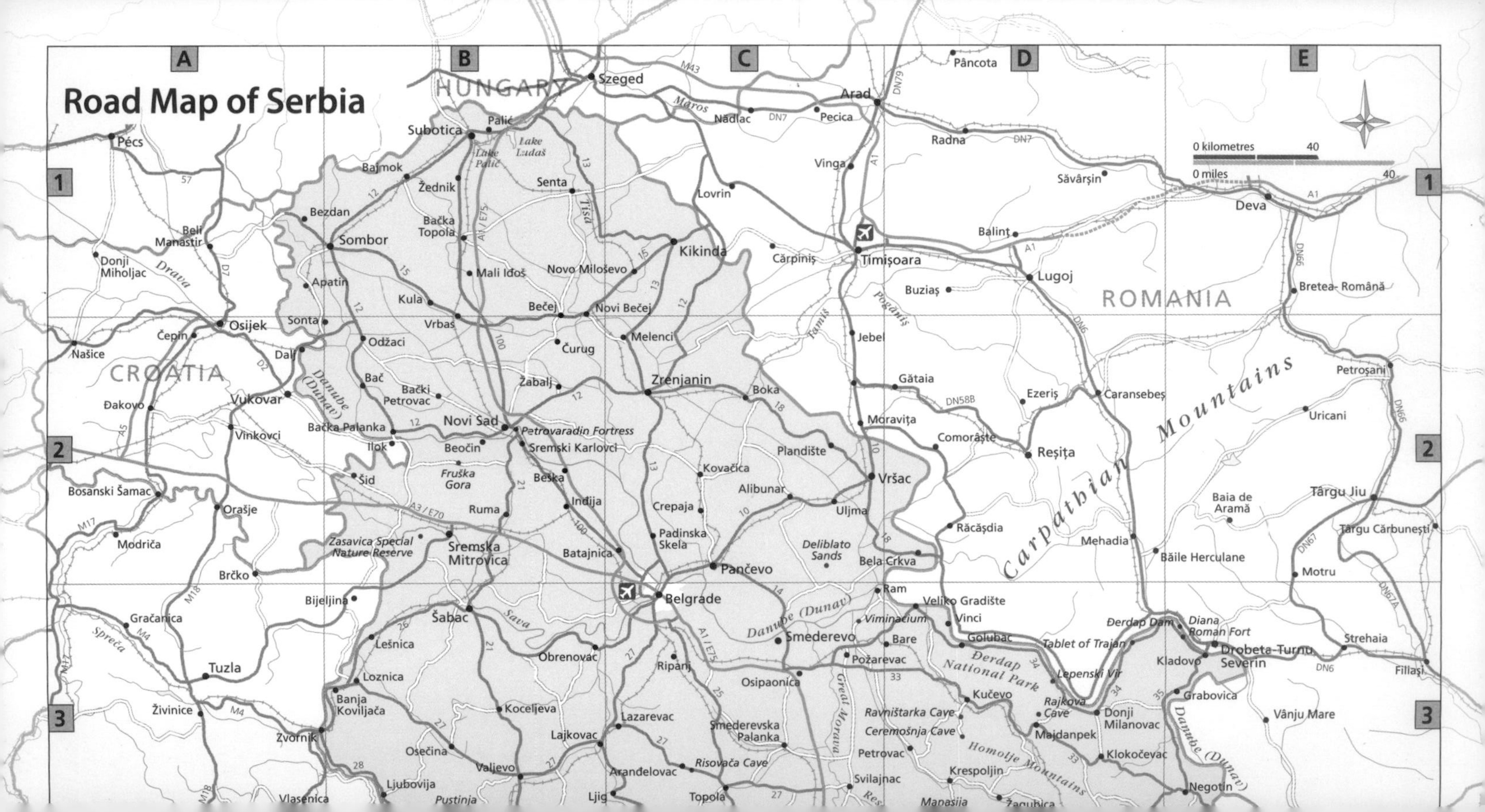